Free Your Self

A Self Awareness Handbook

S Beasley

DEDICATION

To my sweet wife Renee, whose own mindfulness and patience has steadfastly helped me to find and stay on my own true path.

CONTENTS

ACKNOWLEDGMENTS

To my awesome, wonderful and inspiring children; Edward, Marian and William, thank you, for you have taught me so much about myself.

To all of my friends and acquaintances who have shared moments of their life with me, thank you, for the sharing of a moment with a true friend, is priceless.

To Dr. Chris Bell, whose insights on psychology and self awareness have been instrumental in connecting all the dots. The insight on attachment to outcome has been especially significant.

Thanks to William Beasley who designed the cover page

To Steve and Debbie for the heartfelt support and assistance. Your help has been so very much appreciated. Also to two cats named Yin and Yang who are Ambassadors from Consciousness, bringing harmony and balance to all who come into contact with them.

To Kim and all the wonderful people at The Balanced Body Spa, who work so very hard to bring peace and harmony to all that walk through their door. This Spa is truly a positive energy zone and is an oasis in a desert of unconsciousness.

Introduction

How to Free Your Self and Get Your Life Back

'The mass of men lead lives of quiet desperation." Henry David
Thoreau

The intent in this book is to keep meditation as simple as
possible so that the average person can use the practice to gain
self awareness. Since self awareness and mindfulness are the
states of consciousness to be realized, it is important to not
have too many "rules" or "instructions" to cloud the path to
realization. And most importantly, do not feed ego whether it
is yours or mine.

This book is written by an ordinary guy who found a way to
get his life back. This is just a guy attempting to live the
American dream. And like so many Americans, the attempts at
the dream are what got him into so much trouble. Some years
ago, I found myself in a self destructive pattern that led to a
miserable life and a final melt down. At middle age one day I
realized that I was broke, chronically ill, miserable and
contemplating some type of end to it all. Through years of
insight meditation and self awareness I came to understand the
nature of my self destruction.

When I had finally suffered enough and caused the suffering of
others, the time for change was realized. My former existence
was transformed into something extra ordinary. Because I was
ready to listen, ready to commit to change, the right teachers
and the right lessons appeared on my path. Finding balance
and harmony, I now reach out to others who are seeking a way
out and feel they have run out of options. My message is that if
an ordinary person like me can find balance and harmony, then
so can you. It is never too late to start.

The journey of waking up and remaining awake has been a
process. There have been set backs and failures. However,
being committed, I stayed with this new path until I realized

inner peace. There has been a lot of research and exploration which is not something most people would devote themselves to. Part of this success is due to what one of my psychology friends describes as "intellectual sensation seeking". Intellectual sensation seeking is still just another form of chasing a desire, yet in balance, it helps lead to wisdom instead of misery. Transcendence is not a term commonly used in the Heart of Dixie which is where I grew up and currently live. Nor is it a common concept with many other residents in this modern culture. Everyday folks from all over do understand about waking up in the middle of the night unable to sleep due to common worries of all people. Many millions of us, where ever we are, experience heartache and longing. Unless we are able to awaken to be our true authentic self, it is inevitable that we will find ourselves searching.

Perhaps you find yourself at an intersection or crossroad in your life. Or perhaps your path is fairly smooth and you are not seeking relief but a deeper understanding. Sometimes when we are relatively free from problems we have an opportunity to sense that there is something greater going on in the background yet we are not quite able to bring it into focus.

How to use this book

This book is written in an easy conversational tone. The chapters have been arranged in such a way that the reader may pick out behaviors that they would like to change. To find specific problem areas, please use the index at the back of the book. As you will come to understand in the chapter on ego, many of us have very little patience and want instant gratification. This will probably mean that you will skip over everything and go straight to the chapter that relates to your problem area. However, I strongly recommend that you read the chapters on Self Awareness and Ego first. Then you can go directly to the chapter that describes your problem area. These are insights for realizing change as it pertains to a particular behavior or issue. Each specific insight is there to help you realize what you are doing and why you are doing it. These insights overlap each other and each supports the other. So if you are not inclined to read this book from cover to cover, try reading the first couple of chapters and then go directly to your particular area of non harmony. You may feel inclined to read other areas to help reach further understanding.

This book is an attempt to create a guide that the western mind can identify with or relate to. Individuals from the Far East, have been studying, practicing and developing these spiritual practices for thousands of years. Most of those cultures absorbed and embraced this form of spirituality way back in history, and thus each view or concept has evolved in a separate thread. So there are many variations. There are many monks, gurus, yogi's, priests, scholars and experts who all feel that their understanding is the one that works best. Here is but one voice from an everyday guy in our modern culture.

I am the first to tell you that I am no expert. Well, maybe I am an expert on how to get your life messed up by living the life of ego. Yet, I hope you can learn from my mistakes and enjoy a life as I have learned to experience. Here in the south we have a saying that goes like this. "Even a blind hog can find an acorn every once in a while". So even a stumbling bumpkin like yours truly find his true path. It can be so very simple, but it can take a lot of work letting go of old habits and behaviors. You will learn that will power comes from acceptance. Acceptance is very hard to practice on a momentary basis. So is patience, yet if you can bring these into balance, you can transform your life. This book is not about becoming a Saint or a Buddha; this is about just bringing your life into balance. While enlightenment is a worthy goal, it may be better to just work on some of the big problems first. If you can learn to be happy moment by moment, the enlightenment will take care of itself. In this book you can learn that when you are awake and aware, you have created the space for choice. In wisdom you can choose a path that leads to balance. Balance is a very special unity where the sum is greater than the parts. This is living your true self in a true authentic life. This is true living.

This book is a gathering of various insights by various teachers that are a lot wiser than I am. In truth you may not be ready for these teachings. It may be that more misery is in order, so that you finally are willing to listen and change. However if your life is a mess, then you might be ready to allow balance and harmony to return. Being ready, means that you can set aside the impatient part of your mind, and the skeptical part of your mind long enough to allow awareness to open up new possibilities. Being ready means that you, that is the authentic you, the higher self you, is ready and able to embrace choice. Being ready means that you are willing to be honest and accept things as they are and to become your true self ...again. It means that a part of you is willing to transcend to become a spiritual being. It is the willingness to change from old habits and thoughts, and to let them go. Being ready will make it possible to realize choice. It is a choice of infinite possibilities that awaits you. Not being ready, is to be lost to that part of the mind which refuses choice, through an unwillingness to see all of the possibilities that are before each and every one of us.

If you are not ready to face your moment of truth, then put this book back on the dusty bookshelf or sell it or give it away. Being honest with our higher self is an absolute must and nothing will change until we embrace self honesty.

If you choose to return to the unconsciousness of ego and the materialistic path, then you are not ready and must suffer more. But try to remember this book just in case you do become ready to awaken to your true purpose and life. Try to remember there was some guy from Georgia saying that there is way to untangle the knotted life that you may find your "self" in. When (not if) life becomes a steam roller, and you feel that you have suffered enough, then find this book.

So, dear reader, are you ready? If so, then let us get started on the path to infinite possibilities and a truly amazing life.

Free Your Self

"What is necessary to change a person is to change his awareness of himself." Abraham Maslow, Psychologist 1907 – 1970

We will all have a moment of truth. For many people it is the rare occasion when something is either so very good or so very bad that we stop and become in tune with reality. That moment of truth is as unavoidable as your next breath. It can be the defining moment of your life. It may be the moment you experienced a birth. It may be the moment you experienced a death. It may be the moment of love's first kiss or it may be the first time you experienced a significant lie. Whatever the circumstances, it is one of the rare moments we become fully awake and experience life with the psyche fully engaged.

The message in this book is that life does not have to be so complicated and filled with stress. We do not have to wait for one of those rare moments of truth to wake up and set our compass in the right direction. This book is about realizing that every moment is a moment of truth. The authentic life is the living in one continuous moment of truth. The truth is that life is simple and joy is abundant when we can awaken from the unconsciousness of dwelling in a materialistic world.

This is the original truth. The teaching of this truth predates recorded history and has been taught from culture to culture over the eons. It is just as true today as it was in its original understanding. We, as modern humans have forgotten who we are. We have forgotten that we are in essence spiritual beings having a physical experience. In every generation of every century, humans become lost in the pursuit of the next thing. Humans have forgotten how to live. Life has been replaced with a type of waking unconsciousness that cannot satisfy an insatiable hunger. Life has become the journey of desire fulfillment, and living has been postponed until the desire is met. In this dead zone we become addicted to the fulfillment of desire and we come to know suffering and unhappiness.

The spiritual beings that we are can become lost to the superficial sense of the faux self. Our identity as our authentic self is lost. Our true sense of self is imprisoned and our identity is taken over by the false sense of self and that is where everything becomes complicated and we lose our peace. Our authentic self is pushed into the dungeon of unconsciousness and is so grounded in ego that we forget who we are.

It is not supposed to be this way. We are supposed to be happy, fun loving people living simple lives of abundance. As a species and as members of the human society, we have forgotten what normal is and have come to accept the most outrageous of behaviors as no big deal. We actually entertain ourselves watching misery and drama unfolding in other parts of the city, country or world. We kid ourselves into thinking we are the most advanced sentient species on the planet. Yet unlike any other we cannot refrain from killing each other.

If you are living a life of misery at any level, and you are ready to change, then this book is for you. If you have had a moment of truth and are choosing to remain awake and aware, this book is for you. If you are ready to free your "self" from the unconscious path that the others are going down then this book is for you. This moment of truth is for you. In this moment it is time to free your "self". This is done through meditation, self awareness and the practice of mindfulness. Read on dear reader and welcome to your true life.

The Self (true self vs. ego self)

"Be vigilant ana guara mina against negative thoughts"

Form is not self. Ij form were the self, this form woula not lena itselj to disease"

The Buddha

"The sincere aspect of who you are" S beasley

Who are you?

Early on in the exploration of self, the question gets asked. Who are you? At this juncture it is best to simply discuss who you are not. Self awareness is self discovery. There are many wonderful aspects or components.

You are not:

You are not your thoughts. Thoughts fall into the tool category.

You are not your name. That is what you are called.

You are not your job. That is what you are paid to do.

You are not your many roles. You role may be a Father, Mother, Wife, Husband, Friend, Mentor, but these are just roles. They are not who you are.

You are not the identity that ego has you to be at this particular moment. Ego is always changing identities and if you are ego then you are illusion.

If you are not any of these identities who are you?

This is a self discovery that you must undertake. It is not an answer that this book will hand over to you. So let's put the "Who Are You?" question aside for now and begin the process of rediscovering your true self.

Being just a guy and not a Buddha or Psychologist, I just try to keep things sort of simple and focus on the two basics of self. Those would be the authentic or higher self and a sub entity, the lower self. Our eternal spiritual core that is ever present but often not realized or ignored, is the authentic self. Most of life's' "problems" are encountered by the lower self also known by many as "ego".

Most people who have not awakened are experiencing life as a physical being that has a temporary identity know as ego. This plane of existence is defined by material terms and aspects of the ego (lower self). This identity is based on and defined by memories and experiences. Somewhere in early childhood enough memories of experiences have been accumulated and a kind of critical mass develops. This critical mass begins the self sustaining identity known as ego. Who we are becomes defined as our auto-biographical identity. We become identified with our experiences. As we get older and accumulate more experiences we form a stronger identity. When someone asks who you are, you begin to fill in the blanks based on what you have been told and what you have experienced. Along the way, the ego, which is always judging will define these life experiences as good or bad. Each experience is labeled depending on how ego feels about it. For those who live a strictly materialistic existence, this is their reality.

Quality of life is defined by how ego judges life experiences to be. Moment by moment, day by day, and year by year, layer after layer of definition is laid down. Moment by moment we make minute decisions in life that directs us along our path. Each decision is based upon previous life experiences which become the determining factor for all things. Each decision creates a cause that will mature into effect down the path. Course changes along the path are made based on the previous experience and result. After years of coping with the experiences we deem either good or bad, we become conditioned. Conditioning is like being on auto-pilot, where decisions are made unconsciously or in the back ground where we pay very little attention. We end up being and doing things without even thinking about it. We know many of these as habits. Habits are the conditioning for cause and effect. Good habits can lead to good effects, and bad habits can lead to undesirable results. Feelings and mood can be a result of conditioning and many times define the quality of each day regardless that one day is pretty much like other days when observed from beyond ego.

This conditioning, is part of the motive behind the phrase "we are what we think about." We create our reality based on what we are thinking and how we define events as they rise. This thinking reality based on conditioning is an illusion. One has to understand that it has been created by living within a false identity of ego, and that it is possible to wake up and be your true self or higher self or spiritual self. You are not your thoughts, emotions or feelings. The aspect of the self that associates identity with the history of experiences and the roles it has in social structure calls itself "me." It is the lower self known as ego. Ego's sense of existence is based solely on its self story. The accumulation of life experiences can make up an auto-biography that may compel you to believe that this is who you are. You may even feel that without the memory of those experiences, you would not exist.

Once a student told me that without memories they would not exist.

I asked, "Who would not exist?"

The student answered, "Me". "I would not exist".

I asked, "Can you not observe your own memories?"

The student thought about it for a moment and said, "Without memory, there is no me".

I asked, "If you developed amnesia, would you not still exist?"

The student answered "no, that 'me' would not be here

anymore".

This dialogue is good at getting your mind working on the concept of "I" and "me" and the higher self. For some it is quite difficult to conceptualize being without the concept of "me". Yet it is this identity which can cause so much confusion. As is sometimes the case, there was no success in drawing the distinction of being that which observes the memories, the higher self, and the memories for which the lower self, or ego finds existence.

What needs to be understood is that there is the higher self that observes all things even the memories. Your memories are not the higher self, or your authentic self, they are just memories. People with amnesia who cannot remember their past do not stop existing, they just lose their ego identifying memories. Life goes on and they start over with new memories. The consciousness that observes never left and never leaves. And that is your higher and eternal self. Read the chapter on ego for an in depth look at this aspect of "me".

So if we are not our thoughts, emotions, and all of the other descriptions that arise, then who are we? We are the Knower. Different cultures and belief systems attach various labels such as spirit, soul, higher self, pure consciousness and the many definitions of God as a name of our true being. Try not to get caught up in right or wrong here. That would be a function of ego and you will come to understand that futility later. Right now just take a look at what is being shared here without judgment. Just consider that there may be another aspect of our "self" that we have lost connection with. Identity is a funny thing really. There is some human (ego) need to place all things, under a label and identity as this or that. As far as any of us know this is strictly a human characteristic and a feature of higher egoic function. Self-awareness in this book means being detached from ego and the obsession with identity and just being. Self awareness is the waking up from the illusion of ego and being pure consciousness. Self awareness is becoming unchained by the content or details that define the egoic identity and becoming the observer and the knower.

Self Awareness is the true realization of being. It is an understanding that we are not all of those labels that we attach too and define as our life. While it is true that aspects of our life may have a momentary truth and help place us in the society in which we dwell, they are just features that are perceived. The adjectives that describe our existence to others are a convenience that other minds can use for categorization. It makes for useful conversation and discernment between individuals. The mind perceives but the discernment of the content in perception is where things go awry. In awareness (higher or true self) a person is not attached to definition. Opposite to this, ego is addicted to content and judgment is always made to be good or bad. Reality is manifested based on which entity is in control. So whatever aspect of your mind has control over the definition of perception also has control over your identity. Your true identity is that as a spiritual being.

If you can concede that you are a spiritual being, you can begin to *know* that this physical experience is but a transient moment in infinity. The wisdom of sages teaches us that we are just spiritual beings having a physical experience. It is important to begin to realize that many if not most of us have become lost in a material orientation of the world as we perceive it. The agent of materialism is the sub-entity of your personality called ego.

A shift in identity has to take place. Many inappropriate behaviors are sourced in the egoic entity. No debt reduction plan, no diet plan, no change can take place unless you can get control of this aspect of the self. If it is the ego that makes the decision to change, it will not happen, because ego has a much different agenda than the true self.

The true self is the pure orientation. I am reluctant to say that it is who we truly are because it reverts back to identity. Identity needs quantifiers to establish existence. Pure consciousness needs no quantifiers because it is the source for all things. Ego can still play a necessary role in how we interact with each other and how we chose to perceive. Yet ego must be kept under control and managed. Life would be pretty weird if we decided to speak without using the term "me" and "I". It would especially be boring if we dismissed all emotions and lived a determined life of neutrality. The dichotomy does play a role in defining good from bad and contentedness from misery. So a healthy balance with moderation is the key to a less problematic life. This is quite doable.

Being oriented with the true self, the higher aspects of love and compassion become the direction to which we can point our moral compass. Instead of finding purpose within the framework of materialism and sensation seeking, we can really enjoy the simple things in life. Life is best enjoyed when unified with balance and harmony.

Being aligned with pure consciousness is being aligned with all there is. It is a knowing that all things are connected and that separation is illusion and ignorance. Being detached from ego is to become in tune with the universe. It means realizing that we are the universe. This is heady stuff and at this moment your ego is probably rejecting it as too much. This notion may conflict with your brand of religion whose rules only allow specific beliefs. All I can ask is that you see how that is working for you. Look into your heart, that is, become in alignment with your definition of God and know what your truth is. Being in alignment is being balanced and in harmony with all things. It is the putting aside of "me" (ego) and just being.

Some people are more materialistic than others. The most conservative view is that the only thing real is that which we can touch, feel and manipulate. At the other end is the view that all things are metaphysical. True awareness or pure consciousness transcends all of this and the being perceives things as they really are. It just depends on where you place your self and what you believe. Your belief shapes your reality. If there has not been a shift in the realization of who you really are then you are still a prisoner of ego. Life will always be defined as a series of struggling with problems.

Exercise

If you are having a hard time de-identifying with content in your life then try this exercise to draw the distinction between the observer (true self) and the observed.

Take a moment to sit quietly then focus you attention on how you are feeling. Now simply explore your feelings. If you are not feeling anything special, remember the last bout of demonstrative feelings that you had. This exercise may be more revealing if you recall negative feelings or are experiencing negative feelings.

Notice any detail about the feelings, emotions, memories or thoughts involved with these feelings. Now consider, which part of me is observing those feelings. Notice that while observing, we are not that which we observe. The observer is the subject and that which is being observed is the object. These feelings and emotions are what is being observed and not the observer which is your true self. It is important to realize this misidentification. We are not our feelings. When we realize this, we can realize that choice is available. Can you now imagine what it would be like to be able to be free of immobilizing emotions and feelings? This is the power of self awareness. With practice we can begin to choose how we want to feel. The greater the grounding in self awareness the greater control we can have. It is not necessary to become non feeling gurus to transform our lives. As everyday people, we can transform our lives by assuming some non-attachment to the myriad of thoughts and emotions that surface in the egoic mind. In Meditation, we become aware of our true self. This is the first and most important step in being able to free your "self".

Self Awareness

"Everything that irritates us about others can lead us to an understanding of ourselves".   Carl Jung

What is the self awareness?

Self awareness is defined differently across various cultures, religions, spiritual paths and the academia of psychology. I am going to define Self Awareness as realizing your "self" as the observer in all things. Self awareness is being conscious. Being unconscious is the state where we are lost in the mind stream of ego. Our physical existence or life as we know it, has two aspects. There is the authentic self or true self and the lower or egoic self. The authentic self is the essential being that you are at your spiritual core. It is your essential being, the knower and the observer. It is your eternal spirit that is joined with the tapestry of all things and especially life. The true self is your true identity. The opposite of your true self is the lower self also known as the egoic self or just plan ego. Ego is the false identify that forms as life experiences become memory. Ego and thoughts are temporal and form as the physical experience follows the path of time's arrow. The chapter on Ego will go into great detail of how this mind entity can capture your identity and assume command.

In the chapter on Meditation, transcendence is discussed as the rising above or moving beyond the identity of thought. Specifically, transcendence is the awakening from the domain of ego and into self realization. This waking up and realizing the true or authentic self is transcendence to self awareness. To be fully alive is to be fully conscious and aware as a living being. As you will learn in the chapter on ego, the opposite of being in a state of pure awareness is to lapse into a type of waking unconsciousness. I call it a waking unconsciousness because even though the lights are on, nobody is home. The eyes may be open but the attention has been absorbed by the stream of thought.

To keep things as simple as possible it will be easiest to just consider the basics of sentient life. This living being that you identify as "me" can get up and go to a mirror and correlate the image in the mirror with the being that you *feel* "inside. This is a very basic sense of self awareness.

Ancient sages teach us that complete transcendence is pure consciousness. Pure awareness is a state of consciousness which even transcends the living body. The concept is that pure awareness or pure consciousness is spirit and that which remains aware even after the death of the body. It could be considered to be joined with the continuum of the mind and together this pure consciousness survives the physical body. I will leave it up to your religion or spiritual path to define what is experienced after the dissolving of your physical body. That is a subject for great debate. This book is about being in the here and now as a living being. It is about transcending time and living in the moment. In the chapter about the illusion of time we will look at the present up close and personal. Hopefully you will come to understand that the present moment, the now, is all there really is and all we ever really have. The present moment is eternal as is our true self.

Self awareness is being awake and aware (conscious) in the present moment. For beginners this may be a fleeting experience. Yet with practice we can learn to transcend or to wake up from being unconscious and experience life in ways never before known. In self awareness or awareness of the true self, we can observe and manage the lower self. Ego is the dominant presence of the lower self and assumes dominant control for the unconscious person. In this unconscious state, identity is known only through identifying through memory (your autobiography) and those stored away experiences. In ego, your life story becomes you. In the higher consciousness of pure being and the observer, we realize that we are not our memories. Memories are just experiences that have been stored in the organic brain. As the observer we are not them. You are the observer and memories are the observed. In alignment as the observer, we are transcended from being identified by the experiences in memory. Since memories and experience shape our behavior, our false identity is defined by the mind entity known as ego. In ego, reality is defined as good or bad as it is compared to previous experiences. When we leave the false identity to become our higher and true self, that ego identification and meanings no longer apply. In this transcended state of non ego, we are just being. This is our spiritual core, or our true self.

In the fully conscious state of being in the true self, the higher self, we can learn to manage ego and create balance. Not being self aware is to be lost in ego where one dwells under the illusion that you, your identity and reality are defined solely by feelings and thoughts.

A life that experiences problems is one where all events perceived are defined strictly by ego. Problems are created by two aspects of unconsciousness. One is Ego identification and the other is being fettered in mindstream. As any given event arises, the mind perceives information through the senses. Thinking processes the information through the various centers. Ego, the dominate aspect of the lower self will give it emotional meaning based on previous memories of life experiences. When life is experienced or filtered through ego, reality becomes heavily influenced if not imprisoned in this one domain. This sense of "Me" becomes who you think you are. This identity forms slowly over time beginning in infancy. It is the biography you build by each experience. Each moment of perception becomes part of the experience, and each experience becomes a layer as we develop identity. We build up layer after layer. This identity builds along with it. It develops the identity of who you *think* you are. Along with this identify are the survival strategies which get layered down into behaviors. Many if not most become automatic and unconscious. We are unaware of what we are doing and why we are doing it. To become aware and observe and pay attention to what is going on both internally and externally is to be fully conscious. This is the state of meditation and self awareness. Since we cannot spend all of our time sitting on a cushion or sitting in a chair we must learn to carry our state of awareness into the business of living. We can learn to remain awake and aware as we go about our lives. This balance of being awake and aware of what we are doing no matter why we are doing, it is known as mindfulness. This balance of being awake and paying attention to what we are doing and why we are doing it is where the rubber meets the road. See the chapter on mindfulness.

You are not your thoughts.

As mentioned, we are not our memories. It is just as important to realize that we are not our thoughts. So what are thoughts? Dictionaries define thought as the product of mental activity. Ok let us go with thoughts being mental activity of the brain. In the brain neurons are firing along neural networks. Words appear in the mind expressing feelings and ideas. These powers of the mind or capabilities are faculties that help to make up the many working parts. They are tools for the higher self or consciousness to perceive through. So if we are not our thoughts then what are we? We are beings. We are consciousness observing the thoughts and other parts of the self. This means we are not our experiences, we are not our memories, we are not our eyes, and we are not our ears, or our name or our occupation. We just are. We are beings. We are beings that transcend identity. Collectively we differentiate ourselves as unique specie of being we have named as human. As human beings we have the unique ability to become aware of ourselves as a separate from others of our kind. We also have the capacity to transcend the living unconsciousness and to realize the higher self or pure awareness or pure consciousness.

There is a lot of dialogue and debate about whether humans are alone in their uniqueness of obtaining self awareness. There is no real tangible way *to know*. That is a debate and discussion for a different book at a different time. The knowing that all animals have awareness is the basis for many who are vegan and vegetarian. Those whose compassion includes all creatures are passionate about not causing suffering to any animal or creature.

Who are you?

In my meditation class, I ask the students the question of "Who are you"? Their homework assignment that week is to contemplate that question. I tell them that whatever they come up with, that is probably not it. The exercise is to help them realize the illusion that they think they are the things they identify with. This false identity is at the heart of the illusion.

When one contemplates this question, the first and obvious answers arrive.

My name is Sam. I am Sam

I am a male.

I am a Meditation and Tai Chi Instructor

I am a husband

I am a Dad

I am so many years old.

I am this and I am that.

Notice the "I" (with a capital I) in this thinking. There you can see the function of identity at work. This begs the question of who is this "I". The answer to that is that it is the controlling authority we referred to earlier called Ego. See the chapter on Ego.

Meanwhile, if we are not our thoughts then who are we? What are we?

As mentioned earlier we are the original and essential being, the true self. There are ways to get a glimpse of this perceiving and existing. Let's take dreaming for example. If you are able to remember your dream experience, consider who it is that is observing the dream. That part of you that is observing is not the dream itself, but the observer. You are not the experience, you are the experiencer.

When you recall a memory, and can replay it in your mind, that part of you that is observing is not the memory. The memory is not awareness yet it comes into awareness for your true self to observe. The memory is not you (true self). It is just a recording of an experience. When memory is allowed to be the identity, that is to say, when a being identifies themselves as the memories they have stored, they are living in a sense of false identity. Memories are just data. As a spiritual being you are not data, you just are.

By being lost in thought is to become unaware. I call this continuous and incessant flow of thoughts and feeling as *mindstream*. Mindstream can be considered to be like a stream of water moving along with the arrow of time. Depending on how much the mind has been stimulated, the mindstream might be a lazy pool one day and then a raging torrent the next. See the example of driving the car while unconscious in the chapter on balance and harmony.

In mindstream, thoughts, feelings and perceptions are a continuous flow across the surface of our consciousness. For most our waking lives we are completely captivated inside this state. Being completely captivated by it becomes our prison. We think that this is all there is. Imagine growing up in a single structure with only a few windows. The only thing you might know is what little occurs within that domain. There is a strict limit on what can be perceived. Reality becomes defined by only what you sense in front of you.

Your identity would then be defined by your experiences from within that prison. Your identity is defined only by what you can gain through thought.

Or another analogy would be when one is lost in the torrent of the raging waters of mindstream. Carried away by mindstream and the flood of thoughts and emotions, we either feel like we have no choices or the choices are severely limited.

Self Awareness is the waking up from the unconsciousness of mindstream and realizing that the identity through thought is an illusion. Now do not get me wrong, having an identity and plenty of adjectives to describe your physical trappings to others is a necessity. So don't freak out. I am not saying you are to cut your hair off and join a monastery. What I am saying is that when we become completely absorbed in this illusion, an imbalance is created.

When one is able to detach from the river of thought, one can experience transcendence. This is when we enter the state of being. Being is the observer. Being is awareness. Being is the higher self or the soul or spirit. Being is infinite, eternal and unlimited. As described before, becoming self aware is an awakening.

Meditation is the transcendence into self awareness. The *practice* of meditation is the doing activity that detaches your higher self from mindstream or it could be considered that it creates a space for self awareness to arise. There are numerous techniques for detaching from mindstream. These techniques use a focal point of awareness to pull out of thought and become ultimately pure observer or pure consciousness. I use the word ultimately, because meditation takes practice. It is hard work. It may be the hardest thing that you ever tried to do. In the chapter on Meditation, you will come to understand the distinction between Meditation and the practice of Meditation. Many people fail when they are not ready to commit to the practice. Yet those who have had enough, and have suffered enough, realize on some level that this is the only way out of the prison of thought.

The best technique is the one that works for you. The one that can help diffuse the mindstream enough that a space between the thoughts becomes apparent. It is in this space that awareness arises. With practice, the space become larger, that is, awareness becomes greater and broader. The more awareness is allowed to unfold the greater the ability (not an adequate word) to perceive more insights about the true nature

20

of things. To fully transcend into awareness is to become fully enlightened. I am of the belief that enlightenment is a matter of degree of balancing states of being and doing. It seem that the further along the path [to enlightenment] one is, the more enlightened they become. The more enlightened (wise) you become the less suffering you will experience.

But enough about enlightenment right now. Right here and right now, there is plenty of work to do to untangle the knots. Constantly striving for enlightenment can be a function of ego and a trap that beginners can fall into.

It is better to start with simple steps and work on one issue at a time. The more you practice the better it gets.

Because this concept of self awareness and that you are not your thoughts is so complex, the practice at first is kind of redundant. In my classes, I approach it from different directions over and over so that over time and with practice it will begin to gain cohesion. You will see that the different aspects all overlap each other.

Most people reach a point where they are either suffering or they are feeling unfulfilled. Their lifelong pursuit of sensation seeking and seeking distraction has brought them to a point of life dysfunction. They may be considering suicide or just simply cannot find authentic fulfillment. Eventually the misery gets to a point where something needs to be done. They reach their moment of truth. It is one of those cross roads that people eventually arrive at. Usually they are suffering from some type of imbalance and are making an effort to sort it out. Usually they have tried other things that did not work long term. They are unconsciously searching for their authentic self. Their egoic life is just not working. Hoping to find answers, they give meditation a try. As each student has the experience of these insights I watch their internal battle between ego and consciousness and wonder where it will end up. Will they wake up and find their authentic self? Will the wonder and beauty of a true life be realized? Or will their need of sensation seeking or distraction take over and they become lost in the world of thought and doing again. There is this point where you will reach a moment of truth when it comes forth and you will have a glimpse of awareness and how simple and wonderful life really is. Or as the moment of truth passes, the powerful ego resurfaces and finds meditation boring, too hard, and not thrilling enough. Having read this far into the book is a good sign. At least ego has not put it aside and gone looking for some other unconscious pursuit.

More often than not, the power of ego and unconsciousness prevails. I am frequently told by students that they are dropping out of meditation and the message is that they do not have time. But sometimes I can see the light go on and the being in front of me begins the awakening process. Sometimes it is because they were able to use one of the techniques to remain asleep all night. A full night or even better a full week of good sleep is transforming in itself. Or many times the relaxation technique is very helpful in helping them relax. Somewhere inside they remember what feeling good feels like and they want more of it. Sometimes the moment of truth arrives with a short experience of the true self. All it takes is a glimpse and you will be changed forever. For a moment you see how it is all connected. In a timeless moment of perception you are at one with the universe. You sense your place in this wonderful tapestry and understand how it all works together. After that, it just becomes a matter of getting back there. And that is meditation.

The first big milestone is when people really understand that they can chose how they feel. That was a big one for me. The day it sunk in that "you mean I don't have to feel this way?" was like lifting a 200lb weight off of my shoulders. I was sick and tired of feeling sick and tired. I was absolutely done with the cycle of fear, anger, explosion and depression. I hated myself for many reasons, but mostly for abusing and hurting others. I knew that deep down inside there was a good me. The "me" that was before I became the jerk looking at me in the mirror. I hated myself, and I feared that that I could not change.

The moment I realized, and by that I mean I realized with a sincere knowing, that I had a choice of how I could feel and act was a supreme moment of truth. This was my first insight. I realized this insight because I was able to see my egoic behavior from the perspective of awareness. After practicing meditation long enough that I was able grasp that there was this space that my higher self could reside in. In this space I could realize the power of choice. I grabbed onto that like a drowning swimmer does to a life ring. In this now, people who know me are quite shocked when I describe the old "me". In truth I was never that "me", but I was imprisoned by the false identity of "me". That false identity of ego even had me believing that was who I was. It even argued that this mean aggressive, let's kick some ass character was good. My kids called this behavior going "Wal-Mart" because of a meltdown in a Wal-Mart one day.

Here is the important part. Being self aware of the emotions beginning to arise in the continuum of the mind, allowed me to remain detached from those behaviors. It allowed me the choice of 'if' or 'how' I might respond to any given situation. Over time and with practice I came to realize that more often than not, no action at all was needed. Or if action was required, there are often many options to choose from. I cannot express in words how empowering that choice is. Being aware is to experience the power of choice. Being able to choose is one of the most powerful and enlightening aspects of self awareness. It just never dawned on me that it was possible to choose to let negative emotions go. If you are suffering in some emotional bondage right now, can you imagine that you can break those chains and allow joy to arise spontaneously, independent of what is going on around you? It is not easy but it can be done. This is transforming in the truest sense. This might be your first insight. This is the insight of choice.

In the previous chapter on the self we practiced the exercise of discerning between the observer and the observed. Here is an exercise to help further that state of consciousness by becoming aware.

Exercise

Part one. Recall the last time you drove a car or truck. Note how and where the mind went when you had that experience. Now recall how after you got the car in motion, your mind began to wander off. Typically you probably were lost in mind stream and your thoughts far away. So there you were, driving a 2500 to 3500 vehicle among other heavy steel vehicles oblivious to what you were doing. This is being unconscious and absorbed by mindstream. Every traffic cop or highway patrolman can recite how many people die each year because they were not "paying attention". Being self aware while driving means that instead of being lost in mindstream, you (your higher self) would be paying very close attention to what you are doing and why you are doing it. Did you stop at red lights and stop signs? How do you know? In one sense the focus on driving becomes a practice in mindfulness. Being mindful of how your attention wanders away, you bring it back to the here and now to be fully alert and aware of what is going on.

Part Two. Take a short trip in your car or truck. Rather than allow your mind to wander away, make sure to pay very special attention to where you are moment by moment. Note important detail about how the vehicle is performing. How fast are you going? What and who is around you in traffic? Turn off distractions that might hinder your practice of paying attention. Things like talk radio or cell phones can cause you to be completely lost to where you are and what you doing.

Self Awareness is never far away. However since most of us are not monks and cannot spend our lives in meditation we must find a way to live our active lives yet keep self awareness close by. This is done by the practice of mindfulness. In the chapter on mindfulness we will discuss how to remain in a state of awareness as you navigate your waking life.

We should practice self awareness as if our life depended on it. In the case of driving our car it makes complete sense to do so.

Being self aware is the living of life and paying attention to it. Anything else is just being lost in distraction and avoiding life because it is too boring or not sensational enough. To be able to change our behaviors and conditioning we must first become self aware. In awareness we can observe and know what we are doing and why we are doing it. You must first become aware to free your "self".

The Mind

"Age is an issue of mind over matter. If you don't mind, it doesn't matter. "
Mark Twain

As I sit here and write this, there is a person pacing up and down the side walk across the street talking very loudly to himself. To the outside world his utterances are nonsense. This fellow is a regular in the neighborhood and I no longer even get up to see what the commotion is about. Now I hear him shouting away at his demons and know who and what it is. He is one of the homeless in our area, lost in his own world. Our first reaction is to label somcone like that as crazy or insane. Yet with a little introspection maybe we are all not so different.

Once during a Dharma teaching I was attending, our teacher gave us a homework assignment. She said that one way to become aware of all the crazy thoughts that continuously come to the surface of our mind, is to imagine a loud speaker on top of your head. Imagine every thought being broadcast to the world where all could hear. This wonderful insight revealed that the only difference between my egoic mind and the guy across the street was that his thoughts were out loud and vocal while mine were kept secret. So just imagine if your thoughts were being verbalized out loud all of the time. The very narrow margin of vocalizing and just letting the mind bounce around quietly inside is a very fine one indeed. In fact how long has it been since you last talked to yourself? Think about it and ask who was talking to whom? My point is that the egoic mind bounces around like a football. It can be and often is chaotic. So for many of us there may be only a matter of degrees of separation between normal and not normal. If our stream of thoughts were broadcast out loud we might be classed as a lunatic.

So what is the mind? I am not going to get caught up in any of the debates about whether the mind is in the brain or existing everywhere. For now let's just say it is the realm where perceptions arise. The things we can perceive are observed as they come to the surface. It may be data provided by the senses, it may be data by other processing aspects of the mind that handle problem solving. It may be emotional content. It is all to be observed on the surface. Below the surface of the mind is the dark realm of the subconscious. A typical state of awareness can only realize a small percentage of what is taking place on and in the mind so a lot is going on that we are not aware of.

The insight here is to understand that all phenomena being perceived on the mind is something that is observed. Self awareness is being aware of what is playing out on the surface of the mind without being absorbed by it. Remember in the chapter on the Self, the question was asked who are you? There was discussion on what you are not. And here the same question gets answered by stating you are not your thoughts. You are not the content being observed, you are the observer.

The mind can be observed to be in states or conditions. States of mind can change suddenly or slowly depending on conditions. This conditioning occurs gradually over life experience and as we become absorbed by this conditioning of the mind, it becomes who we think we are. Since most of us are never taught to remain aware of our true self, the conditioning takes over and assumes our identity. This is the prison of the ego identity (see the chapter on Ego) in which we live our lives absorbed in whatever is occupying the mind. We forget who and what we really are and we become identified to the emotional conditioning of our life experiences. So trapped in this mental state, with whatever is playing out on the mind, we are forced to live it.

It does not have to be this way. In awareness, we observe the functions of the mind and remain unattached to its state. One way we can do that is by taking control of meaning. When the higher self is self realized our consciousness is no longer absorbed by the thoughts of egoic thought stream. This is an important insight to realize.

In meditation, the person lets go of the attachment of thought stream through self realization and identifies as the observer and the knower. More specifically, in meditation we can anchor ourselves in awareness by use of focal points and each time we begin to be absorbed by the mind we can pull ourselves back into awareness. When we are lost within the mindstream of emotions and desire we are no longer observing but have been absorbed by this lower aspect of self. Events arise in the mind, and the first reaction of the unconscious mind is to judge the event and give it meaning. (See the chapter on Judgment). All meaning becomes based on painful or happy memories of the past. *Emotional* response becomes the criteria for meaning. Conditioning is the mindset that sets in to form behavior. It does not take long in life for behavior to start forming habits which affect decision making. By the time we reach adulthood, we are doing things without being aware of it. The alternative is that we can develop self awareness where we observe those events without being absorbed. We can exercise choice because we are no longer controlled by conditioned behaviors. We can have a lot more control over our emotional responses because we remain unattached.

It does not matter if you broadcast the crazy or inappropriate thoughts of mindstream outside and vocally or just let them bounce around inside, it can drive you crazy. All you have to do is to open the newspaper or turn on the news and you can see just how crazy people really are. Reality should not and need not be experienced in this unconscious manner. We don't have to inflict nor experience so much anguish and disorder. This book is about making the shift from being lost in continuous mindstream to being awake and aware. You are not your thoughts. Thoughts work for you and are there to be observed. Breaking the chains that bind us to thought and mindstream is necessary to free your "self".

Ego (It's all about me)

Every normal person, in fact, is only normal on the average. His ego approximates to that of the psychotic in some part or other and to a greater or lesser extent. Sigmund Freud

You are not your Ego. As discussed in Self Awareness and Mindfulness, ego is the culprit that causes so much mischief. So who and what is this Ego (that is ego with a capital M for [me])

Ego is the portion of the mind or the self that gives perspective of identity. Ego specifically establishes the individual self from other parts that make up the aggregate self. It is a necessary component, otherwise our species might congregate in hives and become like bees. Pure awareness is your higher self and Ego is the lower self. When Ego assumes control, identity problems arise. This is a very important distinction.

As events arise and are perceived by the mind two things can happen. They can both simply be observed and discerned without unnecessary meaning or they can be judged according to emotion and life experience and be labeled as good or bad. The dichotomy of good and bad is a very limited perspective. It precludes the infinity of possibility that can be accessed through awareness. Ego is the sub-self entity which assumes the responsibility of determining if things are good or bad. Ego experiences life as good or bad. It is obsessed with sensation seeking (good) or distraction seeking (bad). When it becomes attached to that which is perceived as good it believes that happiness resides in only experiencing "good" things. This can be observed when the words "I'll be happy when…" come out of the mouth of ego. In Ego, happiness cannot take place unless good things are happening or about to happen. When things are not "happy", Ego does not approve of the present moment, the present now, and seeks to avoid life in the unpleasant moment by seeking distraction. By being distracted, which is a type of unconsciousness, Ego does not have to experience life during the state of not being happy. (See the chapter on Distraction and Sensation Seeking)

Moment by moment, Ego is either sensation or distraction seeking depending on how it defines the current situation. Moment by moment, experience by experience, and day by day, ego puts down layer after layer of defining moments to create an aggregate of experiences. These experiences become who we think we are. These many layers of experience make up the ego identity. Ego becomes conditioned after awhile and behaviors are set. Life through Ego is one where our behaviors rule the path we follow. And Ego follows the path of sensation seeking or distraction. It is the path of materialism.

The alternative is of course being grounded in the awakened state of awareness.

When Ego becomes the sole means in which we interact with others, it takes over identity and controls what the outside sees. It becomes our agent that engages other individuals and their egos in a larger collective of egos. When one has this perspective, the crazy behavior of people can be better understood. This identity theft is not too different from those criminals who swipe all of your personal information and decide to become you. While you are unaware, the identity theft criminal is out on a spending spree living the life they think they were meant to live. This is all at your expense. Ego is much the same. Sometime early in life, it slides in taking over your "self" and assuming control. During childhood years and especially during adolescence egos experiment being different personas. When the aggregate of life experiences have created a critical mass to establish an identity, a "me" is created. They feed off of different experiences, selecting those that give a sense of gratification, self worth and fulfillment. By the time the ego is a young adult, it thinks it knows who and what it is. Unless something intervenes to awaken the self, ego stays firmly in identity control. When asked, the ego will, with great gusto, tell anyone who will listen all about who they are. The story they tell and the story they feel are often two different stories. What they share with the outside world is all about how they want others to perceive them. They will deceive others and especially themselves in creating the façade they place outside for the world to see. Internally, egos are very insecure and constantly seeking validation and security of who they think they are. At other times, egos are simply sensation seeking as a means of emotional fuel.

Since egos define happiness by the sensations they experience they need to feed on emotional energy and are constantly seeking that which will stimulate the pleasure centers associated with the senses. This is sensation seeking. When they are experiencing pain and suffering, or what they define as pain and suffering, they seek distraction. They are in a constant pursuit or striving for the next stimulating experience or trying to avoid those which are deemed unpleasant.

The Ego Identity is shaped by experiences. As it quietly assumes control of identity, it also assumes control of the meaning of all experiences and most importantly, it falsely defines what we perceive. The basis of meaning depends on the life experience of the ego. Each experience forms a layer of emotional pain or happiness and is defined as good or bad depending on what ego got out of it. As each layer of each experience gets laid down, it becomes a defining reference for future use. While being wise to things that have caused problems in the past is a good survival technique, it can create some problems when it comes to defining one's identity.

I can use myself as an example.

When I was growing up, the term "attention deficit" was not used much if at all. My academic life suffered a lot because of my propensity for day dreaming and not being able to pay attention for very long. I spent many hours in detention and in the principal's office because teachers just did not know what to do with me.

I spent most the third grade lunch period alone because I

could not remember to "not talk" during lunch. For me, talking was synonymous with breathing. It was pretty hard for me as an eight year old to be mindful of keeping quiet. So my teacher made me sit alone on the other side of the lunch room where I simply had no one to talk to.

I was labeled as stupid because I just could not function like other students. Being a kid, I believed what I was told. So I grew up believing that I was stupid. My position became one of just letting go of any ambition to learn things like the other kids because there was no point. I thought I was stupid, so I just became that way. It actually paved the way for following a smoother path. Society does not expect much from stupid people so I found my place as a stupid person.

There was a point in the sixth grade when my parents took me to a specialist who tested me. I scored quite high on the IQ test which prompted him to inform my parents that I was not stupid but very bright and just lazy and not motivated. Yet somehow, the message did not get to me until much later, so I maintained my stupidity as the place where I fit in.

I did not find out until I went into the military that I was not stupid. The rigid structure and extreme fear of disappointing my boot camp company commander provided the motivation for concentrating in a manner I had never experienced before. The military encouraged me in ways that I had never experienced. They took my identity apart and rebuilt me into a new person. When I begin to excel at military life, I came to the realization that I was not stupid.

My point in this sordid tale is that my ego formed through many painful layers of experience. My many experiences of being defined as stupid became who I was. Ego became me, and I was stupid. I became my experiences. If asked to identify myself in those days, I would, with all seriousness have answered that my name was Sammy and that I was stupid. It was who I was. My Ego formed around this identity and took over the "self". Other aspects of my "self" faded to the back ground, and I became my thoughts or my experiences. So dear reader, this is the part where you realize you are not your experiences.

Ego and emotion

Some teachers say that Ego and emotion is the same thing. Others claim that Ego is the emotional result based on the meaning given to a given event or potential event. Many of the aspects of ego overlap each other, so when it is examined several areas can come into play. One must explore the nature of each emotion. It is my perspective that negative emotions arise in Ego and positive emotions arise in the stillness of awareness. Now, having said that, it may be observed that a type of happiness or joy may be experienced within Ego, but the distinction should be drawn that positive emotions within ego are always conditional. It is a kind of weird illusion that ego is trapped in. Ego is always seeking energy to feed on. It particularly loves emotional energy that preserves its sense of identity. By that I mean that ego, having its own identity, develops its own sense of self. Being lost in Ego, it is quite common for an ego to look at you and discuss its self even using the word self.

Have you ever found one part of you talking to yourself? Ponder who or what it is having the discussion. That is a good one for contemplation meditation. Perhaps it should be a part of the assignment of asking yourself, "Who am I?"

Ego, considering itself the ultimate protector of the self, is very emotional. One of the dominant emotions it dwells in is fear. Ego uses previous experiences to evaluate everything that could possibly go wrong. It looks for problems to arise and therefore creates them. Even when things are relatively smooth, ego, having experienced the constantly changing aspects in nature, is always concerned about a painful experience of the past, being repeated in the future.

Ego and the Now

It is the nature of ego to resist being in the present moment or the now. When ego finds the present moment with not enough sensation or unpleasant and desiring distraction, it will avoid the present moment. It feels that this now is unsatisfactory and will seek a new and better now. Not understanding that now is all there is, it lives within the illusion of how things were or how things will be. Most importantly, ego does not accept things as they are. Ego does not accept life as it flows. Ego does not realize that all things are connected and it cannot place itself in the fabric of life. It must by nature continue sensation seeking or distraction.

Exercise

Take a moment and consider your life and how you live it.

- Are you able to accept much of it (life) as it is?

- Are you able to just sit still and observe what is going on around you without experiencing an immediate sense of boredom?

- Are you constantly defining each moment as good or bad?

- How much time in each waking period do you seek distraction. That is how often do you need to tune out? [Hint: how much TV do you watch?]

- How often do you sense that there is not enough time?

Many of us avoid life as it is. Because ego does not want to surrender identity with what it considers to be life, over to awareness. When we understand that awareness is being in the now, in the present moment, and observing rather than doing, ego becomes lost and without power.

As the dominant entity, ego resists the now and consistently orients in past experiences or future expectations. Neither of which exist. The past is over and done with. The future has not occurred yet. Yet ego needs to fuel its existential nature, and it does it with emotional energy. So, a concern about the past recurring in the future arises out of habit. Concern then becomes worry. When the event is finally manifested, worry becomes full blown fear, then anger, then sorrow and depression. This is suffering.

In star wars, the character of Yoda says,

"Fear is the path to the dark side. Fear leads to anger. Anger leads to hate. Hate leads to suffering."

Ego and Emotional Energy

Emotional energy has been the most destructive force that humans have ever been associated with. Negative emotional energy has destroyed more lives than any other force known. We claim to be the most sentient, the most self aware, and the most advanced specie on this planetary body, yet we cannot refrain from killing each other, both individually and collectively. Does that not strike you as amazing? As a specie, we can calculate the speed of light, yet we cannot refrain from killing ourselves. Ego is the answer to the obvious question of why.

Ego can even override the preservation of the self. As I write this, I did a check at the National Institute on Mental Health. The NIMH reports that in 2007, 34,598 deaths were attributed to suicide. That is the equivalent of a city the size of Bentonville Arkansas, (the home of Wal-Mart) doing themselves in each year. How can this be?

It is because of the nature of ego and its *inability to accept things as they are*. Even when presented with the perfect scenario it soon becomes unsatisfied. With ego, satisfaction is only a temporary state. Ego, constantly needing more, will always see the grass as greener on the other side of the fence. This constant pursuit of more and better, almost always results in an imbalance. The imbalance may be in the form of any number of abuses. It may be food and any number of substances such as drugs and alcohol. The imbalance is a result of a continuous cycle of sensation seeking and distraction. Never happy and always needing to feed, the ego becomes obsessed with seeking that which stimulates a happy sensation. Or, when not being able to accept things as they are, it seeks distraction. Ego can cycle through sensation seeking and distraction for a lifetime.

Ego can also feed off of positive emotional energy. Happiness and joy are powerful energy sources. Happiness and Joy can be the catalyst for inspiration through self awareness. Ego greatly enjoys the energy from positive emotions. Therefore it seeks it out. Yet ego can seek out happiness in all of the wrong places. Ego is quite happy when it gets attention. When we are talking about "me", and when the spotlight is on ego (me) it swells with pride. It gives great credence to ego's sense of identity. It says "look at me", "see me and how great I am". Attention getting feeds ego with emotional energy and it gives this identity a much needed validation. The self esteem of ego is very thin skinned. Its self esteem is very fragile and constantly requires reinforcement.

 Pride is the slippery slope of ego. It can become the motivating factor of great effort. If the end justifies the means then it is an efficient tool. Yet it is a doomed endeavor because nothing will last forever in a world of impermanence. Happiness that is associated with the rise of egoic pride will eventually lead to an equal or greater sense of failure. Ego is not limited to the individual. Again, we can look at history for examples of the rise and fall of collective egos. Whether they were empires, or sports entities, or individuals, in the end they will fall. And with them, so will their egos. In modern times, we have seen sport fans that have rampaged because their team simply lost a competition. When these egos get together in a collective they feed off of each other's energy and create a storm of uncontrollable emotion. The emotional storm passes and the next day some of them will awaken and they will shrug their shoulders and wonder why they did what they did. Incredibly others will feel pride at their outburst and seek to boast at their own insanity.

Some people have a natural balance between self and ego. Somehow they manage to keep things in a balanced perspective. Hopefully our society will never reach a point where the ego oriented numbers shift the balance of sanity. If so, we will surely destroy ourselves. Seeking energy in collectives, egos will congregate collectively. They can be recognized when one know how to see them. Perhaps an example would be to consider Adolph Hitler and the collective group that were known as The Nazi Party. We can see how wrong things can go when a collective of ego's become too powerful.

Right now, even as I write these words, the country of Syria is undergoing a painful chapter in their long history. The majority of people in that country no longer want their current leader in power. So what is it that causes the dictator in power to hold on at all costs and to destroy everything in the process of holding on? This may be over simplifying things a bit, yet I cannot help but see ego at work here. It is so typical that ego will say and do anything and everything to maintain its position. In the leader's mind other areas such as reason and logic have been suspended. A type of insanity prevails that cannot lead to a beneficial ending. The Higher Self has been shunted from decision making. That means that of all the many aspects of the mind, only ego is involved with orienting the compass. Each decision is simply about what is in it for "me".

Sometimes these melt downs are on a smaller scale. The term "going postal" brings to mind the results of individual egos going over the top. Sometime the egos are young and would seem to have reached the point of no return. Think of the Columbine Massacre in Colorado years ago. When we see the final break down and shake our heads, and we wonder why and how this can happen. Now you know. At the heart of the matter is a mind entity called ego. It is never satisfied. It is the residency of evil.

Below are a few basic questions one can ask about any given ego including your own. When contemplating whether something is sourced from ego or awareness you can try several means to test it out.

Exercise

Ask yourself some of these questions? Is this action that is being contemplated?

- Going to cause pain and suffering of others?

- Going to benefit me at the expense of others?

- Going to benefit others regardless of me?

- Sourced from compassion?

- Sourced from greed?

- Sourced from anger?

- Sourced from a need for revenge?

- Sourced from love of others?

- Going to relieve the suffering of others?

- Based on any negative emotion?

Fear was just one of the many negative emotional agents in the collective that sought to dominate the world and remove unwanted, undesirable, inferior egos. History is replete with ego gone awry. It is alive and well even today. Just open the newspaper or turn on the television news for insights into ego's gone wild.

Several chapters in this book are devoted to the emotional energies that ego thrives on. Ego is the source of the very problems it seeks to avoid. The solution to all of this of course is for us to become detached from ego and realize awareness and identify as the authentic self. Well managed and behaved egos need not dominate. Ultimately we should all orient completely in awareness. Yet very few of us have ever done that. These very special people are wonderful and rare. You may recall them in history. The Buddha, Jesus, Gandhi, and others stood out as those who followed a higher path and devoted their life to help relieve misery. There are many who have reached a higher degree of self awareness, yet perhaps they are not in the full stage of enlightenment. These folks are wonderful to be around as well, and the chances are good that you may have met one. They just seem to have it all together. Perhaps you too can already sense the shift in perspective from ego to your awakened self.

This course is titled "Free Your Self" because it is about being free from the chains of ego. Being free from ego means being free to become aware of choices and then being free to choose from them. Being free to change how you give meaning to each and every experience will quite literally change how you define an event or potential event from being a problem, a non event or an opportunity. There is an old saying, "it is not what happens to you that is important, but how you react to it that matters" By breaking free from the dominating identity of ego, one can dwell in the now. The now is infinite and so are the possibilities. Yet infinite possibility will never be perceived while in ego.

Self Awareness through meditation and mindfulness is transcending the world of thought and ego. Let us look at examples of ego and its negative emotional behaviors.

Transcending ego requires a very special and very direct truth. Accepting things as they are is a function of self awareness. Rejecting the truth because it is too painful is a function of ego. No transcendence or transformation can take place until we accept things as they are. One of these truths is accepting how hard ego is to diffuse.

Having read all of this about ego, you may now be convinced that it is time for ego to be gone. That is a great start; yet please understand that something so easily arrived at is so very hard to do. Like diets, it seems so simple. Just eat less and exercise more and bang, weight loss and good health. If you have been there and done that, you know it sounds a lot easier than it is to do.

Ego is sneaky and conniving. It is not going to go away peacefully and silently. It is the great pretender, and even learns the basics of "normal" behavior. Ego can even fake enlightenment and awareness. Just take a look at how egos merge with religion and use it as a means to an end. One can always test for ego by including love and compassion in decision making. We can look back in near history and remember the Jim Jones tragedy to understand how ego can assume control and lead others into disaster.

Unchaining your "self" from ego is a spiritual process, but the battle ground will take place in the realm of materialism. Identifying as a spiritual being rather than egoic identity is the process. Simple but not easy is how others have described this shift unconsciousness to awareness.

I also recommend that you find others who truthfully practice mindfulness and meditation and give it a faithful effort for at least six months. Mindfulness Meditation takes practice. Not only does it take repetition of contemplation, but it takes repeated efforts in meditation to form the supporting neural network that will develop in your organic brain. The more you do it, the better you get. There is awesome research supporting information that you can read online and in books. One such book is "Zen and the Brain" by James H. Austin M.D. So not only do you transform your mind, but you transform your brain. Our original manufacturing seems to be hardwired to transcend the material world and self realize as a spiritual being. Notice how when you consider doing nothing and in the background a feeling of disapproval may arise. Our culture frowns on doing nothing and labels it as "laziness". Yet doing nothing is doing everything. Tuning into the universe, or God or however you wish to define it, is and should be your purpose. Everything else is just detail and content. Be in the flow and realize your place in the great tapestry of life. Just Be.

The next chapter will give a very basic guide for de-identifying from ego. As you read it, frequently return to awareness where you can be honest. When you realize your own truth you can implement changes. If a particular behavior strikes a resonate note, you will then know where your first detachment should begin. This is hard work, and I wish you luck. Yet, as you conquer ego, awareness arises and your true self is set free.

Conquering Ego

"Be the change you want to see in the world" - Mahatma Gandhi

The first step in extricating your true self from the chains of ego is to wake up from the unconsciousness of mind stream. This awakened state of consciousness is meditation and the practice of meditation is the awakening process.
A person in the awakened state can observe things as they truly are. This is opposed to the tainted illusion that is created by the crafty scheming ego. The chapter on meditation will discuss meditation and all that goes with it.

In meditation we become aware and the next step is to be able to carry this awakened state into our daily activities. This is mindfulness. To be mindful, is to be alert in awareness and watchful for the tricks ego will play.

Step one is awareness through meditation.

Step Two is mindfulness. Please read the chapter on mindfulness.

Step Three is to find and maintain a balance between awareness and doing, moment by moment as we live our life. It requires a constant vigilance to keep from becoming absorbed in egoic mindstream. Listed below are some common egoic behaviors for you to become aware of. This is simple to comprehend yet it can be quite difficult implement, so don't give up. It requires that you be honest with your "self". It may be helpful to read the chapter on honesty with the self, for this to be most effective. The degree to which you exhibit these traits depends on the degree to which ego has taken over your identity. So let's begin. Here are but a few common behaviors of ego to contemplate.

Lying

I have started with one of the most sublime and hardest of ego tricks to detect and let go of. It is difficult to be aware of because it is so prevalent. When everyone tells these soft lies, then soft lying becomes acceptable. Our collective egos have made it acceptable to be constantly providing these subtle untruths. There are big lies that all of us find unacceptable, and there are those subtle little "white lies" that seem to be ok. If a person finds themselves to be a chronic big time liar, that is to say, if you are causing havoc and pain on a large scale, then you should seek professional help immediately. This insight here is to be honest about those little lies that we think are acceptable.

Well sorry, but they are not acceptable. The reason they are not, is because of the foundational support that they give to ego. Many of us can tell ourselves these subtle lies so many times that it *seems* to become a self truth. The faux truth as a foundation lends ego permission to go forth and commit all sorts of other untruths and behaviors. These behaviors are the source of the problems and suffering we experience.

Ego and the constant striving for high self esteem will present these subtle lies to impress others. It starts off as a perceived need. A person may want to impress an attractive person of the opposite sex. It may be during a job interview. It may be to avoid criticism. Once told, the ego has a way of appreciating the "new truth" and it becomes a false truth that just seems to become fact.

Lying is absolutely not accepting things as they are but more to the point; it is not accepting your life as it is. (It is important to read the chapter on the power of acceptance).We often lie about the life we have created. The only situation where lying makes sense is when it may save someone from *unnecessary* suffering. For the most part, this situation is pretty rare, so don't plan on using that excuse very often. Otherwise, lying is living the life of illusion. Ego, not being in a state of awareness, often does not even realize it is lying. Sometimes ego just makes it up as it goes. The more that we live our lives in ego, the more our life is non authentic. Some people are pretty honest and lie rarely. A close discernment will reflect that they are not as lost in the egoic life and are more oriented to the authentic self. Egoic life is living a lie, and being aware is being your true self. The true self accepts life as it is, and ego must lie because life is not good enough as it is.

So if you are awake now, consider some subtle lies you have told in the past to impress or protect yourself or to look proper or good to others. Be honest in the assessment, yet not too hard on yourself. This was ego at work, and we all have done it. The work at hand is to just stop doing it. The good news is that if it is not such a huge or detrimental lie, then others will forgive it because down deep they know they have done it also.

Be aware of the ego's need to impress others. In mindfulness be aware of ego rising to the lie and let the lie come and go. In awareness we must accept things as they are and that means admitting that we are quite ordinary sometimes. If the need to feel greatness persists, contemplate the egos need for that. When the need to avoid truth rises, become aware of it and then just let it go. Letting go of the need for greatness will diffuse the need to lie. This is a very powerful insight and allows the positive virtue of love of others and humility to arise.

False Wisdom

Insecurity is a frequent aspect of ego. To overcome a perceived weakness sometimes ego will go to a large effort to impress others with wisdom. Have you ever noticed how from time to time a person will need to let everyone know just how smart they are? They might actually have great cognitive skills and wonderfully functioning ability to reason. Yet it is immediately diminished when ego gets involved. Perhaps it is displayed by the obsession of making high grades. Perhaps it is so they can gain praise from peers or bosses. Paradoxically ego does not seem to be aware of how it looks when being so needy and is constantly working to impress others on how smart it is. One give away is that it is not just a onetime event. It is constant. Perhaps the ego fears that the others just don't appreciate just how smart they are and likes to constantly remind the world around them "look at me, I am so smart". In awareness you can notice that truly smart people have no need to boast. They just are. They just quietly go about doing the brilliant things they do and often reside in a sense of humility.

Drama

Or should it be said "gossip"? There are some egos whose identity becomes that of the source of gossip. Identity is everything to ego. To be needed as the source of information and more importantly the source of emotional energy for egos gives rise to a false sense of power. All reasonable people know that gossip is a destructive behavior and works against compassion. Collectively the egos even become competitive in their abilities to find as much negative information about another individual as they can. The need for gossip is only outranked by the need to share it. It all comes back to "look at me". It is yet just another insecurity of ego. In quiet awareness, neediness and desire diffuse and become as vapor before sunlight. In ego, neediness is the unquenchable thirst that can never be satisfied. Please do not misunderstand the power of Drama in our culture. There is a billion dollar industry of TV drama that has become the opiate of the programming junkies. There was even a cable channel a while back that bragged about how they provided the most drama. Egos love and feed off of drama. This feeding is an unconscious taking of negative energy from raw negative emotion. Drama is the process for manifesting fear, anxiety, stress, worry and addiction. Each day, during the hours between 10am and 4pm millions eagerly go unconscious and allow the programming to enter directly into their minds via an especially virulent and addictive method called the "soap opera". Amazingly most people do not see nor understand that it is a powerful tool used by marketing firms to introduce their manipulative programming known as TV advertisement. The merchants who sell and distribute the product and the marketing groups have the sole purpose of getting into your head to convince you that you must buy their product. This all works because of our addiction to drama and gossip. The egoic need to gossip has adapted the TV drama in a symbiotic relationship where not only do they get to feed off the energy created while being absorbed in the show, but then have it for desert again the next day when they get to gleefully gossip with each other about the characters in the show itself.

There are even complaints when these dramas are interrupted by legitimate news events where serious need to know information is provided for the citizens. There have been times where addicted viewers grumbled when their show was pre-empted because of a serious news bulletin. Be honest with yourself. Become aware of your need for drama and gossip.

Bragging

We touched on a form of this earlier in false wisdom. This section highlights the behavior of bragging. It takes many forms and shapes such as look how smart I am. Here are a few.

"Look how busy I am. Look how many hours I work."

"Look how religious I am. Look how spiritual I am. And even "look how good I am at meditation and self awareness". (I hope I have not portrayed that in this book)"

"Look how much stuff I have. I have more (fill in the blank) than everyone else."

"Look at me in my (car, boat, suit, hair style, tattoo, etc)"

'Look how beautiful I am. Look at my body, isn't it great. Look at me, everyone!"

"Look how much I can eat"

"Look how much alcohol I can consume"

"Look how fast I am"

"Look how efficient I am"

"Look at me, look at me, please whatever you are doing, stop and look at me.

Why is this so bad? It is problematic because it sets up addiction to a false sense of fulfillment that cannot be sustained. These egoic behaviors have a nature of dualism or a dichotomy of two conflicting halves. Things are happy or sad, good or bad, and all of the other yin and yang features of this mindset. When ego does not have the good, they are left with the bad. This creates the neediness of desire. It creates the striving for ego satisfaction. In awareness we can observe this need for things to always be just right. Then by realizing what we are doing and why, we can choose to just let that neediness go. Life is as it is. Instead of trying to control the flow of the universe we can learn to control how we react to it. By defining fulfillment, contentment, joy and happiness as being validated by others through some skill set such as being the best whatever, we set up the eventual fall from the top of the heap to a feeling of unworthiness. This is the false view of ego. Ego can only realize high self esteem when it feels that it is seen as number one.

Sports Fanatics like to hold up their index finger and shout "we're number one". Yet watch what happens when their team inevitably falls from the top. Each ego rapidly collapses, and as a collective group they descend to a very low place. Rabid sports fans have been known to burn, pillage, stampede, fight and even kill each other over a team loss. All because the false sense of self, ego cannot abide the reality of how things are. Ego qualifies life based on the outward definition gained in the material world.

Being mindful of our behaviors and actions, we can begin to release our attachment from the egoic view point. Being mindful, you can see the egoic need to have people look at you as it arises and just let it go. In awareness we realize we are this infinite spiritual being where anything is possible. Placing energy on the pursuit of loving, having compassion and caring for others will take the energy out of the neediness of ego. Yet be careful, for quickly the sneaky and always vigilant ego will get involved. You may notice the advent of ego beginning to envisioning a picture of how it is best at being caring and compassionate. And before you know it, ego is telling the world "look at me", look how compassionate and loving I am. Then you find yourself back where you started. It is the same behavior only different content.

Entitlement

A sense of entitlement must always have a foundation to rest upon. Many times it may be a very realistic illusion. One common example is that just because something is written down on paper, that it constitutes a reality. Therefore when the validation of the paper is no longer present, the basis for entitlement is missing. The item of entitlement is gone, only leaving us with a feeling of judgment, fear, desire, greed, lust, rage, hatred, disappointment, desperation, jealousy and many others

Any time you are feeling a sense of entitlement, you are viewing life through the filter of ego. Life is not about things being fair or following the agenda of our egos. Ego will experience a feeling that it is owed something or entitled to something by the false virtue of desire. (See the chapter on Desire) Entitlement is the bait which is set in ego's trap for Judgment, Fear, Desire, Greed, Ambition , Lust, Rage and Hate , Disappointment , Deprivation , Desperation , Jealousy, and Debt. The sense of entitlement is ego's expectation that life is meant to be in alignment with its own sense of desire. Ego feels that since it is all about "me", then all aspects of life should be all about itself. We are so conditioned in ego that we practice many of the above mentioned inappropriate behaviors without even be aware of it. Yet being aware of what we are doing and why, we can step back from *this illusion of being entitled to something* and be self reliant in our life.

Example

During the recent recession, many of us suffered substantial or catastrophic losses with retirement investment accounts. We all had this false sense of security, feeling that because we believed our savings were untouchable. We received monthly statements showing how much money we had acquired over the years and how much it had grown. These paper or electronic statements along with our past experiences gave us a feeling that we had plenty of financial resources sitting in funds around the world. And then, the recession hit. Within a very short period of time the value of those portfolios was reduced. In many cases they were reduced enough to cause some emotional and mental suffering. In a few cases, the losses were catastrophic. This sense of security, this illusion of thinking and feeling that we were entitled to that money set us up for a disappointment in the least. Many people experienced deeper and more profound emotional and mental suffering. This is brought on by being attached to the illusion or sense of entitlement that we were owed money because it was ours. The result of cause and effect collapsed the mirage and many of us had our moment of truth. Later in this book, you will read chapters on cause and effect and attachment. They are emotional co-conspirators in this trickery of ego.

In awareness, we are in a state of consciousness where we are able to see things as they really are. Removed from this ignorance of ego, we can learn to be grateful for abundance when it is apparent. In the wisdom of awareness we do not become attached emotionally to the material aspects of our world knowing that it may be only temporary. In awareness we can know that we live in a world that is constantly changing. With wisdom we can realize that change is brought on by cause and effect, and that many times we cause the result that we suffering from.

Ego entitlement can be experienced in other forms also. Our sense of entitlement can grow from the seeds of expectation.

Expectation is avoiding the present moment and looking to the future. Once our egoic sense of entitlement feels like we are owed something, and we expect it, the trap door is once again set to drop us back into ignorance and suffering. Respect is a virtue that we can expect and thus feel a sense of entitlement. Based on our position, title, badge, rank insignia, diploma, or other label, our ego can expect respect. Yet in reality, any reasonably wise person can understand that respect is not a given. Power loving ego, will feel a sense of entitlement and demand the respect it feels that is due. It will demand respect never having earned it. In this, hopefully you can see the illusion. While the rank, position or role of prominence may carry the honor and respect, the individual, in that position, still has to earn respect from those they serve. I have found the best leaders are those who feel a sense of serving to those who they lead. It seems to be that when one does not expect nor feel entitled to respect, it will be them who will receive it most. Learn to be aware and mindful when any sense of entitlement arises. When you can sense this illusion arising you will know you are in ego. Being self reliant you will free your "self" from the egoic sense of entitlement.

Our objective in reducing ego is to return to awareness through meditation and mindfulness. The simple litmus test is check to see if what you are doing is for "me" or truly for another being. History has recorded examples of humans who have exemplified this virtue. The Buddha, Jesus Christ, Mahatma Gandhi, Nelson Mandela, Mother Teresa, and Dr. Martin Luther King Jr. are but a few. But there are others with us now. These modern and local saints go unrecognized because of their degree of enlightenment. You probably know a few of them. These altruistic people pass the litmus test every time. They do very little for themselves and everything for their community. Observe them. Learn from them. These are very special people and are to be cherished. If you find part of you feeling disagreeable to this notion then you have your first insight. Ask what part of you is so opposed to these people and this way of being. If you are honest with yourself you will find that it is ego. Practice on letting go. Start small and work your way up. It may take many efforts over time. Be persistent and patient.

Not only will you be transformed, but you will transform the world around you.

"Be the change you want to see in the world" - Mahatma Gandhi

Conquer your ego and free your "self".

Attachment

Pray to God that your attachment to such transitory things as wealth, name, and creature comforts may become less and less every day.
Ramakrishna

In the Chapter on Distraction and Sensation Seeking the point was made for being mindful of our attachments and how we use them to cope with life's perceived problems. Therefore it would be prudent to take a look at the nature of attachments and how they become the links of chain that imprison us to ego and the false self.

To free your "self", that is to transcend ego and be the higher self that you really are, requires breaking the illusion of ego and the ego identity. If you have not read the chapter on Ego, now would be a good time.

Ego, never accepting life as it is, is always striving to deal with or cope with the present moment by distraction of some sort. When life is problematic, ego will turn to some materialistic or even intellectual item to find happiness and comfort. This usually falls under the heading of distraction or sensation seeking. It is at the heart of egoic desire. For ego, life is simply the fulfillment of desire, and desire is the avoidance of life as it happens, Life as it is.

Ego attaches itself to these distractions or sensational experiences as a means of sustaining its existence. And therein lies the real problem. In other chapters we talk about discernment, acceptance, and choice as options for the awakened being. In ego, these options are not available because it is the nature of ego to reject life as it is and seek avoidance by being distracted or enjoying sensational experiences. Ego lives for nothing else. This need of ego to sustain itself over and over creates an attachment to those things which can continue the illusion of being satisfied.

Each attachment we form creates a link in the chain that

imprisons us to the false self (ego). There is no such thing as a benign attachment. This is because attachments are only a means of avoiding life as it is. There may be degrees of danger with each attachment but they can all lead to suffering and problems sooner or later. They become a feature of dependency. So whether they are sunflower seeds or Heroin, the ego depends on some "thing" for satisfaction.

As you read this, you may have never even considered that there was such a concept as life without depending on "stuff". Yet that is the nature of true contentedness and joy. They require no outward thing or stuff. This ability of being able to simply experience happiness, joy, contentment, and fulfillment are choices that can be made only from being grounded in awareness. That is the nature of the higher or true self.

This choice is only available when we orient our reality and our identity in awareness. When we transcend or become unabsorbed by ego, we lose the neediness of coping and striving. Within our life long conditioning, we have created these coping mechanisms, these attachments to help us deal with life because we knew no other way. That is the nature of the egoic life. Unless we are taught how to transcend and remain in awareness, we live lives ignorant of how things really are. Spiritual paths and religions may or may not help find this realization. It really depends on the effectiveness of the teachers and the personal development of the practitioners. Ego can absorb anyone not grounded within true awareness. It can be recognized by its nature which is grounded in "me" or "us". Ego can throw on the cloak of religious leaders, spiritual leaders, and any self proclaimed expert. They can be recognized by their attachments. If they have them, they are not self aware, or they are bouncing back and forth between ego and awareness. The degrees to which they suffer or cause suffering identify how deeply they are absorbed by ego through discernment. The more they strive, and have attachments the more they are grounded in ego. And since ego will congregate into collectives, the sense of "me" evolves into "us". "My" attachments and striving becomes "Our" attachments and strivings.

In self awareness, as spiritual beings, we just do not need a lot of stuff. We live simple lives because we can accept so much of what is. By accepting so much of what is, that is life as it really is, we do not need to cope and develop attachment for getting by. By letting go of judgment and practicing acceptance, life becomes pretty simple. Love, compassion and service replace egoic self serving, attachments and striving for more.

In relationships, it is possible to become attached to the degree that others become our sole reason for existence, and we can become dependent on them as our coping with life. This is not to say that we should not love each other and serve each other. Each of us should love one another, and bond with those very close to us such as spouses, partners and family members. We should each live our lives as productive beings, sharing our lives with each other, yet not being dependant on others for our happiness and fulfillment in life. That is a heavy burden to place on someone else. No one can be responsible for your happiness. That falls within your domain. When we are grounded as our true authentic selves, we are released from our attachments and free to experience life serving others without becoming overly attached to them. Look for balance in all relationships. We serve each other without being completely dependent on them for our psychological well being. We find joy in being with those we love, without becoming attached to outcome. In each moment, be grateful for them, love them, and let them be who they are.

The degree to which we can be free from attachment will determine our true state of contentedness and fulfillment. When self awareness is successfully sustained through mindfulness, you will find that life is really quite simple. Neediness is a good indicator of the trend of attachment. Be mindful of neediness and the striving for the attachments. You can practice meditation to transcend ego and become self aware. Sustain awareness by being mindful in each moment of what you are doing and why you are doing it. Free your "self" by being free from attachments.

The Power of Acceptance

"Everything can be taken from a man but one thing; the last of the human freedoms—to choose one's attitude in any given set of circumstances, to choose one's own way.' - Dr. Viktor Frankl

In the Chapter on Distraction there was the point made regarding the inability of accepting things as they are. In many aspects of living, individuals find that the present moment is unsatisfactory. We learned in the chapter on Ego problems are realized when inappropriate judgment is applied to events arising on the surface of the mind. When we perceive these problems and strive to avoid them we are practicing non acceptance. The egoic aspect of the mind lives in the illusion that all occurrences should follow its desire. When the ego perceives something in life that does not go according to plan, it immediately labels it as a problem. The egoic view is that problems that cannot be quickly resolved are to be avoided.

Acceptance is the allowing of events that occur around us in life to be as they are. In the chapter on desperation we discuss the reactions of ego when it finds itself in a situation that it cannot be removed from or cannot change. By not being able to practice acceptance, an impossible situation is experienced. This has been the foundation for many personal disasters.

When a person is experiencing the desperate feeling of being in an impossible situation, emotion quickly accelerates into a storm of feelings that quickly spin out of control. The egoic self feels trapped and threatened and sanity goes out the window.

However the antidote to this is found in awareness. By grounding in the present moment and being aware of the power of choice we can unify with the power of acceptance. In awareness we can observe what is taking place, both externally and internally, and remain objective. As stated before in this book, awareness provides the space for infinite possibility. If an event is truly one where we cannot remove ourselves or implement change, then acceptance is the only recourse.

In a state of Ego, acceptance is very hard to implement. For ego, which resides in a materialistic domain, identity is grounded in attachment to feelings and emotion. Feelings are an existential property that defines its identity. You might look at it as "I feel, therefore I am" or "if I am not feeling, I do not exist". Identifying as ego that is, being grounded in ego, acceptance is sometimes impossible because it cannot let go of that which enables its existence.

When details along our life path are perceived, we go through a process of discernment or judgment about how we will be affected. Lost in the mindstream of ego we are not able to remain unattached to outcome and cannot accept things as they are or as they might become. In awareness, we can observe the details arising along our path and allow them to be. This is because our higher self, in awareness, is grounded in the realization that the infinity of now can absorb anything that may arise. In awareness we, as our authentic self, pure consciousness, can *know* that we are that infinity of now. Being present is accepting the flow of life and being at one with it.

The practice of acceptance can begin immediately with our inter-personal relations. When we take an honest look at how we are behaving, we can realize that we often avoid or have deep conflict with other beings in our life. It is important to become awake and to become aware of these conflicts that we are creating. These inter-personal conflicts may be with people at work, family members, friends, bosses, parents, pastors, teachers, children, siblings, community leaders, national leaders, or world leaders. Acceptance can be plural in that we may find our ego not being able to accept whole groups of individuals because of how our ego perceives them to be a problem.

The instant we can accept differences between our self and them, the problem begins to diffuse. Therefore it is reasonable to say that our egoic selves create many of these problems. Conflict arises when ever there is a lacking in acceptance of that which is different. For the ego, difference can be experienced as something unpleasant to something threatening. Ego, being addicted to drama can create a false reality by playing a game of 'what' if and convince themselves of the most amazing illusions. Paranoia may be defined here as baseless suspicion of others. Egos will tell you straight out that they don't like something or someone because they are different or they do not understand them.

In relationships, the ego expects everything to revolve around it. So when something changes, chances are good that ego will immediately have a problem with it. The change does not even have to be sudden. Every day, people pledge before their God and solemnly swear to commit to, uphold, love and protect the person they desire to share their life with. Yet, statistics show that in the United States, they will break those vows and seek separation and divorce. Many times, with close inspection, egoic perspective can be seen at the heart of the break up. It occurs because one being in the relationship cannot accept the change in the other. Ego is so focused on its own need to fulfill desire that it cannot even follow logic. There are some people who will separate from their commitment because their betrothed has simply grown older. In a bizarre since of non acceptance, they are not able to realize that they too have grown older. Some egos are so grounded in narcissism that they will unconsciously trade spouses every so many years striving for a better model. These beings simply cannot accept things as they are, especially people as they are.

In awareness, something extra ordinary is present. In awareness, and seeing other beings as manifestations of spiritual consciousness, they accept and find beauty in their non materialistic aspects. They love the experiences that they share. They are aware of and love the wrinkles, the laughter and feel a great sense of gratitude for being able to share a life together. These higher insights of spirituality have nothing to do with the material world. They are pure. They are simple and they are available to be experienced by anyone who can accept things as they are.

There are Scientists and Psychologists who firmly believe that the modern human being was able to evolve so rapidly because of a unique nature of acceptance. This trait began to surface along with sentience and helped to propel ourselves to the top of the food chain because of a very special aspect of acceptance. That aspect is called cooperation. Those early humans who were able to band together and work together in a cooperative way created the opportunity for growth. By accepting differences in views, opinion, techniques, food, and other innovative ideas our ancient ancestor gave creation to the people we are today. Yet, another aspect we display serves to destroy it all. And that is ego and its inability to accept things as they are. With the creation of nuclear weapons, all it takes are small group egos in leadership position to refuse to accept the different views of others, to release a nightmare that could end our existence or at least return us back to our early starting point. In this present moment, there are those who are striving to do that very thing. There are collective egos that literally give their life to help realize the loss of life of those who they believe threaten them. This has happened before, and before we allow our own egos to create an illusion of self righteousness we must examine our own motives, views and be very honest with ourselves and our actions. In the last century there are many examples of how individual and collective egos would not and could not accept the way they perceived reality and other beings. Great suffering and pain ensued.

During the Second World War, the German leadership determined that they would exterminate a whole race of people that lived in their lands. This is a very large example of collective ego and lack of acceptance. Yet there are stories of heroes who in awareness were able to find enlightenment in the middle of the most horrible of circumstances. One such story is of an Austrian Psychiatrist by the name of Viktor Frankl. In 1944, he and his wife were deported to the Nazi concentration camp known as Auschwitz. Then his wife was transferred to another camp called Bergen-Belsen. Dr. Frankl not only survived but found a high degree of enlightenment through a level of acceptance. His book, an international best-seller, "Man's Search for Meaning" should be on your reading list.

The great power of acceptance is realized when we as conscious beings become aware of what is taking place. Non acceptance is a great burden that most people carry unnecessarily. The first time you are able to practice acceptance you should experience a feeling of having a large heavy burden lifted from your heart. Acceptance can sometimes be the only antidote when you find yourself in an impossible situation.

Distraction and Sensation Seeking

Most ol us don'l realize the value ol life and whal it's really about, we're so caughl up in little distractions thal are 100% meaningless. Author Unknown

Being distracted

Many novices and beginners view meditation as a type of relaxation. Something like quietly listening to music or day dreaming or some quiet activity. These activities are all good at what they do which is relaxation. But these activities are *activities of distraction*. It is important to recognize the effort to be distracted. Think about those words "to be distracted". Being can be defined as existence. Distraction is to divert the mind or attention away from the current mind state. Therefore to be distracted is to seek to divert away from existence. This begs the question of why would people seek to avoid existence? It is because they cannot accept things as they are. They cannot accept the present moment and what it brings, so they seek escape through distraction. In many cases the perceived problem in life is one they created themselves and find that they cannot accept and live with the results. (Please read the chapter on Cause and Effect)

Most people can recognize distraction as a temporary escape of life's problems. What they are not aware of is how destructive being distracted can be. The disastrous aspect of distraction hides just outside of our attention. One only has to remember the last time there was a life lost to the driver of a car being distracted. The distraction might be applying makeup or it might be trying to send or receive text messages. Relationships have foundered when one or more of the participants have become too distracted. Distraction is not benign. It is seeking to be separated from life because one cannot accept the present moment.

Being unconscious, that is diverting the mind away from the realities of life, is an unconscious attempt to detach the higher self from the world of thought. This temporary detachment is just an illusion and reality sets back in very quickly. (Please read the chapter on acceptance)

Individuals seek to divert their minds from reality quite often. It may be as much as every moment of every day. Distraction seeking can even become our purpose in life. Everything we do can be for the purpose of supporting the state of being distracting. Whether it is sitting down in front of the television or sitting down at a bar to numb the mind with alcohol, people are seeking escape. This continuous intention to escape life is an unnatural phenomenon. It is a characteristic of not being (not existing as) our true authentic self. It is living a life in a dream of unconsciousness. This unconscious life is directed by a sub division of the self called ego. Please read the chapter on ego to understand how this false identity takes over our lives.

Individuals seek distraction because they have lost touch with their spiritual core or their higher self. Without the practice of meditation and becoming aware individuals do not realize that reality has become shaped and defined by this unconscious aspect. Seeking distraction is the becoming attached to those things which help us "cope" with events in our life that become defined as unpleasant or "bad".

Distraction seeking is the non acceptance of reality as it really is. In awareness we can realize that we are not our experiences. Therefore, our memories do not have to define how things are based on what has happened in the past. Events arising before us are just details. Details get defined as good or bad by comparing this 'now' with past 'nows'. Being unconscious in ego, individuals expect life to be a certain way. When the egoic sense of life is out of sync with reality we deem it as problematic. Also in unconsciousness we quickly forget that circumstances we find ourselves in are many times the result of the cause and effect we created. When we are living life through the illusion of ego, all events unfolding in life are determined as either good or bad. When they are defined as bad, ego wants to escape. Ego seeks distraction from the illusion of bad. When ego deems something as particularly good and enjoys the sensation, it desperately seeks more of the same. This becomes sensation seeking. Depending on how painful the illusion is, egos can even self destruct searching for the false sanctuary of distraction.

Sensation Seeking

The higher form of distraction is sensation seeking. When life is perceived by the egoic mind to be unsatisfactory, then it seeks out distraction in the form of a pleasant sensation. The physical feeling that results from the stimulation of one of the sense organs is sensation. The ego adopts the stance of "if it feels good, then do it". This cliché was popular on bumper stickers back in the 70's and 80's which gave rise to phenomenal sensation seeking. Pleasure seeking through the sensation of the senses has been around a long time, yet has become quite sophisticated in modern times. Take a moment to consider how many trillions of dollars go toward the industry of fulfilling desire through sensation. Perhaps it is not too untrue to make the statement that most people are addicted to some form of sensation seeking. Seeking a sensational experience is just another form of not accepting the present moment as it is. In a given now, the ego does not accept the state of how things are and pursues the desire of making life better by experiencing something sensational. When ego perceives pain as a result of a problematic life it seeks to cope by the distraction of some pleasant sensation. The more the pain, the more stimulating the sensation is required to be. Since all dissatisfaction with life and especially a painful experience is the result of cause and effect, a cycle of pain and coping is created. The perception of events as being either good or bad tends to be the illusion of ego, the coping that arises is just another part of the illusion. Many times the coping sensation seeking creates even more problems (debt, bad health, depression) and more coping is required. Ego, never being satisfied, dwells in a spiral that can end in disaster.

This can be seen readily in individuals who destroy their lives with the over use of anything. Addictions are the basis of distraction seeking gone too far. Excessive distraction can easily be seen as the imbalance in the lives of those around us. These imbalances show up in many forms. It becomes easier to understand how we find ourselves in the messes we are in.

Before you are quick to judge someone you know, it would be better to look at your own life and take an objective assessment of the balanced life. Distraction and sensation seeking can be seen by taking an *honest* look in just a few areas. When you answer the questions below and know you have a problem, consider how the need for distraction or sensation seeking is playing a role.

Debt How much debt are you responsible for? How are you coping with it?

What did you use it for and why?

Health Is your weight normal? How are you coping with it?

What are some obvious warning signs you are ignoring?

What are some obvious behaviors that are inappropriate to sustain your life?

Mental Health How much stress are you experiencing? How are you coping with it?

Do you ever experience hatred?

Do you have fantasies of revenge or hurting others?

Relationships How healthy are your important relationships?

Is it easy to love you?

Is it easy for you to love others?

How likeable are you?

These are just a few basic categories and they often over lap. If you are not able to be sure or not able to face up to the true assessment, then ask someone that you trust to tell you the truth.

If you obtained this book because you have already begun to face up to the situation you find yourself in, the chances are good that you will have a lot to consider in the questions listed above.

If you have doubts about being able to untangle the knots by yourself, by all means seek professional help. A trained professional can help be your guide out of the perspective you have and help you begin to untie some of those knots.

To choose a path other than distraction and sensation seeking, we must first become aware of what we are doing and why we are doing it. Paying attention to what we are feeling and how we deal with those feelings is called mindfulness. Being mindful of unconscious behaviors as they arise provides the space to break the attachments we develop. These attachments are how we cope with the many illusions that we get caught up in. Illusions are assumptions made by ego based on past experiences. Illusions can be assuming that things are good or bad because it is what we are worried about.

In awareness we can at times chose from an infinite amount of other possibilities. Rather than react on the assumption made by ego, we can practice patience and acceptance. Reaction is often not required in the first moment of perception. If we can resist the first knee jerk reaction and discern the fact without emotional filtering the possibility of a truer perspective exists. There are times when immediate action is required. Most professionals will advise us to resist panic when an emergency sets in. Panic is uncontrolled emotion of fear and can lead to even more harm. More often, events arise that do not require immediate action. By being mindful of what is arising on the surface of the mind we can learn to choose the appropriate response. Even no action is a response.

By avoiding many of the illusionary traps of emotion we can experience less pain. The need for coping and distraction is less and life is easier to maintain in balance. Perhaps you can remember being told to "count to ten" by someone while you were feeling an emotional storm rising. This counting to ten is serving the purpose of slowing down your automatic reaction and stress. The counting to ten gives you an opportunity to avoid the attachment of emotional response. It can create the space to consider how to exercise choice, including and especially how you chose to feel.

When we feel good about life we no longer need to seek distraction. When life is good we no longer want to avoid living. This moment by moment experience of life can be so very sweet *if we choose it to be*. Living life is actually very simple. It only becomes complicated and problematic when we create unnecessary problems through cause and effect. Practicing self awareness and mindfulness through meditation provides the space for choice. In awareness we can observe and discern events as they arise. By accepting life as it happens in each present moment, we do not become absorbed in the effort of avoidance and escape. Living in pure awareness, we no longer need to distract or divert our "self" from living the true experience of living. Free your "self" from distraction in self awareness.

Feelings

"We experience ourselves our thoughts ana feelings as something separate from the rest. A kina oj opticai delusion oj consciousness. This delusion is a kina oj prison for us, restricting us to our personai desires ana to affection for a few persons nearesi to us."   Albert Einstein

Feelings are there to be observed. In self awareness we can tune in and become aware of feelings as they arise. This observation is not an action where one tried to seek out, avoid or change the feelings that arise but to acknowledge them. This is extremely important when seeking truth and being the authentic self. There are different aspects of feelings and it is helpful for the student who is working on self awareness to develop a road map for not taking a wrong turn. The foundation for understanding feelings must come from the high state of self awareness. Anything else is an illusion generated by the emotions of ego.

We use the word feel and feelings so often that one must be careful of what context they mean.

"I have a very bad feeling about this"

"I don't feel like eating hamburger"

"I'm not feeling it"

Feelings play such an important part in our lives that it must be included in this book. You the reader must come to terms with feelings and learn what place they have in your life. It is important to not become attached either the good (positive) nor the bad (negative). As the observer, we observe them and accept them for what they are. Importantly, in awareness we neither accept the positive feelings nor do we reject the negative feelings. We must realize them for what they are if they are to provide guidance.

Feelings are a kind of consciousness/awareness affected by emotion. Feelings as a sense drive intuition are an important aspect of perception. A person must be free of mindstream to be able to focus on feelings and intuition. Feelings and intuition must be accepted as they are. There must be not an attachment to outcome. Feelings and intuition are a vital and important source for the expanded awareness of perception.

What is it that shapes thoughts when they are forming? It happens when we give value to the information that comes through the senses. In the chapter on ego we talked about how ego hijacks our identity. Ego uses previous experience to form this pseudo identity through thoughts and previous experiences. As each experience is given its meaning and assigned to memory, the identity is structured. Experience can play an important role in learning. Perhaps the old saying, "don't throw the baby out with the bath water" is applicable. A long life of experience can lead to wisdom.

Feelings from the egoic perspective, as you might expect, are quite different than how they are observed by your higher self. In Ego, something different evolves when thinking defines new occurrences and things through negative emotions. Critical thinking can very easily be manipulated and influenced by emotions. Whether positive or negative, these emotional values will taint and shape the experience. Thus the memory gets filed away with the label of good or bad.

Problems occur when perception and thoughts are implicitly controlled by the egoic mind. The ego is a thought based entity that is very narrow in its spectrum. Its value system is also very narrow and the term of what is good and bad is based on the sensational quality of the experience. The first evaluation that ego performs is to judge what is in it for "me". The sensation seeking ego is always fueled by desire, its primary emotional energy. The ego makes a quick judgment based on previous experiences. Ego's discernment weighs the good or bad of the previous experience and arrives very quickly with a feeling of whether it will benefit "me" or not. There is a threat assessment to determine if it may be good or bad or how it might make "me" look.

In each and every moment, events arise in perception. Our five

68

physical senses and feelings detect and perceive information to provide context and order to the nature of events. In Ego, events that are judged to be a threat or lacking in potential to satisfy desire will not be accepted. Since there are so many things that ego cannot accept, there are many things that are deemed threatening or unsatisfactory. Therefore in each given moment there is an opportunity for choice. In awareness we are not attached to outcome so choice is readily available. Existing in the illusion of Ego, because of conditioning and set behaviors, the opportunity for choice will often be missed. Even if choice is available, Ego narrows the possible choices because of its discriminating nature. Fettered to past experiences and grounded in the false identity, Ego must pursue its mandated path of sensation seeking or distraction. When our consciousness has been absorbed and confined by ego and egoic feelings, choice is directed by whim of the false self. Therefore we, our egoic self, are guided only by false feelings.

Opposed to this is Awareness and higher self. Grounded in our true self, we are aware of choice and are able to choose. In awareness, the higher self has an infinite amount of patience. Moment by moment in the now, the primary choice is often to discern if action or no action required. Is action or acceptance required and how soon if at all. In awareness things can slow down dramatically and the calm abiding nature of awareness can avoid emotional reaction that is often not necessary.

The higher self is able to perceive in a variety of choices through an infinite perspective. Unemotional discernment provides the space for selection of options for action that might be available. Or, in the unlimited patience of now, no action may be required at all. Evaluation can be postponed or even dismissed completely. Meanings are defined by positive emotions such as compassion, love, serenity, amusement, inspiration and others. Since our pure being is not obsessed with "me" then the perspective is completely different. As events arise in awareness, time has a completely different meaning. Often time is not even a factor. Ego thrives on action and negative action. It demands instant gratification and seeks fulfillment ignoring the ultimate cost to those around it. With its focus always on itself or ME, that is the only compelling carrot for it to strive for.

In meditation, awareness of the self includes being aware of feelings. It is important to not become attached to good feelings or to run from and avoid bad feelings. Good choices are made when we can observe, discern, and consider acceptance. By staying grounded in awareness we do not become absorbed by or controlled by our feelings.

In awareness, discernment is practiced more often than judgment. Discernment is a discriminating function for distinguishing differences or changes and are not necessarily influenced by emotion or feelings. After discernment, comes judgment. (See the chapter on Judgment) Judgment forms opinion. The higher self will judge from the space of awareness and not so much influenced by emotion and ego. Through awareness judgment is neither the first nor the only perspective to which meaning will form. While the higher self will sometimes have to make a judgment, it is usually through observing through awareness first. When the judgment comes, the value is based on a much broader range of values and perspective. For the higher self, judgment is easily postponed and requires no sense of urgency. The higher self resides in the infinity of the present moment. It does not have the constant need of evaluating everything as either good or bad. Ego is impatient and therefore quick to judge. Always influenced by its nature of fulfilling desire, or being carried by the current of emotion, it is almost always impossible to be impartial in its findings. It is especially influenced by negative emotions such as anger, revenge, greed, and frustration. The higher self accepts things as they are. It doesn't carry the needy disposition of sensation seeking or distractions. The higher self is satisfied with the simple things in life. The higher self, through awareness sees the positive possibilities of things as they are. When the higher self thrives in faith and confidence of the ultimate source then through awareness, the higher self accepts what will be, will be.

We can summarize feelings as a function found in perception. We must remain in awareness, neither seeking certain feelings nor avoiding certain feelings. Feelings are information that is provided by internal senses. It is the single most important factor in discerning truth. To have to be able to truly free your "self", you must find your own truth and your true self. This requires exploring your feelings through pure awareness.

Behaviors, Conditioning and Habits

"Habits Change Into Character" Ovid (Roman Poet, 43BCE to 17ACE

When I was growing up there was a favorite Aunt who used to ask me "Are you being Have?" That is southern colloquialism for are you behaving, or are you refraining from mischief. Not yet deep into ego and earnestly wanting to please my elders I would always reply with sincerity that I was "trying". Somewhere along the way when my personality began to mature and ego began to arise, the sincerity for trying to maintain balanced behavior went by the wayside. And so it does in all of us.

As sentient humans who accumulate personal experiences we also begin to develop our personal history. Experiences, coping and adaptation become consolidated into behavior and conditioning. At some point these modifications become so engrained with who we are and how we conduct our lives that it becomes just something we do without being aware of it. It can become our character and personality.

Each moment of each day we are faced with decisions. Making these decisions creates the reality we find ourselves in. So it would seem that if a person would want to create the reality they desire, then great care would be given to each and every momentary decision. Yet we all know that it does not work that way. We place a lot of the little decisions on auto pilot and place our attention on some point in the future where we anticipate having a better experience than the one in this moment (this now).

As soon as we get into our car to go to work we go into auto pilot with our attention already on being off work and being back at home. In auto pilot we continuously look to the future which does not exist and completely ignore the life we could have and should be living right here and now.

So what about this auto pilot mind we fall into? It seems to be a sort of software program that makes decisions for us so that we can obsess with what might be or should be. The unconscious decision making behavior makes assumptions based on past experiences and is defined by the conditioning that is a result of repeated experiences. The easiest way to see how well this is working in your life is to be honest and see how well your life is in balance. Please see the chapter on honesty before trying this exercise. Without being honest, this exercise will be a waste of time. Next read the chapter on balance and harmony.

Having read the chapter on being honest with your "self" and assessing balance in your life you may not have to even read any further. It is important to connect the dots of your subconscious behaviors with the level of imbalance in your life. If you are out of balance in any way, you should contemplate the underlying behavior and conditioning to see how the cause and effect has produced your condition.

Cause and effect has been highlighted by the Buddhists for millennia, yet it has barely scratched the surface of Western culture. For many of us with the western mind orientation, being mostly occupied with life in the material world, cause and effect is usually understood only by those who genuinely follow a spiritual path with its strict adherence to morality or those non spiritual beings who adhere to human ethical guidelines. For many it serves only as a sort of warning sign to avoid major calamities. In the 1970's there were bumper stickers and tee shirts that announced "if it feels good, do it". In this current western mindset of the last twenty years, living in the present moment equates to being impulsive in the now without any regard for what the consequences may be down the life path. Please see the chapter on Cause and Effect.

Perhaps the Butterfly Effect can best describe the result of this moment by moment unconscious decisions that the person living in ego experiences. We often find ourselves in impossible situations and facing disaster with no apparent resolution. When our position becomes precarious enough or we have suffered enough we sometimes contemplate how we got in the spot we are in. Yet even then, the moment is quickly absorbed by ego which is eager to get back to the business of sensation seeking and distraction. The smallest of unconscious decisions can lead to the most disastrous of consequences. Many times the decision is not even a conscious one. Yet all action creates cause and effect.

Ego likes to blame these unfavorable consequences on bad luck. Sometimes it is convinced that the world is out to get them. Sometimes is becomes easier to blame some deity or another person for our failures. Being honest we can look back and take ownership of what we have reaped based on the seeds that we have sown. Being in debt, overweight, alone, disliked, late for something or behind schedule are usually results of cause and effect. Inevitably we create many if not most of our problems.

These consequences lead to bad experiences. These experiences lead to behaviors and conditioning which shape and form future decisions. Life becomes a downward cycle of misery all because we cannot seem to be aware of what we are doing. Most people do not desire misery. When is the last time you met someone who sighed with desire and hoped for suffering and bad luck? So why do we continuously do it to ourselves over and over? It is because of being unconscious in ego. Being unaware of what you are doing and why you are doing for years at a time creates a life time of cause and effect. These behaviors and habits operate deep within the current of mindstream and push the buttons for us. It is like a preset auto pilot that follows the course that has been set. Unconscious of what we are doing and why we are doing it, cause and effect continues to create havoc in our lives. Unconscious, it is impossible to change behavior when we cannot *observe and know* what we are doing and why we are doing it. And even if we do, in our unconscious state we have a brief glimpse of what we are doing, ego quickly resumes control and resumes the path of fulfilling desire regardless of consequence.

The antidote of course is self awareness. In awareness we pull out of egoic mindstream and become aware of being. We become aware of being in the now. In the now, the present moment, we can observe what we are doing. In the space created by being removed from the mindstream of thought we understand why we are doing it. In our daily lives we can be mindful, that is, we can pay special attention and remain alert for these little minute decisions. We can be alert for the conditioning that we had previously been unaware of. In each moment we can realize and utilize choice. These choices can dramatically change your destiny. Good choices are the planting of good seeds that will bear a sweet fruitful life. It is all so simple once you have changed your conditioning to be aware, rather than chained up in the prison of ego.

Simple does not equate to easy. It takes dedication and practice. An individual has to embrace the willingness to change from awareness or spirit. Wanting change from ego is weak and without true meaning. Ego will eagerly try something when it thinks it will look good or get some new sensation from it. But ego is relatively lazy and will give up quickly when the hard work begins.

It is something instructors of meditation see frequently. Students realize the concept that they can feel better and suffer less. Their egos see opportunity. Their egos will be thinking about how cool it can be to tell all their acquaintances of how they are now meditating. Or they like the idea of being empowered somehow. To ego, having more choice means having more options for sensation seeking. Ego can envision invigorating the senses so they can experience a heightened sensation. So having said all this, it is important to hear it stated that meditation, self awareness and mindfulness are hard work for the novice. It takes practice and diligence. If you have spent a lifetime developing conditioning, it does take some practice to detach from that conditioning.

Here is an exercise for exposing a deeper condition of a bad habit. Sit in a comfortable chair or meditation cushion and relax for a moment. Now ask yourself these questions. Be honest and take your time to discern the answers.

- Where are you most out of balance in your life?

- What is the biggest worst habit or behavior you should get rid of or bring into balance?

- What are you doing and why are you doing it?

- Have you tried before and why did you fail?

- What are the deeper feelings that might be the foundation to this habit?

- Do you even know why you are doing what you do?

- Are there strong emotions involved with your behavior?

- Can you recognize that you are not your emotions?

- Can you face those emotions?

- Can you let those emotions go?

- Why not?

- Be honest, are you willing to change?

- Are you willing to make the continuous effort for change?

- Do you sense part of you wanting to avoid making the effort to change?

- Can you recognize that you are the observer and not that part resisting change?

- Can you recognize how you are unconscious when you are doing something and not being aware of it?

- Are you willing to wake up and become aware of what you are doing, and choose a more appropriate response?

Read the chapter on Meditation. It is important to be able to observe this feeling yet stay unabsorbed by it. Note how often we participate in a behavior without even thinking about it. This is the conditioning that was spoken of. Ego is conditioned to have things it desires quickly. Understand that once you begin the practice, ego will be impatient to be doing something else. Doing nothing is something that ego cannot do. So to embrace meditation, you must find that part of yourself that is patient and is willing to detach from the conditioning and let go.

Can you do it? Are you ready? Or are you still so attached in ego that it is just easier to make some excuse and return to being unconscious. Are you really ready to be carried away again only to cycle over and over through a life of suffering?

Success lies in being in each moment. Live your life one small moment of perception at a time. In this moment you be still and quiet. Forget about the future, it does not exist yet. Forget about how you will feel five minutes from now; just be alive and aware here and now. By truly being in the now, we let go of this incessant and impossible illusion of controlling everything that presents before us.

To change your path, you must be here, now, to be able see and feel now. In each now, opportunity and possibility arises.

Here and now you get to choose. Here and now choice does not have to be controlled by egoic conditioning. In awareness time is on your side allowing you freedom to consider what cause and effect might mean. Be here, now. Free your "self".

Action and Reaction

"I am not what happens to me. I choose who I become."
~Carl Jung

Karma can be understood in one way as the culmination of
action or reaction. In every moment we decide on our course
of action, there will be a reckoning when it matures into its
result or reaction. See the chapter on cause and effect. To
break the cycle of problematic results, we must exercise
wisdom with our actions. Wisdom is realized when we learn
from our mistakes. The life of problematic results is
experienced as a life of imbalance. Unhappy lives are those
being lived by the non authentic self. The degree to which one
experiences discontent and unhappiness is where there is a lack
of balance. Living the life of ego is one lived by the continuous
reaction of ego.

When events arise in awareness we are able to discern and then
we can exercise choice. The choice might first be whether to
act or not. Action is how we fulfill an intention that is
grounded in awareness.

Reaction is the egoic response which is spontaneous and
without regard to choice or awareness. Reaction is what ego
does and an emotional response without paying special
attention to discernment. Discernment is the insight of
understanding. This reaction is the automatic response by ego
which is *unaware* of choice.

Strong emotional reactions are frequent when consciousness
has been absorbed by ego. Anger, fear, hatred are all strong
negative emotional forces that limit our ability to remain free
from the current of mindstream of ego. The automatic
responses are driven by a great negative power, a virtual storm
of emotional energy which creates an irresistible desire to
respond. Crimes of passion are common and take place every
hour of every day in our country. People go "postal" or
experience "road rage" quite frequently. This type of
temporary insanity is a common "reaction" which almost

always results in something catastrophic.

After you read this, be alert for the next news article you become aware of where someone did something horrible. Discern where loss of 'self' control was demonstrated by a strong inappropriate reaction of ego.

The antithesis of reaction is action. It is important to draw the distinction of action and right action. Right action is a doing activity that is premeditated in awareness. In awareness, action is the choice of two options, action and no action. As we become aware of events or phenomena arising, we can discern detail without being carried away by the mindstream of ego. Unabsorbed by mindstream, we can choose whether action is appropriate or not. In our awareness we can evaluate acceptance or not, and then action or not. We can evaluate whether we want to change, remove or accept the circumstance we perceive. If the circumstances are not too urgent we can contemplate what action might be best, if any. Awake and aware, we are not absorbed back into the distraction of emotional ego mindstream, we can then perceive a variety of possible choices. Not caught up in the push for instant gratification, or trying to "fix the problem" right in this now, we can allow consciousness and source, guide us to the best solution. Then, if we remain awake and aware, we can perceive the right path when it is apparent. Patience is the insight of allowing things to be as they are while you watch for the right action to take, if any. See the chapter on Patience.

If you practice this 'allowing', you will find that mosaic of our life has its own big picture and that so called "problems" will solve themselves. It is the nature of the Universe to be constantly changing. Moment by moment we are to be awake and aware of what is going on around us and in communion with this flow of change. When we go against the big picture, or the flow, we have replaced "what is" with what the ego wants. When ego does not get what it wants, judgment defines the event of what simply is, as a "problem".

To fulfill our intention, we must initiate action in accordance with "what is". Right action is taking action when necessary and within the framework of the flow of things as they are.

Grounded in awareness, discernment is simply recognizing these changes without emotional judgment and accepting that "it is as it is". When we undertake reaction we are jumping into the flow of life and endeavoring to move against the current of what is. We can reside in the illusion that we are in control, yet the payment of cause and effect will come due. Cause and Effect will work its way around to us sooner or later, and effect is dependent upon the degree to which we have moved against the nature of things being as they are.

So many of the insights we have looked at in this book overlap with this feature of reality. Let's look at Ego (ignorance) vs the true self (wisdom)

Ignorance of ego:

- Ego: the sub-entity of self and false identity (false self) of non acceptance

- Non-acceptance: not accepting things as they are

- Judgment: not accepting and placing inappropriate meaning to what is

- Cause and effect: the result of action and reaction

- Reaction:

  o Distraction and sensation seeking: reaction of not accepting

- Experiences - Rage, Deprivation, Hatred, Jealousy, Embarrassment,

- Discrimination, Apathy, Desperation, Manipulation, Stress, Sickness and poor health, misery.

Pure Consciousness:

- The Higher/True Self,
- Accepts reality as it is because in *wisdom* the higher self realizes its place as part of the universe and that all things are connected.
- In awareness, observation and discernment take place as opposed to judgment.
- Cause and effect are the result of being grounded and in alignment with all that there is.
  - o Action:
  - o The higher self may or may not take action
  - o Action is based on the perspective grounded in awareness, not ego
  - o Action is grounded in love and compassion
  - o Action is guided by - Honesty, Patience, Joy, Gratitude, Serenity, Calm Abiding, Peace, Harmony, Balance, Abundance,

Fulfillment, Good Health, Strength, and

good health.

Action, Reaction, Cause and Effect are the underpinning for reality. It really comes down to being in alignment with our non materialist spiritual core. One leads to enlightenment which is the end of suffering and the other leads to ignorance and the cycle of suffering. As you read this it may be beginning to dawn on you that you have a choice in all things. Perhaps in this moment, this now, you are having a moment of truth, an awakened moment of awareness and find that you are committed to change. As in every moment you face a fork in the road where choice is available. Awake and aware you can choose to begin to practice awareness and transcend the life of ego. Transcendence is the freeing of the self from the false self of ego. It begins with the practice of meditation. To transcend to the true self, living a true life, you must free this self from the traps of ego. In meditation, that is pure awareness, you realize who and what you are. Awake and aware you navigate your path, moment by moment, mindful of what the tricky ego and mindstream are up to without being absorbed. This is mindfulness. The next step is to find a good mindfulness instructor and begin your practice of sustaining an awakened reality. This is it, your chance to free your "self".

Judgment

"If you judge people, you have no time to love them"

Mother Teresa

In earlier chapters we learned about discernment, choice, action and reaction. In discernment the observer distinguishes or recognizes that which is being perceived. In awareness we choose action or no-action and in ego illusion we most often react without unemotional discernment. Judgment is the egoic reaction guided by emotion through perceiving and defining a thing as good or bad.

In awareness we discern information without being overly influenced by emotion. In judgment we form an opinion. Judgment in itself is not so problematic, but becomes so when the opinion is guided solely on feelings and emotion. Discernment is observing in such a way as to not react to a given event or detail as it is perceived. Typically in ego we react to content that arises with a mental action known as judgment. This is a mental action where an opinion forms and is based on a previous emotional memory. This is where ego can assume control. In judgment we form opinions and conclusions which are highly influenced by ego through emotions and feelings. Please read the chapters on Behavior, Ego and Feelings to see how the lower egoic self quickly becomes absorbed by emotion.

Most if not all of the ancient sages warn us about the dangers of judgment. Judgment is one of the higher functions of ego and is driven by our personal life story. It is the habitual reaction of ego that occurs so many moments in our life that most of us are not aware of it. This comparative function that our minds are constantly engaging in allows us to perceive differences which help us navigate life in a safe manner. It is a necessary feature of discernment which places humans at the top of the sentient pyramid. Yet when discernment gives over to the illusions of ego, judgment arises. Whatever is being perceived is now defined as good or bad. If emotional ego judges the information to be bad, a "problem" is born.

In the first chapter, reference was made to the "ego illusion" from which many of us create a reaction. This illusion is created when a false reality is formed based on facts that do not exist. Typically the illusion is an emotional response based on a negative emotion such as fear, anger, hatred or any of the other negative states of ego.

Here is an example.

You are driving down the street and late for work. You have been late before several times this week and your boss has already spoken to you about it. Worried about being late you drive a little faster than the speed limit allows. Your thoughts are captivated by scenarios of trying to explain why you are late one more time. As you play out this stressful daydream scenario in your mind your foot unconsciously presses the accelerator a little harder.

Suddenly you see a police car coming in the opposite lane. You glanced at the speedometer and see you are 15 miles over the speed limit. You tap your brakes a little, hoping that your brake lights are not seen and hoping you have not been caught. A feeling of desperation begins to creep in as you realize that this could have all sorts of bad ramifications. It might mean an expensive ticket to pay, you might get reprimanded or fired, and ultimately you might become unemployed during a recession. In a split second your stress level has elevated dramatically and nothing tangible has even happened yet.

Then, sure enough, the police car turns makes a U-turn and turns on his blue lights. Now your elevated stress level rises even higher and you begin to experience fear, anger, and frustration. As he approaches from behind you maintain the speed limit careful to obey all the driving regulations waiting to see if in fact what you fear is indeed true. As the police car moves over into the lane behind you, you are convinced that he has nailed you and you decided to turn into a side street and just wait for your punishment. You feel sick and disgusted with the predicament and yourself. You reach for your license and insurance to give to the policeman and glance in the rearview to see if has turned into the street behind you. You watch as he continues on past the street where you turned and sit astonished as if some great miracle has occurred. For the last few minutes you have been existing in an illusion of what might have happened because of the way you were incorrectly judging the situation as something other than how it really was. This is a true story that happened to guess who?

As you can see, judgment is not relegated to just interpersonal relationships. Judgment or the emotional conclusion that is drawn strictly by the ego can influence anything that is perceived. We can choose action over reaction. The cause and effect of this choice will create a result that can either become ignorance or wisdom. As discussed earlier, in awareness we have choice. In awareness possibilities rise and surface in a spontaneous fountain of perspectives. So when making a judgment on a given situation, we should remain awake and aware rather than allow ego to run away with our thoughts and emotions.

When ego reigns unchecked, judgment is frequently an emotional characteristic that provides a source of negative energy to feed on. Always jealous and critical of others around it, it quickly judges to find fault in that which is not it. It gains esteem through the perceived weakness of others. It gets a thrill of energy when someone else makes a mistake, suffers, and is embarrassed and thus egoic judgment is the height of arrogance.

Egoic judgment can be the height of arrogance because it likes to assume that it can do no wrong. Busy in its "look at me" routine, it will go to great length to push attention on those who are weaker and on itself when it is stronger. The arrogance extends from always forgetting its own limitations and assuming it is never wrong and better than all others. When the light of judgment shines back on ego it lashes out with indignation saying "how dare you criticize me".

Sometimes the bi-polar nature of ego will swing the other way and experience itself as inferior. In this illusion it suffers from a low self esteem because of how it compares itself to how things "should be". It can falsely judge and conclude that it is a failure and not worthy of a high esteem from others. It extends the illusion to define the quality of life it has created as "bad" and will suffer. All because the emotional judgment of ego defines the present moment on previous emotional experiences. It does not have to be this way. See the chapter on worry:

When judgment is a part of decision making, it should be done through awareness and free of ego. Seeing things as they really are, that is, to observe without judgment, makes sense from several perspectives. Analytically, observing without the emotion of ego can allow decision making to follow logical conclusions. Practicing Wu Wei, the action of no action is a great way to allow judgment to diffuse and for possibility to arise. Notice the distinction between analyzing and judgment. One is observing information, the other is emotional decision making. What you will find is that more often than not judgment is just not required for decision making.

But let's not throw the baby out with the bath. With balance and harmony as our guide, some emotion may be proper. Love and compassion can mean the difference between heaven and hell for those on the receiving end of your analytics and judgment. Ultimately the enlightened being can refrain from all judgment and accept all things as they are. Along the path, it helps to have a spiritual direction to aim our compass. Love and compassion are those emotions that we can steer towards.

Often we are coached on how to gain and maintain a healthy self esteem. Yet I submit that self esteem is more often than not just a feature of ego. The esteem to which we evaluate the self can be arrived at by choice. When self esteem is discerned to be low, the ego is simply placing judgment on itself and letting doubt and disappointment create the illusion. Low self esteem is the path to depression, yet may be avoided if we can remain in awareness.

In awareness, we know what ego is doing, yet remain in charge and do not become absorbed by the illusion of low self esteem. In awareness we may be able to exercise choice and choose the feeling that is appropriate. Self judgment is unnecessary.

Mindfulness is the function of awareness of paying attention to the activities of the mind. Being aware of what ego is up to, we are able to remain un-attached to the devastating illusion that the emotional ego will manifest.

Being free from the reaction of judgment is a necessary step in freeing the self from low self esteem which is experienced in a state of egoic dominion. Be here, in this now, and avoid this painful unnecessary state. Free your "self" from the judgment of ego.

Fear

"The whole secret of existence is to have no fear. Never fear what will become of you, depend on no one. Only the moment you reject all help are you freed." The Buddha

Fear arises when there is a perceived threat. Fear is an emotion that is not exclusive to only sentient beings but is a primal function of survival in all animals. We can even sense fear in insects when they struggle to escape harm. We all experience fear as part of our survival instinct. So as a survival skill, fear played a role in helping us to avoid discomfort, pain and death. However, as in all things, there must be balance. Fear can help avoid catastrophe, but excessive fear can cause panic. Panic is an extension of fight or flight and can quickly escalate to a loss of control. Panic is certainly a state of emotion that should be considered out of balance.

As human beings, we have a desire to avoid pain and suffering. A low grade but sustained form of fear can move in and reside in our consciousness. This type of stress is one of the most devastating forms of negative emotions. There is a wide range of fear factors and these can lead to an unpleasant experience.

When Ego functions through fear, it goes beyond discernment and begins to judge many issues from a threat perspective. This threat perspective can permeate the egoic view in such a way that it begins to control all thoughts. Illusion takes the place of normal discernment and fear begins to create possible scenarios for what might go wrong. Fear can control our lives and create a massive amount of stress. Stress is a killer, so managing it is a must. Please see the chapter titled "Stress Kills".

In awareness we can observe fear as it begins to arise and avoid being captured by panic. As fear arises we can learn to not be absorbed by the emotion and its associated reaction. Again, in awareness choice becomes evident along with the many other options that may be available. By not becoming absorbed by the fear, we can transcend this emotion and exercise choice. We can still be very aware of what our instinct is telling us and if we need to take action, we can do so without being controlled by the fear. By controlling fear, we can eliminate a lot of the stress. Managing fear can be a formidable task at first. You may want to seek professional help to learn to manage this all powerful emotion. If the practice of meditation and self awareness are not helping or if the fear has already become too destructive, seek help immediately.

Worry

Be careful what you water your dreams with. Water them with worry and fear and you will produce weeds that choke the life from your dream.
Lao Tzu

Worry is a type of low grade fear that settles in for the long haul. Unless brought under management, worry will form the foundation for most of your decision making and through cause and effect create a self fulfilling destiny. If you focus on something long enough, there is a good chance that the "thing" will be produced. Anticipation of problems can produce the feared results. When Ego perceives everything through fear, it will continuously look for the scenario that it fears. Eventually conditions will be right for the worry to be actualized. Once the worry is realized it will escalate quickly into fear. If not brought back into balance, fear can become panic.

Long term worry can erode our quality of life. It taints our moment by moment perspective and becomes the limiting factor that we can become trapped in. Worry is a barrier that traps us in a negative mindset in which we remain lost from our true and authentic self. Through meditation and the practice of awareness we can become aware of being in the worried state and learn to transcend the feelings that limits a fully functioning life. As stated above, worry and fear have a way of becoming a self fulfilling prophesy. Dwelling in a state of worry and fear wears a person down minute by minute, hour by hour and day by day.

Exercise

Think back to a recent worry/fear day that you have experience or one you may be having right now. Sit still and allow yourself to relax and focus on your breathing for a moment. Become aware of where you are and what you are doing. Be alert for the next thought and try to count ten breaths without losing concentration. When you are relaxed ask yourself these questions:

- How does your energy level feel? (Are you or were you tired?)

- Are you experiencing worry or concern?

- What was the event, thought or worry that triggered the fear or worry?

- In awareness can you see the nature of the fear and worry without being swept away by it?

- Try to realize the root of the fear. What is the source that is causing concern?

- Do you detect your mind playing the "what if" game where it is creating all sorts of negative scenarios of what might happen.

- Can I change it, remove it, and move away from it?

- Can I just accept it? If no, why not? (see the chapter on 'The Power of Acceptance'

- In this quiet stillness, what are other possibilities for solutions?

- What are other possible actions are possible?

- Is there any actions necessary right here and right now?

- If not, ask why in this moment, can you not go ahead and experience peace?

- If the problem is not apparent right now, why can I not adopt happiness or contentment for the time being or until a resolution is realized?

- Can you see the thought or feeling of fear and allow it go its own way and keep returning your attention to the present moment without being absorbed.

If we practice staying calm during an emotional storm, we can become strong with our grounding in awareness. At first it may be very hard but with practice many of us can learn to just let go and be in the present moment and to let the fear or worry subside. In order to not become absorbed by the ego, we must realize that these emotional storms will pass. It becomes a matter of hanging on in awareness until the energy is depleted. Remember, we are not our fear or worry; those are just emotional states that ego resides in. If you cannot detach your "self" from these worries, seek help from a trained professional who may be able to help you break its grip.

Worry can run in the background like one of those power draining applications on your computer that applies a continuous drain on the battery. When we stay busy multi-tasking with many activities on the surface of our mind, and have an energy draining worry in the background, the result will be exhaustion. This is known as stress. Please read the chapter on Stress. Generally, stress causes a slow degradation through constant misery and just using up to much energy. With stress comes the constant cascade of caustic hormones along with the energy drain that leave no room for the immune system. Worry, Fear, Anxiety and Stress just sucks you dry mentally, physically and spiritually.

Fear and Anger

Fear is the antithesis of hope. Ego, the vigilant protector of me, is always on the lookout for either what can go wrong or what it can benefit from. See the chapter on attachment. Fear of loss is one of Ego's many aspects unawareness and is a path to anger.

As it was mentioned earlier, unrestrained worry can evolve into a "what if" scenario. This illusion is created where fear begins to get creative and generates an illusion of "what may go wrong". In this present moment everything might be just fine, but looking to the future it can become hyper vigilant in trying to protect itself from the suffering of *what might be*. Since the future has not happened yet, it does not exist. It is just one of an infinity of possible futures. Yet ego treats the future with a false certainty that often does not justify the panic which is being experienced right now.

Once during a discussion on illusion, a person argued that the fear was justified because of the certainty of the following events. Let's look at this example.

The example given was one where it was stated that if we do not pay our power bill, the power will be cut off. Let us imagine that today there may not be enough money to pay the power bill that is due in one week. In awareness we can ask those questions from this exercise.

Exercise

- Do you detect your mind playing the "what if" game where it is creating all sorts of negative scenarios of what might happen.

- *What if* there is not enough money to pay the bill

- Can I change it, remove it, and move away from it?

- Can I change it? Maybe, call the power company.

- Is there any chance that the money will come in?

- Can I borrow from someone?

- Can I remove it?

- Can I move away from it?

- Can I just accept the situation

- Can I accept it temporarily while I explore possible solutions?

- We can accept that things are as they are. Feeling deprived, resentful, worried or angry will not solve the problem. It only makes things worse both internally and externally.

- In this quiet stillness, what are other possibilities for solutions?

- Practice this and see what you can come up with?

- What are other possible actions

- Practice this now?

- Is any action necessary right here and right now in this very moment?

- No, in this moment the power is still on, so things are ok

- If not, ask why in this moment, can you not go ahead and experience peace?

- In the quiet stillness of this now, other than ego, what is stopping you from satisfaction with life, what part of you is worrying? (Ego)

- Can you see the thought or feeling of fear and allow it go its own way and keep returning your attention to the present moment without being absorbed.

Observing the feeling of worry and fear is being mindful of what is going on within your egoic mind. As the observer you can choose how to react or feel. Why not choose calm in this now and take the action of resolution in a calm manner.

Possible Action Step

In a calm manner you can contact the power company, or call family or friends and explain your predicament. People will be more likely to help you when you are calm and not expressing fear and anger. They will also be more likely to help someone who is trying to help themselves rather than presenting the pitiful self entitled mindset of ego.

- In awareness we can contemplate what we can learn from experience and use wisdom to avoid creating worry again.

- What action steps can I do to prevent this in the future

- What are other possibilities for resolving this situation?

- Be open to possibility by remaining in the calm abiding of awareness

The 'what if' scenario is an illusion created when we substitute the current now with something that has not happened yet. In this moment we can take action or not. Sometimes no action is an action. If we cannot do anything or change anything, we can accept it as it is. But by not accepting the present moment (each now) we set our self up for illusion. By being in awareness we can put fear aside and consider the choice of action we might want to take. In awareness, possibilities arise and solution can become evident. In worry, fear and panic we lose the ability to see outside of the box. We find ourselves experiencing an impossible situation where we cannot accept life as it is. This is suffering and it creates stress.

For someone with chronic fear, everything they do in their conscious life is oriented towards fear of things going wrong and experiencing pain. And since this is a reality of impermanence, things are always changing. The worry and fear of losing the things we are attached to provide one basis for anger. To not accept 'what is' is to not accept our life as it is while it is unfolding. Worry and fear is simply not accepting what is and giving in to the emotional reaction to ego. (See Action and Reaction)

Fear dominated egos have a filtering system whose spectrum resides completely in problems. For them, there is nothing but problems. So the filtering spectrum is set to allow only problems. On any given day, they are experiencing only a few problems or they may be experiencing a lot of problems. They are either experiencing a lot of emotional pain and fear, or only a little. There is always something there, because that is how their reality is defined. .

If one believes in the old adage that we are what we think about, then when we only think of problems, problems are what we will perceive. Fearful egos will manifest their own self fulfilling problems. It is as if they need to validate their problematic existence by having the problems they envision always come true. You may have encountered these egos and recall them telling you "see, I told you something would go wrong". And then for them things did go wrong. Sometimes they almost seem happy that they were happy to prove just how bad they have it. Read the chapter on 'Cause and Effect' to better understand how we plant the seeds to our future.

It makes a weird sort of sense when you think about it. Egos love attention and one tried and true method of receiving it is to share their many problems with others. When faced with skepticism, the fearful ego is only too happy to prove how bad they have it, so that then they can fulfill their sense of entitlement through attention from others.

I submit that sometimes even when things go extraordinarily well, some egos will not be satisfied and will cause a problem just so things will seem normal. These egos will even worry when things are going too good. They will even tell you "things are going too good, something bad is going to happen". If you find yourself in this position try the exercise listed above.

Fearful ego's have a hard time understanding or conceiving that actually life is usually pleasant and good with only the occasional bump in the road. If you suffer in this way, then there is a clear indicator that your ego is hard at work dominating your perspective. What you will find out is that through self awareness those problems you perceive are often unjustified. Through self awareness and changing your perspective, you will realize choice. You will come to be able to choose from a number of responses on how to define events as they arrive in this ever changing world. Often we can accept things as they are and avoid an unnecessary meltdown.

Sometimes Anger results from *unresolved fear* in Ego. The ego's sense of preservation will gather everyone around it for support. When the fear gets too great and cannot be satisfied, it will mutate into a higher level of negative energy. Anger is one of the highest forms of negative energy. Anger is one of the most destructive forces we as humans have ever experienced. I will use the metaphor of a volcano to help demonstrate the destructive nature of Anger. As in volcanoes, sometimes anger smolders quietly fuming slowly building pressure. Perhaps the mantle of reason can weight it down for a time until the pressure becomes too great. Then there is a massive eruption and bad things can happen.

Other times the pressure builds quickly and erupts quickly. Things can escalate so quickly that we can find our selves in a blind rage of unrestrained egoic anger. And like a volcano it blows up with immense power and destruction. Then the ego/volcano becomes dormant for a time. Having spent all of its energy, the anger demon goes to sleep until the next eruption.

"Fear is the path to the dark side. Fear leads to anger. Anger leads to hate. Hate leads to suffering." Yoda, from Star Wars Episode 1, The Phantom Menace

With some egos, anger is followed by a sense of remorse, guilt and even self hating. One's self esteem falls down very low. It may become so low that the individual may feel depression. They feel remorse for what they do and will promise anything and try everything not to repeat it again. The ego even believes it has learned a lesson and will lay low for a while. As the ego regains a little energy, it feels better. All is forgiven as a false sense of happiness surfaces and for a little while everything is wonderful. But before long, the hunger pains of ego begin to rumble. The dissatisfaction of the present moment leads to fear of what may happen to it or resentment for what it is being deprived of. This leads to anger. Unresolved, anger can lead to many other unacceptable mental conditions including depression where the cycle begins all over again.

The fear may be rooted in tangible or intangible concerns. A tangible concern may be worrying over a legitimate issue such as financial problems. Fear over becoming homeless often led me into the cycle. Before self awareness I never realized that the fear did not really help anything and only made things a lot worse. It can be a real and qualified concern. Yet fear in itself will not solve it. I believe the best one can hope for is that fear can motivate one into action. Yet reaction based on fear, is by far less effective than action based on inspiration.

Sometimes fear is rooted in the intangible. Some of these can seem very benign, and then they can turn into something quite extraordinary. Probably one of the silliest yet profound examples that you will recognize is how egos worry over what other egos think about them.

If you are trending towards the fear and anger cycle, yet are still aware enough to be seeking help, it is not too late to turn back from the dark side of an ego dominated life. If you are in a deep cycle of fear and anger, it is never too late to begin breaking the chains of bondage. The longer you have been lost, the harder it is to remove yourself. So the sooner you begin, the sooner you can free yourself and get your life back. Freeing yourself requires a willingness to make the changes necessary for results. If you or someone you know is yet unwilling to make the commitment to change, then more suffering may be necessary and is on the way. Unfortunately that means not only will they suffer more but those in their domain will suffer along with them. If it is someone you know and love and want to help, the best thing you can do is strengthen your practice of self awareness. In awareness you can choose compassion, forgiveness and understanding while practicing a qualified refusal to participate in the egoic activities.

As Gandhi said, "become the change you would like to see in the world" However be careful because ego is threatened by awareness, consciousness and love. It destroys those things when it feels cornered or threatened. Ego despises peace. Look at what happened to those enlightened leaders who were the change they sought to see. Gandhi was assassinated, Jesus was crucified, and Dr. Martin Luther King Junior was assassinated as were others who manifested peace yet were perceived as a threat to the collective ego.

In mindfulness we can watch for and pay special attention to how we are feeling and what behaviors we are experiencing. We can become mindful of dark emotions as they arise. By being mindful of dark emotions such as worry and fear rising, we can then avoid being caught up in the tantrum of fear and anger. Being aware we have a choice. The choice is about letting these feelings go and choosing an alternative action. See the chapter on Mindfulness.

Practicing mindfulness meditation will allow you the space to see the trends of behavior as they are building. Even during a busy day you can practice active mindfulness and being aware of what your ego is up to. Be aware of how it is pacing in its cage ready to jump out and feed. Being mindful you can starve ego of its dominance and let it diffuse into a background noise of no importance. There is a great power in being free of negative emotions. Of course ego will argue that fear is a great motivator, or that anger is good energy for defense. Being wise and aware, you will know that flirting with ego and all of its trickery is akin to stepping through a mine field. In mindfulness meditation you can learn to just let these thoughts come and go. With the practice of daily mindfulness you can learn to let egoic reaction go, as you balance being with doing. Through wisdom and awareness you will have a knowing, that love and compassion, the components of light and spirit will ultimately prevail and then you can free your "self".

Desire, Greed, Ambitions, and Lust

Desire

"Do not spoil what you have by desiring what you have not; remember that what you now have was once among the things you only hopea for." - Epicurus

"...The wise man attends to the inner significance of things and does not concern *himself with outward appearances. Therefore he ignores matter and seeks the spirit.* Verse 12 Tao Te Ching

Desire has been the subject of discussion since humans have been recording history. Aristotle has his observations in ancient Greece. The Buddhists consider striving for fulfillment of desire as one of the primary causes of suffering. Descartes calls the passion of desire "an agitation of the soul". Ultimately, the end of suffering [enlightenment] only happens when we can let go of desire and just be. But life is a long path with many lessons to learn. I believe that the more immediate goal should be to bring desire into balance. After all, the desire to improve your spiritual life through self awareness is a step in the right direction. Trying to remove all desire is like quitting cigarettes 'cold turkey'.

The basis of desire is sensation seeking. Sensation seeking is different from satisfying our basic needs, which are those things required to sustain a healthy and normal life. Notice I did not add the word "style" to life. Desire is wanting. This constant wanting or striving for the fulfillment of desires leads to trouble. Striving is the opposite of acceptance and each moment we should be grounded in awareness and accept life as it is. We can learn to enjoy all the wonderful aspects of life as they come, or we can be lost in egoic pursuit of desire which is grounded in materialism. It is one thing to desire the basic necessities of life such as food, shelter and peace. It is quite another to not be satisfied with what you have and always strive for more than is required.

Desire is a part of life and when balanced with awareness it can play an important role in development. Yet without awareness, desire quickly becomes the fuel for ego and will evolve into greed. Ego's addiction to greed (that neediness of excessive sensation seeking) is closely associated with another negative aspect of ego which is fear. The fear of not getting the desires met can lead to a whole host of problems. See the chapter on Fear and Anger. All of the negative aspects of ego overlap each other. They form a tapestry of failure at life that is experienced through suffering.

It *does not* have to be this way. It is NOT supposed to be this way. If after reading these lines, you find ego at work in your life, NOW is the moment to point your compass in a different direction. Now, this present moment, is all you have. Make sure to read the chapter about the illusion of time. In each moment, in awareness, you can find the simple joyful life that you, the higher self, are meant to experience.

Let's examine just a few different aspects of desire and how it gets us out of balance and into trouble.

Greed

"*Greed is Good*" Gordon Gekko from the 'Movie Wall Street 1987'

As I write these words the economy is struggling to make a rise out of a very bad economic recession. This experience has been very hard for some and the suffering has been wide scale. It has been one of many recessions in a succession of hills and valleys. One has to wonder when or if it will ever level off. The answer of course is no, it will not. That is, it will never change *unless we all change collectively.*

Our economy, and thus the world economy, seems to be dependent on sustained growth. It is the mantra spoken on Wall Street and board rooms across the world. While there is a natural growth in any society where a population is increasing, the problem arises when the growth is grounded in an imbalance of desire and consumption. From awareness this can be seen quite easily. The problem of desire and consumerism is both individual and collective. Originally the American Dream was based on freedom and the pursuit of happiness. And now the American Dream has been redefined by the collective ego and conspicuous consumerism. The American Dream is now the unrestrained pursuit of fulfilling every possible desire which is grounded in materialism. Materialism is a virtue straight from the heart of ego. As discussed in earlier chapters, ego falsely searches for contentment in material things. And then even when it gets "it", ego is never satisfied for long. As ego dominates the self, we as individuals and collectively as a society, covet and search for happiness in all the wrong places. Never satisfied with having enough or even having an abundance, ego is always striving for more. It is only through self awareness and the practice of gratitude can one begin to reign in the greedy ego

Here is how it might work. You are at your place of employment supposedly doing the work you are paid to do. You (your ego) are bored because the labor you agreed to do is not inspiring or meaningful. Rather than being conscious and focused on what you are doing, (your job), ego slips into your identity and assumes control. Your mind, now ego begins to wander. On the radio playing next to you is a commercial that is very effective at persuading your ego that you (ego) will be happy, look cool, be envied, feel the wind in your hair etc … when you buy this new car. The higher self accepts things as they are and realizes that the car you drive is just fine. It may also be nudging you that you have already maxed out your budget and there is not room for more outgoing money. Quickly ego swells with the desire of filling this perceived need of a new car and ego now feels that it has to have it. It is now in the forefront of your mind. Your thoughts continuously revolve around how you are going to get this new car. Other thoughts are daydreams where you envision the envy of friends and co-workers of you with your new car.

Later, at home, in front of the Television, a commercial comes on. It is a commercial about the car of your dreams. Earlier during your commute from work, the radio programmed your egoic mind for desire fulfillment. Ego, upon hearing, the radio ad was only too delighted to hijack the higher self and begin the 'what if' scenario. Ego builds mental pictures of you and your new car. Now with the Television directly linked to your optic nerve, there is a two dimensional feed into your mind. The mental picture of your dream car has been enhanced with a realistic, moving, color display of the very essence of your dream. The obsession intensifies. You (ego) must have this car.

Later in bed, just before falling asleep, the vigilance of ego has weakened. From somewhere far away the notion of whether you can afford this large purchase slides into focus. You briefly feel a bit of panic and resolve to think more clearly about it in the morning. In the morning when you wake up, you (ego) begin to think about your day. Immediately you (ego) determine that it is going to be another boring uninspired session of drudgery. Then it occurs to you how you could so live with this burden if you were just driving that wonderful new car to and from the salt mines where you are employed. It occurs to you that maybe you (ego) could just drop by the car dealer on the way home and just take a look at the object of your desire. Another day is spent in the new car obsession. You watch the clock all day, and when the time for departure arrives, you gleefully hop into the painfully boring car you currently have and set out for the car dealer, full of euphoric anticipation. You arrive at the dealer, park in front of a selection of those dream cars. A friendly salesman greets you and ready to manipulate you. And here you come, already preprogrammed and ready for being manipulated. The process of negotiating is a sham. You (ego) only want to be seen as being a shrewd buyer. Ego has no intention of driving away in nothing less than the dream car. Ego senses that victory is so close now, and determines that nothing can stand in the way. All the through the process of making the purchase, warning sirens are going off. Ego is efficiently turning off the sirens and flashing lights, keeping the focus on the prize. Soon the purchase is complete. You are handed the keys to your new dream car. You float on joy out to your new vehicle on a cloud of ecstasy. You are en route home living what was just a few hours ago a fantasy. Ah, life is sweet and life is good. The illusion is wonderful.

Until a month later and you realize that you don't have enough money to pay all of your bills. Stress begins to build up as you put aside one of the lesser bills you cannot pay. Stress follows you to work the next day and you (ego) suddenly realize that you hate this job. And you (ego) realize that it does not pay enough. You feel trapped and miserable. You (ego) leave this crappy job for a better job that pays more money. The new car is still great, but the love affair has cooled to a being a necessary status symbol. The new job is not what you thought it would be and to cope with the added stress you decide to buy a new home theatre system. You max out your credit card and your checking account and go home to set it up. A week or so later, you find you cannot enjoy the new toy because of the incessant ringing of your phone. It is all of those people to whom you owe money and they will not go away. In fact they are quite rude and even make threats about the things that may happen if they are not paid right now.

The spiral continues until we experience the moment of truth of what we have created. See the chapter on cause and effect. We collapse mentally, physically and spiritually. Perhaps there will be a moment of awareness, where you suddenly wake up and realize what you are doing and begin changing your path.

Imagine this scenario in the collective sense. Imagine millions and millions of citizens living the life of illusion. The illusion is not just cars, but everything that desire can possibly conceive of. Unless we all wake up and become conscious of what we are doing and why we are doing it, we will all have this experience again. What is that saying about doing the same thing expecting different results?

Exercise

Let us have a moment of truth. Look at some of the areas of

your life where you might perceive problems and imbalance. This requires self honesty, so be very honest and do not lie to your "self".

- How much unnecessary debt do you own?

- How much stuff are you surrounded by?

- How much of the stuff was purchased on credit to which you have not paid off?

- How much stuff do you no longer use but just keep around?

- Why do you keep it around?

- How much of this stuff that you don't use is part of the debt that you owe?

- How long ago did you experience the feeling that if you just had _____ everything would great and life wonderful?

- How much of your stuff is a result of being unhappy due to some aspect of your life such as job, relationship, self esteem etc?

People search for and come to these courses on meditation, self awareness and mindfulness when they have had enough and want to find peace of mind. They either sense they are in a downward spiral, hit some low plateau or maybe even hit bottom. It is sometimes apparent during the first few minutes or first several sessions when ego asserts itself and snatches the individual out of the course to resume the never ending cycle of sensation seeking and distraction. Most often the reason for leaving is that "there is not enough time". Ego never has enough time, for it is never satisfied with the now and must set desire fulfillment as a higher priority. Learning from our mistakes creates wisdom. Repeating our mistakes, expecting a new outcome, creates ignorance and misery.

People who are able to break this cycle, come to realize they do not really need much in life to bring forth the happiness and contentment that was being sought. It is because in awareness they are able to understand what they are doing and why. In concentrated meditation, they can peel back the onion layers of their behavior and get to the why they are doing what they do. It takes a very personal honesty and truth to realize one's true nature. Sometimes, maybe a lot of times, it may take the help of a professional counselor to help get to those truths. If you dear reader, are one those, do not let ego stop you from seeking that help. If you know you need help unraveling the knot, become aware of how ego may want to block the effort. Ego may feel embarrassed. Ego may feel it is a waste of time. Ego will not want to surrender its existence and allow your higher self to get to the truth.

The others, especially those who have suffered enough, will come to a moment of truth where they take ownership of what has been going on and commit to changing it. There may be a kind of fear that without the pursuit of sensation seeking or distraction, life will have no joy. What they often find is that in awareness the honest and profound joy will arise on its own. This kind of happiness and joy can arise from the simplest of things. It is a joy that almost always requires no action or monetary requirement.

Sexual Lust

This Desire based aspect is complex and dynamic. We are stimulated on several fronts that are both physiological and psychological sources. Young people in the prime of their life have an abundance of emotional energy and hormonal longing for procreation. In other situations, lust is sought as a sexual release or a sensational coping mechanism. It sometimes becomes a coping mechanism for the stress that we develop due to the many problems that we perceive. In many cultures and religions physical intimacy is considered to be a gift that couples can share with each other. This is true, but I offer caution. It remains a gift when it is a mutual sharing that is mutually given between couples. But like many powerful sensations, sex can quickly become something our ego becomes dependant on. Desire becomes lust when a coping ego becomes dependent on the sexual release. What begins as the gift becomes the fix. The original intent in the activity becomes something else and eventually both parties will realize it.

When one in the relationship no longer desires participation, the other is left with the unfulfilled desire. If the desire has become too strong, ego will suffer and begin seeking yet more coping to resolve the new source of pain. Ego, never empathetic or compassionate, may demand its share or perhaps seek release somewhere else. Thus begins the downward spiral. Sometimes it becomes an obsession which leads to all kinds of problems that I will let your imagination handle. Relationships are sometimes started and finished with foundations based on sexual lust. Male egos are notorious for agreeing to any condition to fulfill sexual desire. Later if that desire cannot be fulfilled, they may break all rules of ethics and decency to fulfill this powerful neediness. Sexual lust can become an addiction to which individuals will go to all sorts of extremes to satisfy. Sexual lust is just another striving for a powerful sensation in which to escape the realities of life. In awareness we can observe and know this sensation for what it is and choose a different path to take. It takes willpower to sustain from inappropriate behaviors. Willpower happens when we accept things as they are, lets go of the attachment (sex), and do not give into the illusions of ego. Desire is best managed with the harmony and balance that can be realized in self awareness.

Ambition

Ambition is the desire for achievement. This aspect of desire requires balance. Ambition is considered a positive virtue and part of the American dream. Many consider ambition to be the opposite of lazy. I have known co workers in the corporate world who were so absolute in their ambitious views that they only perceived two categories: Forwards or backwards. And that dear reader is pure ego.

Ambition becomes an aspect of ignorance when it is co-opted by ego. Egoic ambition can be characterized as an aggressive pursuit of sensation satisfaction. Ambition can be realized as part of not being satisfied with what you have, where you are, and where you are going. It can be an aspect of being impatient. Ego that is never satisfied and hungrily seeking instant gratification is constantly pinging the environment for an advantage. For ego, this advantage may be at the cost of anything and everything. Nothing is too sacred for an ambitious ego. A few years ago my wife introduced a new word into my vocabulary. The word was "frien –enemy", or "frenenemy". Frien-enemies thrive in the world of office or group politics. You can find them in board rooms or churches. Frien-enemies will pretend friendship as they use you as a stepping stone for achieving their ambitious goals. These egos will sell you off at the first opportunity with a smile and a shrug, never caring for a second what it means on a personal level.

Other Egos form collective groups of like ambitions. They create a synergy of power that may or may not be helpful to the corporate agenda. There is always a strong ego at the top whose ambition is greater than all others. But usually a slightly less established ego just below it. This hierarchy is formed with the weaker team members filling a pyramid like structure with the weakest and least ambitious on the bottom. The base of the pyramid is the foundation and the stronger and more ambitious egos step all over the weaker on their way to the top. This temporary assembly ambitious go getters will only hold their collective together long enough to fulfill their goals.

Ambition as a positive virtue, is characterized by grounding their motivation on compassion and love. These are individuals who practice self awareness. They are content to evolve in a timely manner in accordance with the natural order of things. Their compass points them in a direction that empowers as many people as possible which may include customers, co-workers and their bosses. In awareness they are aware of greed and ambition as they arise but also know to let them go. They can practice patience and take a moment to consider what is best for all concerned. They are good listeners because they are not focused on egoic needs, but truly listening to what others are saying. They have a knowing of how and what a person puts into the world, through cause and effect, and this will come back bigger and stronger. When these people get together in awareness the sum is greater than the parts and a true synergy will unfold. They help to build and lead teams of like minded individuals. They fully understand that when a person allows the elegance and beauty of source to be the guide then productivity increases. When a grouping of aware minds focus together, then miracles can happen.

When ambition is a positive motive, when it is grounded in compassion and love, the community truly benefits. When the need for profit is balanced with the delivery of a wonderful product or service everyone benefits.

For examples, just look at history through past news articles where the ambition of a collective either helped or hurt people or the environment. As you look over the facts of what happened, filter it with the question of what the intention of this organization had.

Exercise

Think about the organization that you most affiliate with. Ask yourself these questions and *be honest* with the answers.

- What is the organization's goal and in what ways does it serve and empower others? Who benefits most from its actions?

- Regardless of stated intentions are the actions in reality ethically and morally sound?

- Even if a lofty mission goal is stated, is it followed?

- What is your part in this effort and are you participating in an ethical and morally sound manner?

- Is anyone discriminated against as a result of organizational policy? (be honest)

- Are you supporting any discriminating actions or behaviors?

- Is ambition a positive or negative aspect of your behavior?

- Is ambition a positive or negative aspect of the organizations behavior?

- If you know that negative ambition and unworthy behaviors are present, what are you doing about it?

These are just some questions to alert your higher self to ego at work. When you answer these questions with awareness and honesty you are having your moment of truth. In this moment you can choose to do the right thing. Be present and aware of egoic feelings and thoughts that arise.

Ambition and greed are present in every aspect of modern life. When negative ambition is in a state of imbalance, suffering will be experienced. The most obvious example we can look at is the current economy. The recession that we just went through was a direct result of greed and ambition out of control. It is the result from individuals as well as businesses, being out of balance. In just one segment of the recession it is obvious that the housing market became an environment where greed and ambition went awry. There were many individuals who wanted more than they could afford and more than they needed. And a lending industry which was also experiencing a fever of ambition was only too happy to comply. We, as a collective of egos, were all too quick to borrow and too quick to lend. We will be working through this problem for years to come. I hope through awareness, enough people will realize what has happened and not repeat the behavior. History shows that it will cycle around again. The depression of the last century and the great recession of this one are opportunities to realize what we as a society are doing. Once again we have a chance to turn failure into wisdom if we can just become aware of our feeling emotions and actions. All we have to do is become aware of what we are doing and why we are doing it.

We can go on and on examining our feelings and emotions. As you have seen, greed and ambition can create havoc. Compassionate ambition can be wonderfully creative. This is something you do through meditation and mindfulness. As you become aware of what you are doing and why you are doing it, the opportunity for change will be apparent. The more you can do this, the more balance and harmony you will realize in your life. The path becomes smoother and the opportunity for joy and happiness will have a better chance to arise on its own. We must be able to manage our desires and bring our lives into balance. When we are able to be in balance we are being our true self. We can free ourselves from the suffering brought on by greed and negative ambition by becoming self aware. Free your "self".

Wealth and Debt

"Chase after money and security and your heart will never unclench" –
Lao Tzu

Constant striving for gain through ego is the path to suffering.
Ego, never satisfied with simply just being, is constantly
sensation seeking or looking for distraction. These two
endeavors can be the entire premise for existence for some
who live entirely in ego. Money is the common item of
exchange for which to obtain those sensation seeking thrills,
and ego can never get enough of it.

Wealth is a subjective term. Some of the happiest years of my
life have been during times where my financial status fluctuated
below and above the established poverty line. Wealth should
not be categorized as something only relevant to money.
Money is just a means to an end. For the self that is free from
the prison of ego, joy, happiness and contentment arise from
the simplest of things and wealth may or may not include
money.

See the chapter on ego to understand how the egoic cycle of
striving for "stuff" is a never ending pursuit. There is no end
to the journey because ego will never be once and for all
satisfied. The ego can create such a deep desire for false
happiness that it will push through all reason and logic and do
the most self destructive things. I once knew of a business
acquaintance that could not control his gambling fever. In one
last crazy attempt to win it big he wagered his life's work, his
business which was everything he owned and lost it all. It was a
devastating blow to him, his family, his business partners, his
bank and countless others who depended on him being the
captain of the ship and providing leadership. All gone in the
moment five cards were turned over.

While the average citizen may not think they would ever
gamble away their life, they do it every day. Part of this last
severe recession we went through was the striving and greed
exhibited by good law abiding people. Pursuing the "American

Dream", these everyday hard working people ran up their credit cards, bought too much real-estate, and gambled on the stock markets, borrowed money with no tangible means to pay it off. It was the perfect storm for individual and collective egos on both sides of the lending industry. Individual egos always wanting more, being put on the hook by collective ego's willing to loan them the money. Debt is like a cancer, slowly building until it gets a grip around the heart and mind. It is a cumulative, day by day, item by item gathering and collecting of things and experiences that were made on borrowed money. The sad thing is that I believe the collective ego behind the loaning of money with excessive interest rates has the full intention of getting people on the hook. The perfect position for a credit card company is when the individual in debt can pay the monthly minimum but never actually pays it off. In the end, that wide screen HD television that was purchased on credit will take years and years to pay off. You borrow $500 and pay back $2000. It may be that payments continue even after the item has long gone to the land fill. We have been living in the illusion that a material possession brings about true happiness. The momentary high that the ego experienced for a few weeks or months is now long forgotten with only a monthly reminder of the payment due.

Eventually the debt can become your singular life struggle. Like a cancer, it sucks out everything you can manage just to keep your head above water. The more suffering from debt an ego experiences, the more it seeks sensation or distraction, which leads to even more entanglement. It is a downward spiral that ends in disaster.

Money is not evil. Wealth is not evil. Money is just a means to an end. Financial wealth is just an abundance of money. We all need certain things to maintain a healthy life. As always balance is the way. The balance must be maintained between the spiritual and the material. Free from ego, in awareness, one can realize what they are doing and why they are doing it. Sometimes awareness is simply taking care not to spend more than we make, and to borrow only what we can pay back promptly. Living within a good budget does not sit well with ego, because ego seeks to satisfy desire at any cost. As you will note, I have been advocating living in the present moment. This means being aware of and accepting things as they are moment by moment. What this does not mean is to live in the moment with ego and the pursuit of instant gratification.

"He who knows contentment is rich" Lao Tzu

Only through self awareness and being mindful can we see the egoic hunger arise. Being mindful of these rising desires, we can acknowledge them then let them go.

Exercise

Here are some questions to ask your "self" to see if ego is at work in your unconscious life. As always, you must be honest in your answers.

- How much debt are you responsible for that was created for non essential items?

- Just how do you define "essential"? How do you define excessive? Does the item meet your basic need other than ego definitions?

- Is your purpose in life to make money?

- If you answered yes, to what end does it serve.

  o Who benefits from the money you make? Is it mostly for you or is it mostly for serving others?

- o If it is mostly for you, what part of you requires the striving for becoming wealthy?

- Ask yourself why happiness requires money?

- If you can be happy without money why would you pursue it?

- Ask yourself why can you not be happy in this very moment without the need of a material thing?

- Contemplate why a simple life is not satisfactory?

By being in awareness we can observe this neediness of sensation seeking and contemplate just how necessary it may really be. When you can practice patience you can see if the object of desire can wait, or ask "do I really need it"? It is amazing how often you will quickly determine that this is just another sensation seeking ploy by ego to get yet another thrill.

Abundance is everywhere when our eyes are open. By eyes open, I mean in awareness. By being at one with the flow of life, very often the things we need are close by. When reality is shaped by ego, you get what you place all that energy and attention to. When you become fixated and experience constant craving, eventually if not right away, you will be rewarded with yet more craving.

Being at one with life is accepting things as they are. It means you are aware of things as they arise and have a *knowing*, an instinct or intuition about how to proceed. Ego would have its own magic bottle with a genie in it, giving instant gratification to all its desires. But life does not work that way. There are rules of engagement about getting what you are seeking. Dr. Amit Goswami proposes that consciousness is the source of all things and that to get what you want has to work within the framework of things as they are. He explains what he called the green light rule. You cannot have a traffic light both showing green lights because it would create catastrophe and disaster. Many faiths use the term "thou will be done". We discuss more about this in the chapter on manifestation. Here in this chapter regarding wealth and debt, the focus is on understanding and is about *just being*, without regard to how much material "stuff" you can surround yourself with.

Wealth and abundance certainly have their place. Society is well served if we can learn to share our resources, whether it is knowledge or money. Yet along with compassion and sharing, balance is found with self sufficiency and joyous labor. Constantly striving for reasons we cannot quite pull into focus is the nature of the desperate struggle. Heed the words of the transcendentalist Henry David Thoreau…

"But men labor under a mistake. The better part of the man is soon plowed into the soil for compost. By a seeming fate, commonly called necessity, they are employed, as it says in an old book, laying up treasures which moth and rust will corrupt and thieves break through and steal. It is a fool's life they will find when they get to the end of it, if not before".

Being your true authentic self is to be free from the illusion of a life of materialism. To free yourself, you must let go of the dependency of ego and the life of striving. Life just is. Free your "self".

Rage and Hatred

"People who fly into a rage always make a bad landing." Will Rogers

Rage is the full evolution of anger. As anger gains critical mass and become a runaway emotion it becomes Rage. There are no positive attributes to anger or rage. I have heard some people refer to something called "good anger". I am going to respectfully disagree with those positions and say that anger and rage have no place in a life of balance and harmony. I also believe whole heartedly that to fully evolve spiritually, anger and rage must be reduced greatly. Anger and Rage is one of the most destructive forms of emotional energy and cannot occupy the same dominion as love, compassion and light. When anger has been considered in some fashion to be good, it seems it is because it is a motivating force. I submit that it is a motivating force of ego whose results will not be in spiritual alignment. I also believe that motivation inspired by love and compassion are more elegant, comes from spirit and will endure longer and serve more people in a more positive manner than anger motivation results ever will.

Rage is a runaway, out of control negative emotion whose desired result is destruction. It is the culmination of fear, worry, greed, impatience, anger, annoyance, shame, insecurity, feeling trapped, dread, or embarrassment. Rage is the explosive result when those feelings gain critical mass and reach a point of ignition. Rage uses so much energy that it runs its course and then leaves the person with feelings of low energy and depression. If the motivating factor for rage is left unchecked it will ignite again and again until there is nothing left to destroy or nothing left of the individual. Usually there is no happy ending for rage.

I consider rage so detrimental to us and others that I am telling you right here and right now that if you are experiencing rage you should put this book down and immediately seek professional help. It may be that you sought this book out and hope to find an easy fix for your rage. Usually it is not that simple. Sometimes our lives get tied up into knots so complex, that only a pro can help you sort things out. Do us all a favor and go see someone.

If you are experiencing continuous negative feelings that lead to rage, meditation can help and you should get started as soon as possible. It is not a quick fix and it is not going to be super easy. Yet in itself the practice is very simple. Over time and with dedicated practice you can free yourself from these devastating negative emotions. When you are able to let the inappropriate thoughts go without becoming embedded in them and the emotions they generate, the space for love, joy and happiness will spontaneously arise.

Hatred

"Hatred does not cease by hatred, but only by love; this is the eternal rule".   The Buddha

Unfortunately, not only have I experienced rage, but I have also experienced hatred. Hatred is the evil twin of rage. They skip hand and hand straight out of hell and into the waiting arms of the egoic mind. Like rage, hatred is a super negative emotion that is the desire of destruction. It is a poison that kills the owner as well as the victim. Strangely, or not so strangely when you can understand it, many people justify and relish their hatred. Pick any hate group that comes to mind and notice how they are proud of their hatred and want everyone to know about it. Three immediately come to my mind. Religious, Racial, and Sports related hate groups rejoice in their solidarity of hate. As of this writing, we have been fighting wars that began as a religious based hate initiative. I grew up in Civil Rights Mississippi of the 1960's and 1970's and can attest to the hate based consciousness that prevailed in those days. It was not too long ago that I saw in the news where a soccer game escalated into a fully engaged battle where people died as a result of hatred of the opposing team. I mean wow! I have discerned that as a world culture we human beings have forgotten what it is to feel the positive emotions of love and compassion. Ego will even brag about how enraged they can become and how much they can hate. This is just wrong.

Experiencing rage and hatred can create some of the most stressful conditions to be experienced. The damage that these extreme emotions cause cannot be over looked. The experience of rage and hatred is akin to absorbing poison. In the literal sense it acts as poison due to the excessive wash of harmful hormones that saturate the bloodstream when undergoing stress. The more often we experience these super negative emotions the more poison we experience. Stress kills; ergo rage and hatred are killers. Not only are they a potential killer for victims, these emotions are self killers.

In closing this purposely short chapter on rage and hatred, I urge you to wake up right here and right now and see where these two poisonous emotions may live in your heart. If you are feeling either these emotions for any reason, please seek help from professional counselors or your spiritual leaders. Should you find that there are those in your life who dwell in the domain of rage and hate, then you should run like hell. Rage and hatred beat in the heart of evil.

Disappointment

"The wise man therefore not attempting to form things does not mar them

And not grasping after things he does not lose them" Verse 64 - Tao Te Ching

Disappointment occurs when ego fails to fulfill its expectations. Disappointment is once again, the failure to accept things as they are. Disappointment is one of those negative feelings that can quietly slip into consciousness and become your mood. As a prisoner of mood, feelings and emotions, the sensitive egoic personality can let a minor disappointment define the quality of any experience. Expectations set the groundwork for disappointment. Ego believes it is entitled to have nothing but perfect days throughout a perfect life. In this aspect, ego is that part of you that expects and demands that things just go your way. Yet any reasonable person in a moment of awareness and honesty will admit that things often do not go as planned and that the universe has its own agenda.

Disappointment is one of those stress creating feelings that is not as benign as it may seem. See the chapter on Stress Kills. Stress being the by-product of disappointment, accumulates if left allowed to move in and take up residency. Ego loves to share its disappointment and wants everyone who will listen to know just how disappointed it is. By staying focused on disappointment it can create even more opportunity for disappointment. It seems to be the nature of ego to need the negative energy, drama, and a sort of validation of always being right. The attention seeking aspect of ego will manifest the opportunity for disappointment to render. There are individuals with egos that will complain about how unlucky they are and then go to great effort to prove it to anyone that pays them attention.

Disappointment can lead to anger. How many times have we experienced someone desperately trying to rip the steering wheel off of the column in their car because of a traffic situation? Or pounded the dashboard, or honking the horn excessively. Egos do not like to be deprived of the thing they want. What starts as mild disappointment can build until it erupts into full blown rage. See the chapters on Disappointment and Rage.

Disappointment is always rooted in an inability to change, remove or accept some detail in life. It is an attachment to some expected outcome. Ego always grounded in the unrealistic expectation that life should be perfect, experiences disappointment when the flow of life does what it does. We have discussed in earlier chapters that it is the nature of life and reality to be constantly in change. The inability, neither to understand this nor to accept this aspect of life will always produce disappointment. Expectation is the slippery slope of egoic reality. Expectation that life should follow every personal whim is a recipe for a letdown.

Disappointment can also be experienced in the collective. We have read in the news where sports fans have gone on a rampage over the loss of an event to a competitor. In Awareness, we can accept that reality and the life we experience through it, has a current and flow all on its own. When an individual can be in the now, it is possible to observe and experience this natural flow.

When disappointment is shared by many it can become a frenzy of insanity. Group disappointment and anger has a kind of emotional explosive vapor. It catches fire suddenly and with explosive force. Enraged fans have been known to riot, burn vehicles, destroy stores and even kill people. It is because the only thing worse than an angry ego is a group of angry egos. The evil and destruction combine in a kind of negative synergy that as a whole, the sum is greater than the parts.

The antidote to expectation and disappointment of course is awareness and acceptance. In awareness we learn to avoid expectations and therefore removing the fuel for an egoic response. There is an ancient philosophy found in the Dao Te Ching called "Wu Wei". The best translation I have seen, describes Wu Wei as the action of no action. Wu Wei is awareness of the flow of the Tao, God, the universe, life, nature and allowing things to be as they are. By not placing anticipation or expectation, the awakened self takes no action. Accordingly the action that follows is that of the natural flow of things. It just takes care of itself.

Doing nothing is not an easy thing to do. It is especially difficult during the early period of self awareness practice. Yet determination and devotion to meditation and mindfulness will prove meritorious eventually. As the practice of being present and allowing things to be as they are occasionally become something that occurs on a regular basis, then harmony is reached and the bumps in the road will smooth out all on its own. Being aware and present creates the space for choice, acceptance or a right action. Our reality is constantly changing, and expectations that you know for certain what the outcome will be, is setting yourself up for disappointment. So next time you become aware of expectations arising, try practicing Wu Wei. Do nothing and therefore you do everything, as it was meant to be.

Deprivation

"I live in sin, to kill myself I live; no longer my life my own, but sin's; my good is given to me by heaven, my evil by myself, by my free will, of which I am deprived." Michael Angelo

For the purpose of understanding negative feelings and how they manipulate us, deprivation can be defined as the sense that one is lacking in something important. It is an unfulfilled desire. Like other feelings, it can be quite benign or it can change the course of history.

It is important to first become aware of the feeling of being deprived, and then it can be helpful to uncover the source of the feeling. Of course the source is almost always ego. Within ego, feeling deprived, is sometimes, the precursor to other negative feelings. Feeling deprived we can continue on down the path to experience lust, resentment, jealousy, loneliness and others. Ego, in its arrogant sense of entitlement is never satisfied. It is constantly feeling deprived and gets quite indignant when that which it seeks is withheld.

Probably the most common feeling of deprivation is when an individual decides to change their diet in order to lose weight. The change or reduction in what ego is used to experiencing brings on a sense of deprivation. Ego cannot or will not accept the changes that need to take place. This attachment to food sensation seeking creates a resentful attitude. As discussed earlier, constant sensation seeking and distraction seeking often include coping with stress by eating. When stressed, one may feel deprived on several levels. Because dark emotional energy uses up a lot of calories, they may feel the need to eat to restore energy. Because a satiated stomach and blood stream can give a temporary sense of fulfillment, "comfort food" is sought out. If the higher awakened self has determined that a correction is needed, a conflict arises between ego and the other part of the self. Very quickly a sense of deprivation is felt and frustration begins to arise. A person not trained in self awareness is unable to comprehend the rising of ego and quickly gives in to the feeling of being deprived. The longer one goes without that sense of fulfillment, the greater the urgency of need or want. Soon the individual surrenders to ego and eats even more than before the diet because of the added stress.

Perhaps the most powerful and destructive aspect of desire and feeling deprived is when someone feels deprived of love. Love carries a very powerful energy that can be addictive. Anyone that has felt the joyous energy of new love infatuation knows of which I speak. While this can be viewed as an extraordinary gift, the addictive nature of infatuation, can lead to problems when ego feels deprived. In successful romantic relationships love matures into wisdom and acceptance. When the relationship is based on a *non self serving* partnership where love and caring is shared, a positive synergy develops. Being grateful of the one you love yet not placing dependency on them for your own happiness is a healthy balance. In a balance between sharing and sacrifice, the feeling of being deprived is alleviated.

When dependency in a relationship is out of balance, both parties will suffer. The very nature of partnerships is based on sharing and some dependency. It is when neediness of either side comes out of balance for too long that problems arise. In awareness, where our essential being is centered, compassion and love for the other arises. In awareness, in a state of Beingness, the sense of being deprived is allowed to come and go, to dissolve into the dark mists from which they come. Unconscious and in ego, dependency arises through desire and constant striving. These feelings can get so out of control, that ego will not only destroy the object of its love but itself and everything around it. Perhaps I am over simplifying the case, but it's possible that this is happening in some of the tragic murder suicide incidents that appear in the news. Perhaps it is the nature of egos feeling deprived.

The feeling of being deprived extends into to all areas. Since most of us are not an enlightened Buddha the ability to delete desire is far away down our path. So it is more realistic at this point to try and gain balance in our lives between desire and being. I am not saying that one should not try and achieve enlightenment; I am saying that one should deal with desire here in the present moment. With practice, there will be a natural growth and wisdom that revolve itself in awareness.

Simple frustrations of feeling deprived are quite prevalent in our lives. If you are living a happy life, you are probably not feeling the need to deal with feeling deprived. In fact, if you are mostly happy and content you are probably not experiencing the feelings of being deprived at all. They are the inverse of each other. Thus feelings of deprivation lead to feelings of unhappiness, and feelings of contentedness (grateful for what you have) leads to happiness. It is easy to say yet quite hard to live up to. The degree of difficulty is directly affected by the level of awareness. Being aware of the rise of feelings of deprivation enables the letting go and putting focus on gratitude. Being lost in ego disallows feelings of gratitude in favor of staying imprisoned in the feelings of deprivation.

Removing desire from consciousness is a lofty goal. There is a paradox which questions the desire of removing desire and to to do so would remove the desire of becoming aware. This tangled hierarchy need not bounce around in your mind right now. In this moment, you can become aware and let go of the inappropriate feeling of deprivation and *choose* a different perspective. By becoming aware you can extricate yourself from the egoic paradox of "I have to but I can't". While lost in ego, it will seem like an impossible situation. You could spend days wondering the labyrinth of ego trying figure out what to do. In awareness you can observe this insanity and just let it go.

In mindfulness meditation your consciousness can observe these things arise and rather than get all involved with them you can let them go. Being mindful during your active daily life you can observe these inappropriate feelings as they begin to arise and let them go before they can become established. In the case of feeling deprived you can let it go and choose gratitude. You can choose to let it go or if action is necessary, chose from a variety of possibilities. The point is, you don't *have* to feel deprived. You are not your feelings. As mentioned earlier, this may not be easy, but it is necessary to free your "self".

Desperation

"No man is an island", John Donne, from Meditation XVII

Desperation is the experiencing of life without hope. The root of desperation is despair. It is the bitter end of a life of ego. Desperation is never far away in the egoic life. Ego (see chapter on Ego) feels some level of despair whenever it cannot fulfill its desires. Ego cannot accept things as they are. Ego is lost in the illusion of the material world and the pursuit of sensation seeking and distraction, and has its existence (identity) threatened whenever it cannot manipulate the events that arise in life.

Ego views life in a singular perspective so when no solution of a perceived problem is available, it sometimes loses hope. This loss of hope becomes despair. Egoic reaction while feeling hopeless is desperation. For ego, desperation is as if the life path has reached a conclusion in a dead end alley with no way out.

In desperation we do things that we would never do in normal behavior. Most people understand this but are unaware of what is happening on a deeper level. When we dwell in the unconsciousness of ego, we are unaware and unconnected to the source of all that there is. In desperation all we see is the material perspective. In pure consciousness we are not limited in perspective, because we are connected to our spiritual source. Aligned with source our true selves do not experience the finite view of ego. In awareness, possibilities arise through inspiration and intuition. In awareness, choice becomes available, and one of those choices is to not give in to despair but to reside in hope.

One cannot be grounded in spirituality when they are in ego. Ego *is* the identity of lost consciousness.

Faith is to consciousness as desperation is to Ego. In consciousness, as a spiritual being we experience faith because we know that not only are we connected to it, we are it (the vast continuum of pure consciousness). Not understanding that we are all connected, the ego, in ignorance, cannot reach out. So even though there are an infinite amount of possibilities, ego can only sense that which is resonate with its own desires. For ego it is a closed loop with no way out.

For the awakened person, events do not have finite definition. Events that arise on the surface of the mind (perception) do not have to be defined within the very limited and small domain of the ego. The awakened person knows that we are all connected and have faith in the flow of life and all its participants. As fear arises the higher self remains unattached to those outcomes and observes other possibilities. Feelings of despair may arise, yet without attention they can wither away as does the morning fog with the light of a bright sunny day.

All of this is to say that despair is manifested through ego as an experience of being alone or cut off. Since ego can be experienced as a collective then so can despair. When all beings experiencing a shared event are lost within an individual and collective sense of ego, the manifestations will also be shared. If a group resides within a state of being cut off without hope, they can all experience the same despair. As stated in John Donne's word above, "no man is an island". Individually in ego, you may *think* you are at a dead end. In awareness you know that you are connected to all things, and the effect of synergy is realized when we share our spiritual gifts with each other.

Consider the cliché *"desperate times call for desperate measures"*. A being lost in ego will completely agree with this. It becomes the justification of egoic action. This mindset gives permission for ego to cross the line of acceptable behavior to initiate inappropriate behavior. It does not matter if you are contemplating the burning down of your house for the insurance money or contemplating the removal of a large part of your stomach to lose weight. The end does not justify the means. There is always an alternative. There is always a choice.

If we cannot be in spirit, we cannot become inspired. Being in ego is not being in spirit.

"I once was blind but now can see" from the song Amazing Grace by John Newton (1725-1807)

If being lost and separated from our source and each other leads to despair, then being inspirit, or in pure awareness as the higher self is the quickening of inspiration. Inspiration is the antidote to despair. Inspiration is the answer to hope. One has to be in communion with or connected with the self aware universe to observe the inspiring insight when it present. Being present is the purpose in life. Everything else extends from this orientation.

You can call it grace, inspiration, insight or awareness actualization, it is *the* path or the way. Ego can no more experience this path than "a camel could pass through the eye of a needle". Through meditation, self awareness and mindfulness your higher self displaces the control of ego and despair. When you rid yourself of despair, and you are no longer treading the path of desperation, you are able to free your "self".

Jealousy and Gratitude

"Do not overrate what you have received, nor envy others. He who envies others does not obtain peace of mind." The Buddha

I almost chose not to write this chapter on jealousy. While contemplating the next chapter to be written, the phone rang with an interesting event that arose while talking to a student in one of the classes we share together. This person wanted to warn me that another meditation teacher was very upset about the program that we offer for mindfulness meditation. That teacher saw us as a competitor.

The astonishing irony of a meditation teacher being caught up in ego and using meditation as the object of contention hung in the air like a dark cloud. As the story unfolded, it became a great opportunity to practice calm abiding, awareness and mindfulness, and to let things be as they are. In awareness, ego was observed arising with all sorts of feelings, none of which were positive. Yet victory over ego was to be realized and awareness won the day.

In fact, in awareness, the irony of the situation inspired me to write about how even meditation teachers can allow ego to get the best of them. It would be a good guess that some kind of egoic professional jealousy and fear must have gotten the upper hand in the other being that was having such a hard time. Humor became my choice of reactions. How ironic life can be. A seasoned meditation instructor, teaching mindfulness allowed fear and jealousy to get the better of them. It is a great lesson on seeing how we are all vulnerable to the storm of emotions that can rise in ego.

Should one look in various dictionaries, the definition for jealousy, will include terms like "resentment of someone achieving success", "fear or anxiety due to rivalry" and "even vigilance in maintaining or guarding over something".

As mentioned in early chapters, when events arise, we have an opportunity through awareness, to choose from a myriad of perspectives. Many times, we can allow things to be as they are without taking action of any sort. Always the natural flow of things will resolve itself one way or the other. Action may or may not be needed. The bigger choice is to just let go of the emotions that arise from the responses that ego is proposing. There is always an alternative view point, and the awakened person can allow them to be available in awareness. Being mindful we can see emotion rising and sidestep the first quick knee jerk reaction and allow things to just be. See the chapter on Action and Reaction.

Words in themselves cannot hurt us. They are just sound vibrations from one person's voice box that arrive to the ear and brain of another person. The sound vibrations themselves are not dangerous are threatening. It is the intent behind the words and more importantly the response of the receiver that is important. In awareness and detached from ego, the awake individual can *choose* to let the emotional flaming arrow from ill intent pass by without harm. We can choose how we act or react. In wisdom we can realize that we cannot control the things that happen in life but we can control how we react to them

Jealousy is spawned by attachment and is the product of resentment. See the Chapter on Attachment. Resentment is the feeling of indignation of an event arising in an experience. Any fair minded person can agree that insecurity lends itself to the feeling of jealousy. Being insecure, that is, experiencing the illusion that the flow of life should not be as it is, and worrying about the changes that will inevitably come creates a kind of suffering.

Another aspect of ignorance found with jealousy is the attachment to outcome. When we set expectations on how we think things should be, we are setting ourselves up for disappointment. When we allow ego to control self esteem, our sense of contentment is dependent on how things turn out. When outcomes don't turn out as our ego desired, disappoint sets in. When one feels that someone else received its entitled outcome, jealousy sets in.

Being jealous that another being will experience success is just another needy egoic illusion. Being jealous that another being will pick someone over you is insecurity in motion. Not being aware, ego will suck the individual into mindstream and away they go. They become unconscious and completely imprisoned in the illusion of ownership.

And of course the alternative [to ego] is awareness and being mindful of the tricks that ego is up to. Being mindful of the insecurities, it is possible to just let it go. It becomes possible to just allow things to be as they are. We can be aware of our attachment to some wrongful view and choose the higher path. Ultimately a person must have faith in the flow of life. We must just let it go and simply be.

In awareness the antidote to jealousy and resentment can arise. Several antidotes such as gratitude and humility can become apparent. Being grateful for the abundance in your life does not leave much room for feeling resentment that things did not go your way. Reducing the need for self importance will deflate the ego. Rather than a deflated ego leaving one depressed, it can lead to a feeling of awe and humbleness. It is important to recognize the arrogance of ego. Pride is considered a virtue in our country, yet I submit that pride leads to arrogance, and arrogance leads eventually to a fall in self esteem.

Being in awareness is to accept things as they are. Accepting things as they are is an understanding that all things are connected in this dynamic tapestry of life. Feeling separate, above, and beyond and somehow better is the essence of ego. It is part of that false identity of me. Ego and collective egos expect the content in our lives to go according to our plan. Every day it can be observed how our egos expect nature to comply with our wishes. We never accept weather as it is. We always complain about the nature of it. When it is winter we complain about it being cold. When it is summer we complain about it being too hot. When it is too dry, we complain of not enough rain. When the rains come, we complain about that.

Being lost in ego, arrogance arises with the expectations that life must be as we desire. The lack of fulfillment of those desires leads to frustrations, resentment and jealousy. We live in a world of cause and effect. The cause may be something done, or not done. When others do not follow our agendas, perhaps it is because of what we did or left undone. In awareness we can allow things to be as they are. Acceptance can immediately relive the agitation. See the chapter on The Power of Acceptance. If a different result is desired, contemplate action from a wide variety of possibilities. In awareness the possibilities are endless. In Ego possibilities are reduced to the singular adaptation of emotion. In awareness we can flow with the beauty of life, and in ego we are imprisoned by the filter of desire. Ego is arrogantly demanding that things go "my way". Awareness is an understanding and joining with the creative flow of the ultimate source. You can spend your life in the futile attempt to swim upstream until eventually you tire and get swept away anyway. Or you can merge with the flow of life and become as one with all there is. It is really that simple. At first this simplicity can be the hardest thing you have ever tried to do. With practice and perseverance and through mindfulness, life can be transformed and you can free your "self".

Embarrassment

" So lesson one in embarrassment is to laugh at it with everyone else when possible." S Beasley

We have all been there and done that. One of my most embarrassing moments occurred when I was giving a presentation at a large company sales meeting. Some of the most powerful decision makers of this fortune 500 company were in attendance. I noticed a couple of my coworkers at a nearby table kept giving me these funny looks and motions. Eventually one of them just pointed down to the pants zipper and grinned. It suddenly occurred to me that my fly was open, and I found a way to glance down and confirmed that yes, the old barn door was definitely wide open. I kept on speaking, but my face was beat red and everyone knew that I knew. It was quite embarrassing and I managed to finish my presentation without panic. (See the Chapter on Fear)

What saved my sanity both during and after the presentation was some spontaneous understanding to allow humor take the place of embarrassment. We all had a good laugh at my expense. The good thing was the big bosses would never forget me, and better yet, they got to watch me stay cool while under fire. *Being able to laugh at yourself in times like this is a form of acceptance.* Acceptance is such a powerful virtue that a whole chapter is devoted to it. Sometimes things just are what they are and being aware of your feelings and emotions allow choice to play its part.

So lesson one in embarrassment is to laugh at it with everyone else when possible. It is important to just accept the situation with self humor and laugh. This is just a way of letting it go.

Why is this so important? Because being unconscious in ignorance, ego may react in several negative ways and make the situation even worse. Ego may react with frustration and anger. It may react with embarrassment by crawling under the table. Then later ego may even crawl out from under the table where earlier it was too embarrassed to show itself, and begin to bask in the spotlight of attention. Ego can even go on to create some new event for more attention and pretty soon, ego the clown, has presented itself. So when something happens and you feel the panic of embarrassment rising, be in awareness and just laugh it off, then let it go.

Not all of us are always able to walk away from or laugh at embarrassment. Embarrassment occurs when we perceive a problem and take it personally. Let this lesson be about the embarrassment of ego. Choose not to take it so personally. When I say, not taking it personally, I mean that in awareness, you can remain unattached to emotional conditioning and accept the event as it is, instead of having an automatic reaction such as embarrassment. Sometimes we allow our self to become absorbed by the pain felt by ego. Ego is that part of our personality which places esteem on self worth, experiences the pain of indignity (embarrassment). An ego that always expects the world to be without challenging events becomes very frustrated when it does not look good and feels open to criticism. Arrogantly ego abhors criticism and fully believes it is above such occurrences. Criticism is like acid to the ego. Ego does not care even a tiny bit that a valuable lesson may be learned in the process of making a mistake. So that is lesson number two. Allow embarrassment to dissolve on its own by focusing what you may have learned. In the case of leaving your zipper unzipped, the lesson is to be mindful and in not too much of a hurry. Maybe even taking a quick look in the mirror to make sure everything is in order should enter into mindfulness. The self check does not have to be an ego check. It is simply a check to see that your attire is properly attended to. Straightening your tie or tucking in your shirt (and checking your fly) does not have to be obsessive. You are simply conforming to the dress code of modern social morays. A little embarrassment can be a great teacher.

Then there is someone else's embarrassment. Ego the bully loves it when someone else is suffering. It can feed off the painful energy and participate in the negative humor based on the suffering of someone else. Picking on someone and "having fun "at their expense (their egoic response) is a favorite of ego the bully. However it is important to note that both bully and victim can transcend this behavior by exercising choice and acceptance. The bully can become aware of what they are doing and stop. The victim can realize the bully's ego for what it is and choose to not be affected by the attempt to create suffering.

Trying to cause embarrassment to others by a bully ego is the inverse of compassion and should be let go of as soon as it begins to arise in awareness. When someone else does something embarrassing, we can use empathy to help dissolve the pain of embarrassment. This means that you should not make humor at their expense or if you can, create some gentle humor that gives them a way out. Be a friend and do the right thing.

Chronic embarrassment can lead to over compensating for the suffering ego. If you cannot move on from an embarrassing event, seek professional help. Something like this should not take up residency and dominate your thoughts. If you cannot laugh or let it go, get professional help.

Free your "self" from the suffering of embarrassment by self awareness and mindfulness and free your "self".

Apathy

Scientists announcea today that they have discoverea a cure for apathy.
However, they claim no one has shown the slightest interest in it. George
Carlin, Comedian, May 12, 1937 – June 22, 2008

Apathy has many facets. With regard to ego and how it relates
to others, apathy would be the indifference or avoiding having
compassion for others. Ego is a state of ignorance where
pursuing self gratification is the purpose in living. This
narcissistic path simply has no time for the caring or
compassion of others unless there is some benefit 'me'.

Apathy for Veterans

As I write this chapter, it is Memorial Day. It is a day for
remembering. It is a day we acknowledge the sacrifice of
citizens who have given their lives for the sake of our freedom.
In this country we are free to be who we want to be. It is
meant to be a time that is set aside for contemplating gratitude
and thanks. It is a time that should be set aside for being aware
of the ultimate sacrifice that others made for us. It is a time for
observance.

Yet for many, it is just another meaningless holiday for the
pursuit of sensation gratification. It is a time for indulgence in
the very things that are sometimes taken for granted. Millions
of egos, are lost in the apathy of experiencing some
meaningless sensation. While many of us grieve afresh with
recently lost loved ones, others contemplate the pain of love
ones lost in years past. A lot of people have made the ultimate
sacrifice so that all of us, even those apathetic, can experience
freedom.

What about the veterans who are still living? Many have been
through a hell so traumatic that it is simply impossible to untie
the knots in their minds. Through living and reliving the
nightmare that they went through, some have sacrificed their
sanity for us. Many roam the streets hungry and lost. They
have found ways to cope by turning to substance abuse

because the post traumatic stress is inescapable. You can see them in wheel chairs with limbs missing, dirty, hungry and forgotten. The only thing they are guilty of is agreeing to sacrifice everything for us. In our collective egoic apathy, they are lost and forgotten. They survive on the fringe of our materialistic and egoic society as third class citizens. These are our heroes and should not have to worry about survival. As an egoic society, we are too busy pursuing our sensation seeking and gratification that we can't be bothered to remember them, much less help them. At best we judge them, and at worst we are just apathetic to their fate. There are numerous ways to help and remember them. It usually does not take much. The best thing you can do is to simply become aware of them. Share a kind word or give thanks. Believe me it will mean something. Veterans who are now deceased were once us. Living veterans are us. We are not separate, they are us. Contemplate where we might be as a society, as a world without their service to us.

As you read this, how do you feel? Do you indentify with those desires to just let someone else worry over those things? Or can you take just a moment, a single 'now', and let gratitude and appreciation arise.

The Homeless

Other types of egoic apathy are prevalent in our society. The number of homeless citizens has risen substantially since this last recession. Being homeless is like becoming invisible. In an attempt to avoid the messy consideration of the problem of homeless families, many self serving egos simply remain apathetic to their plight. They will quickly tell you that they are busy taking care of their own families and don't time or resources to help others.

When homeless people drift into our world, we tend to avoid them. We try to not see them. Many homeless people come with baggage such as addictions and mental illness. They smell bad, talk crazy, and ask for our money. There was even one ego on talk radio who once asked "why should I share any of my wealth with you?" Any ego that has to ask that question would never understand the answer. These selfish egos operate under several illusions. One is the illusion that they are separate and in no way connected. The other is their false sense of security. Sometimes they judge the homeless from the arrogant position that they have to pay for their mistakes. They assume that their own situation is secure and will remain so as long as they protect what is theirs. Or they may believe that they are above making mistakes and it just isn't their problem. And that is what ego does. It surrounds itself with self serving illusions. Some very shrewd egos amass huge quantities of resources and do very little beneficial with it. Their resources are simply to guarantee the false sense of security or to use as payment for more sensation seeking or distraction. In some cases it may be to serve egoic greed. In awareness, consciousness can be detached from ego and understand that we are all connected on some level. In awareness, we let go of the narcissism of ego and embrace compassion. As always, balance is sought. We do not have to give away everything we own and give to the poor, but we can share some of what we have. It is not always about money. Sometimes the poor and homeless just want to be recognized as another living being. They simply want the warmth of a kind word of friendliness. Money cannot buy a *sincerely* spoken kind word or a moment of understanding. Balance means that our economy and culture share a vibrant exchange of resources. Balance removes the dichotomy of rich and poor, us and them. In awareness, we can realize that we are all connected through consciousness, compassion and karma.

In awareness we can see how ego has a disregard for those of us who have met hard times and realize compassion in our hearts. In awareness we can realize that they are us.

Apathy for elderly

When my mother was in her final year, it came into my awareness the plight of seniors who are dumped into nursing

142

homes and forgotten. While some seniors are privileged to enjoy a home where conditions are well managed, others find themselves in hell. Sick, tired and lonely, some simply suffer and wait to die. Sometimes the only respite from boredom and loneliness is pain and mistreatment.

Some of our unsung heroes are those dedicated people who love and care for these transient souls. These nurses and aid workers care for our seniors and help them in the last transition. Meanwhile sons, daughters, brothers and sisters remain lost in ego. In their apathy they cannot be bothered to sacrifice a little bit of time and affection. Sometimes it is too painful to do their duty. Not only is ego too busy, but it cannot be bothered with something other than the pursuit of gratification. The opposite of apathy is empathy. In awareness we can embrace the insight of empathy and understand what our seniors are going through. Compassion becomes action as we understand what we must do.

Become a hero. Find a church group or care giver network that operates an outreach to these places and try finding some small way to help. Believe me you have some gift that you can share. In awareness you can understand how our world and reality is constantly changing. Do not be fooled into believing this could never be you. We are not separate from them. They are us.

These are just three examples in our culture where there is some degree of apathy. Apathy is the foundation of hell. You do not have to be religious or dead to believe in hell. Hell can find you wherever you are. Try the simple exercise below and see how deeply your consciousness is embedded in ego. Take the apathy test. For you to transform your life and others, you must be honest. If you are not sure about what being honest means, read the chapter on honesty.

Exercise

- Even if you are a veteran, have you helped a

  veteran?

- On Memorial Day and Veterans Day to you take even one moment to appreciate what they have done for us?

- Are you just too busy.

- What is it you are doing that makes you too busy?

- How do you feel about the homeless?

- How do you feel about helping them in some manner?

- Can you feel compassion for them?

- Do you sense a difference of us and them?

- If you avoid the homeless, can you understand why?

- Are you too busy or is it too hard?

  Do you feel that you should not share even a

small amount of your abundance?

- What is it that makes you too busy to share time or resources?

- Why is it too hard? Do you think of them as separate from you?

- Do you think that it could never be you?

- Are there any seniors you know of that are alone at some facility for long periods of time. It does not have to be a family member; it can be any neighbor or acquaintance.

- Do you feel any empathy or compassion for them?

- Are you doing anything about it? If not, why not?

- Do you feel you do not have enough time or money?

- What is it you are doing with your resources that prevents the sharing of either?

This is a moment of truth. Maybe or hopefully you have had a moment of awareness reading this chapter. Perhaps this has touched your spirit in some way. If so, it is important to understand that this is a moment of awakening and insight. It is important to develop the practice of being this way all of the time. Make a commitment to embrace self awareness and detach from the prison of ego. Not only can you make a difference in the lives of others, but more importantly you will make a difference in own. Free your "self" from apathy.

Manipulation or Cooperation

"There is a paradox with egoic manipulation in that ego not only manipulates but also becomes vulnerable to being manipulated".

S Beasley

Manipulation has several definitions yet generally has a bad connotation. Spiders can manipulate proteins to create a silk thread that is stronger than steel. Birds can manipulate other natural and man objects to create a shelter. So if manipulation is not necessarily a negative virtue why do we find having a negative feeling about being manipulated? It is viewed as unpleasant when we sense that the manipulation happens in accordance with an unfair or inappropriate manner. Simply put, we humans do not like being tricked so that someone else can benefit from us against our will.

Specifically this chapter is about understanding how and why we get manipulated and why we manipulate others. Both actions function within the illusion of ego. First let us look at manipulating others. Remember when you read the chapter on ego, we discussed how this aspect of our lower self, frequently does not accept things the way they are. When a problem arises, ego will use every trick at its disposal to fulfill its current desire. One of those tricks is manipulation.

Ego may sometimes use coercion to reach its goal and often uses manipulation to get others to serve its needs. In the egoic state, which is focused only on "me", the positive virtues of awareness do not exist. Ego does not feel empathy, compassion, or concern for others. It is only concerned with satisfying desire with a platitude of the end justifing the means. So if it can push your emotional buttons to get what it wants, manipulation is a quick and easy method.

Ego is not concerned with cause and effect and does not take ownership of the results that will occur from manipulating. Once the desire is fulfilled it moves on, living in denial about its actions.

There is a paradox with egoic manipulation in that ego not only manipulates but also becomes vulnerable to being manipulated. The same egoic neediness that instigates the trickery, opens the door to it also being deceived. It happens because in ego the use of discernment is not present, but emotional and needy filtering of judgment is. Striving to fulfill its desire in the easiest, quickest, and most convenient way ego becomes vulnerable to the quick fix. Addicted to instant gratification, ego will jump at the opportunity being presented by the ego doing the manipulating. Eager to fulfill desire, it jumps onboard when it hears what it wants to hear, or is offered the object of its desire. One ego is manipulating and the other ego being manipulated. Let's take a look at some aspects in our modern life where manipulation is very prevalent.

Politics

Consider the perspective that our political system uses manipulation to determine the leaders of our country. Our system does not simply make a list of pro's and con's for us to look over and make a decision. The system is geared towards taking the known facts and presenting them in such a way as to cause emotional reactions. They use strong emotions such as fear, greed, love, hate, loyalty, prosperity, hope, worry, anger and many others as a means to evoke a response. This works because of egos striving and neediness to validate its identity, or get what it is seeking. Politicians are famous for telling us what we want to hear. They are constantly accused of being wishy-washy and will justify it by pressing yet more emotional buttons. Even when we know the politicians are just saying what we want to hear, we vote for them anyway. It may be that on Election Day we have to choose between the lesser of two evils because both sides are playing the game. I have often observed some people who cry for straight talk, and vote for the person who tells it like it is. Later I have seen them complain because they did not like what was said. It has been submitted by some that the winner of the political process is the one who was best at manipulating the most people. It is something to contemplate.

The nature of manipulation changed dramatically with the advent of television. Politicians can have flirtatious relationship with truth and lies. They attempt to deceive without downright lying. Some aspects of the media will try to evaluate the facts as true or not and that can help with discernment. However specifically, it is the emotional content of political advertising that manipulates ego. The drama is created when two sides trash each other fees ego and viewership. One has to wonder if television news companies look for opportunities to create drama, not for the sake of truth, but for the sake of ratings. It may be possible that a television company's agenda's favors one ideology over others because the collective ego group running the show has the same agenda. If this were to be true, that would be a very dangerous manipulation on a massive scale. Imagine the leaders of the largest countries influencing voters by the content they program and how they manipulate them. In awareness we can observe who is doing the programming and who is being programmed.

Can you become aware of being manipulated? Can you put aside emotion and judgment and use discernment for just a moment. Let's see. Please be honest with yourself. Try using discernment rather than judgment when answering to understand your own behavior. (See the Chapter on Judgment)

Exercise

- Do you despise one candidate over the others or

    can you appreciate them as good citizens?

- Do you have a favorite cable news channel because they seem to present the news favorable to your opinion?

- Do you find yourself stressed out after watching television news shows or political ads?

- Have you ever caught yourself muttering out loud or even shouting at the television set?

- Do you base your political choices purely on what you hear and see on television without ever doing any other research?

- Are you willing to consider a different point of view or political perspective? Can you empathize with the opposing view? (discernment)

- Do you experience a sense of desperation in having your favorite candidate win?

- Do you feel a sense of fear that all will be lost if your candidate loses? (desperation)

- Do you have an attachment to any one ideology?

These questions do not have correct answers. They are to help you see how you might become manipulated without being aware of it.

Buying and Selling

This is another area ripe with manipulation and being manipulated. People who live the materialistic life of ego are always in the market to buy something. They are who sales people most want to manipulate. Buyers motivated by neediness are plump easy targets for sales people. Sales people who are trained in manipulation know which buttons to push. You may not believe this, but sales people are specifically trained on what to say, how to say it and specific maneuvering techniques to get you to say yes. Ethical behavior can play a role in sales, but is sometimes neglected. Often a successful sales person is defined by how many sales they "closed" and how much money they make. There are lots of clubs where sales celebrities cross their rite of passage by being accepted into the million dollar club. The question is whether they reached the million dollar sales milestone by manipulating people or serving people. I contend that you cannot have both.

Sales people are given scripts on what to say. These scripts are carefully crafted to avoid discerning questions that can void an opportunity. Sometimes they are used to guide the attention of the buyers to their strong points. There is nothing wrong in telling a person all the reasons they should use that specific product, but it is wrong to avoid answering questions and manipulating a person into buying something for the wrong reason.

The buy and sell scenario falls into two dichotomies. One is where the transaction is grounded in awareness and high ethical standards. The other is where both parties are grounded in the illusion of ego and materialism.

When an awake and aware buyer is shopping, they are not chained to the emotional responses of ego. So manipulation is not nearly as effective. They look at the facts and consider the various aspects with what makes good sense. The awake and aware seller is a good listener. The enlightened seller is intuitive in understanding how to the fill the needs presented by the buyer. The awakened seller brings an elegant solution on many levels that satisfies the needs of the buyer and both are very pleased with the outcome.

When two egos get together as buyer and seller all sorts of theatrics come into play. Both approach each with an insincere attitude grounded in exploitation. They both have their compass pointed at "what's in it for me". Now this is understandable for the buyer, but it can be the position of the seller as well. When sellers find themselves preoccupied with closing the sale at any cost, they are not listening or considering the needs of the customer. They are already spending the commission and bragging to the other egoic sales people about their conquest. Like egoic politicians, they can sometimes tell you whatever you want to hear so that you will say yes. They are trained at exploiting emotional vulnerabilities and could care less if the product is right for the buyer or not. It really does not matter if the product is one of quality or not. For the seller it does not matter if their guarantee is valid or not. The only thing that matters is the sale. Just sell it and worry about the details later. One is ready to manipulate and the other is ready and willing to be manipulated.

Exercise

If you are a sales person, ask yourself these questions.

- Do you and your organization have ethical standards for your sales transactions? (honesty)

- How good a listener are you? (patience, compassion)

- Do you get good reviews and are your customers happy for a long time after the sale?

- Do you feel that you need to manipulate buyers to get the sale? (honesty)

- Do you feel that you have to use manipulation to get past poor quality or service in your company?(honesty)

- Would you treat your close family member this way?

If you are a buyer, think back to the last memorable sales experience. Try to remember one where you were very pleased and one where you were very displeased. The idea is to see where you are vulnerable to manipulation and where the sales person could have taken advantage of it.

- Did you walk into the sales transaction with an attitude that you had to have this product no matter what?(ego, distraction seeking, desperation)

- Would you have been willing to walk away if it did not seem like a good idea? (patience)

- Did the transaction go smoothly? Was the decision easy to make?

- Did the sales person seem insecure about any aspect of the sale? (honesty)

- Did the sales person listen to your needs and concerns?(compassion, patience)

- Did the sales person seem confident in their product?

- Did you ever feel uneasy (intuition) about the transaction but went ahead anyway because it just seemed too good to be true?

- Did you ever feel like you were being rushed or pushed into the sale?

- Did the salesperson promise everything imaginable? (desperation)

- Did the salesperson keep their promise? (honesty)

- Do you wish you had thought about it some more before making the decision?(patience, desperation)

- Do you feel like the sales person pushed your buttons or manipulated you?

As a being in awareness you have the power to discern what is going on in your life. When you are no longer a prisoner of ego and emotional attachments, you may be a lot less vulnerable to being manipulated. As a person who is in awareness and grounded in compassion for others there is no need to manipulate others on your path. In awareness we can exercise the power of acceptance and leave behind the egoic actions of manipulation and be free of being a manipulator or being manipulated, you can free your "self".

Cause and Effect (Karma)

"All that we are is the result of what we have thought.
If a man speaks or acts with an evil thought, pain follows him.
If a man speaks or acts with a pure thought, happiness follows him,
like a shadow that never leaves him."
- The Buddha

Karma: the action (or thoughts), which brings about the inevitable results.

This causality is a result created by an initiated action and with an honest look at your life you can realize that you may have caused many of the circumstances you find yourself in. (read the chapter on honesty) Hence, *this* action will manifest *that* result. And when thought initiates reaction then reality becomes what we think about and thus we reap from the seeds that are sown.

As stated many times in this book, ego is obsessed with sensation seeking and distraction. Living the life in ego is living in an ultimate state of distraction. It is a type of unconscious state. Even though we may have our eyes open and thoughts are processing, our attention is being absorbed by our thoughts, feelings and emotions. We may not be aware of where we are, what we are doing and why we are doing it. This is especially true when our attention is completely given over to our emotions and feelings. Being 'lost in thought' we experience life as the striving for the next sensation or distraction. That might sound wrong, but if you take an honest look at how you spend your existence (time) you will find that many, if not most of us, have our compass pointed at arriving at or obtaining the next sensation that might bring happiness or distraction. (See the chapter on behavior). We do not enjoy the journey because we can be obsessed with arriving at the destination. Not being aware of what we are doing and why we are doing it is dwelling in illusion. The reactions we initiate (causation) can bring about results (effect) that may often be defined as "problems". As sentient beings we are creators. We create the paradigm which constitutes the framework of our reality. We can create a reality that is a result of always striving or we can create a reality grounded in awareness. In awareness we are living in each and every now (each moment of perception) and accepting things as they are or initiating actions guided by inspiration. In ego we are bored with the present moment and are constantly seeking sensation or distraction to avoid life as it really is. In awareness we are co-creators with source, in ego we are creators with materialism. In awareness we maintain balance and harmony; in unconscious ego our constant striving creates an imbalance.

As you will recall in earlier chapters, living the life of ego we develop behaviors and conditioning that shapes our lives. Our experiences become memories and memories become who we think we are, which is the false identity of ego. The behaviors or conditioning that develop form the basis for each moment by moment decision. This chapter is about understanding the ramifications of those moment by moment decisions. This is about bringing into awareness how we cause the unwanted effects in our lives. We talked a little about cause and effect in the discussion about conditioning. We looked at how we create cycles of conditioning, decisions, cause and effect and finally back to more conditioning.

We can examine the long term results of this causation cycle in several examples and see some common states of imbalance. It may be helpful to read the chapter on Distraction and Sensation Seeking and cause and effect.

Weight gain

In the American culture, one of the easiest areas to observe the cause and effect of imbalance can been seen in our collective inability to manage our body weight. Most people are very surprised when they realize how much they actually eat. Humans eat for a variety of reasons, least of which is the need to fuel the body. People cope with a problematic life with a wide number of reasons, but there are often only two causes for being overweight. That would be a lack of exercise and eating too much.

Not exercising is due to a number of reasons. It can be perceived as boring, tedious, painful, being distracted and not having enough time. One observation about not having enough physical activity is due to not having enough physical play. Children used to play physically where ever they got the chance. Now our society has replaced naturally inspired physical play in children with virtual play that takes place solely in the mind. Not only do the kids absorbed within role playing video games not move around much, they remain unconscious for long periods of time, unconscious and in distraction. Modern grownups have left physical play behind and assumed sedentary forms of play such as watching TV for hours and hours. It is important to understand that in physical life, atrophy is at work. There is a modern cliché based on Newton's first two laws of motion and goes something like:

1. An object at rest stays at rest.

2. An object in motion stays in motion.

The more you sit, the more sedentary you become, the less energy you will experience, and the worse you will feel. The more you get up and go enjoy life in the physical domain, the more energy you will experience and the better you will feel. We were made to move. The motion *is* the medicine.

Over eating may be because they either use the sensation of ingesting food as a coping measure for stress and anxiety or they use eating as a pleasurable distraction and entertainment purpose. Many times it may be both reasons. The pleasant feeling of being satiated may have started when we were babies and had that first experience with a full tummy, followed by deep sleep. It does not take long before the experience becomes a behavior and we become conditioned to seek food out as a source of contentment. The consequences of mindlessly eating without regard to calorie intake results in an increase in stored fat. It slowly accumulates. The gain is subtle at first. We may not even realize that we have gained a few ounces. But over time those ounces add up. A few ounces each week will turn into 30 or 40 pounds between college and middle age. Suddenly we are walking around with the equivalent of a small child around our waist, all of the time. By the time we are middle age, we are completely worn out and sick. It is all due to the subtle unawareness of constant eating throughout the day and night.

Less physical activity and more food intake has been the cause and effect of being overweight and sick. When self is absorbed by ego which is always sensation seeking or seeking distraction, it is impossible to break the conditioning creating the cause and effect of having a weight problem. In awareness we observe what we are doing and why we are doing it. In awareness we can be released from the emotional fetters (chains) that keep us stuck on the couch and find the balanced life again.

Debt

Debt starts off as a very benign rite of passage into adulthood. We somehow obtain credit and begin purchasing things we cannot afford. Or maybe we can afford them but we choose to use the credit card to lessen the impact of putting a lot of money up front and out of our possession. As we experience the problems in our lives we feel anxiety and seek release through the gathering of material things that we think we deserve. Sensation seeking and distraction has found its financial benefactor and will tap into it until there is no more. Little by little the debt mounts, until one day we realize that we cannot pay everything we owe. Then the true misery begins.

This is cause and effect at work. Over indulging is the cause and debt is the result. Sometimes we find it too painful to deal with life as it is, so in ego we turn to material means to find a temporary release. Then the payment is due and is experienced both spiritually and financially. In awareness we can realize our need to cope and consider the right action to take, if any.

Acceptance can go a long way towards alleviating unnecessary stress which can remove the need to cope. Moment by moment we can side step these traps where we try to buy our happiness with something. Just let it go. (See the Chapter on Coping)

Addictions

Substance addiction is so prevalent in our culture that there is a reasonable likelihood that everyone who reads this book will know of someone who suffers from some type of substance abuse. Do not be too quick to judge these folks if you happen to be free of this particular addiction or misuse of resources. We all have issues and they manifest in different ways.

Substance abuse is rarely benign and harmless. In fact if you can come up with one that is abused yet is harmless please write to me and let me know. Some substances may not be addictive either psychologically or physically, but can cause unhealthy long term effects. Salt and Sugar are two that come to mind, and as someone who suffers from high blood pressure any use of it over minimal requirements can be considered self abuse. Yet salt and sugar abuse is easily overcome with just the practice of self awareness and modifying the conditioning that causes us to automatically reach for the salty french fries or the glazed donuts.

Other substances are psychologically addictive. This means that one has become dependent on a particular substance to help them cope with life. While it may be quite difficult in overcoming the psychological dependence, it can be overcome with the practice of mindfulness and self awareness. Strong will power and recognizing the option of choices will provide other avenues away from the conditioning behind the addiction. Marijuana might be considered a psychologically addicting substance. The state of consciousness experienced while on a good buzz allows for the detachment of those emotional feelings we wish to escape from. It also gives the illusion that it heightens awareness or helps with cognitive function, but this is just another slippery slope lubricated by ego. You don't have to believe the statement in this book, just go read the works by Dr. Daniel Amen where you can see the M.R.I. of a brain on cannabis and see how closely it resembles the brain with Alzheimer's. Further, Dr. Amen correlates the areas of the brain that are being damaged with memory, ambition, and reasoning. Now I can understand why I did so miserably during my first year of college back in 1973. While the short term effects of cannabis addiction can be pretty dramatic, it can be reversed by simply stopping. It is something that you can just walk away from without experiencing dramatic physical withdrawal.

And that brings us to the real problem that substance addictions and that is substance addictions that are both psychological and physical addicting. It's one thing to decide to throw away something that helps you to relax and completely another thing trying to disconnect from a substance that will cause a dramatic sickness when it withheld. These substance addictions are usually chemical addictions which change the original nature of the body, and more specifically the brain. To keep this simple, let me just say that messing around with the chemical and neurological structure of the brain is almost guaranteed to cause you a lot of trouble.

The sensation and distraction seeking actions of ego will over ride a person's innate sense of self preservation and pursue a path leading to permanent ruin. Sometimes ego will reside in the delusion by saying "it won't happen to me", and being disconnected from the true self one steps into the trap. Run away and out of control ego cannot connect the dots of cause and effect. Later at some point you face your moment of truth and find that there is no way out. The more manic ego is to experience that sensation or find that distraction to escape, the more likely you are to become addicted to something. Addictive substances abound in a wide spectrum. It ranges from caffeine which is legal to sniffing something from under the kitchen sink which is also legal to have. So it is not so much about removing the substances from being available, but to educate people as to the source of the problem, which is ego. Imagine how things might be if all people were aware of what they were doing and why they were doing it. Imagine how things might be if they could be aware of the underlying causation of the desire for sensation seeking or distraction and simply let it go.

We should practice meditation and self awareness as if everything including our future depended on it, because it does. We should realize that we create our reality.

In awareness we can be awake to the thoughts, feelings and emotions as they rise and avoid the first knee jerk reaction of meaning that ego places upon the mind. Being mindful of what the ego is up to, we can chose to be patient. We can seek other meanings and possibilities. We can simply let go of the rising emotions and accept life as it is. In ego there are not many choices. In awareness there are an infinite amount of considerations and possibilities. In awareness we can be aware of cause and effect at work, and avoid the pain and misery that will result. We can be aware of what we are doing and why we are doing it. We can sense the warning signs that ego ignores and avoid the pitfalls that will surely await us. We can plant the seeds that bear sweet fruit, or we can plant the seeds for thorny ugly vines that strangle us. (See the Chapter on Action and Reaction; and Cause and Effect)

Being addicted and striving for anything can create a mental and or physical prison. Break those chains of addiction and free your "self" through self awareness.

Stress Kills

"If the problem can be solved why worry? If the problem cannot be solved worrying will do you no good.' Śāntideva, Buddhist Monk (India)

In case you have not heard. Stress is a killer. By that I mean stress will kill you. It is not the benign topic that stressed out people disregard on their way to dying. It is a miserable way to die. It is slow and deliberate. It is cumulative and kills everything tangible and intangible that it touches.
The good news is that it is quite manageable when one learns how. To manage stress, one has to understand what it is, where it comes from, and how to deal with it effectively.

Exercise

Do you show any of these signs of stress?

- Sleep disturbances (insomnia, sleeping fitfully)

- Clenched jaw

- Grinding teeth

- Digestive upsets

- Lump in your throat

- Difficulty swallowing

- Agitated behavior, like twiddling your fingers

- Playing with your hair

- Increased heart rate

- General restlessness

- Sense of muscle tension in your body, or actual

    muscle twitching

- Non cardiac chest pains

- Dizziness, lightheartedness

- Hyperventilating

- Sweaty palms

- Nervousness

- Stumbling over words

- high blood pressure

- Lack of energy

- Fatigue

The next section on Stress Response brings the phenomenon into greater awareness.

The Stress Response

Most commonly known as the Fight or Flight syndrome, the stress response is probably one of the reasons humans have survived as a species in a dangerous world. It is not the only reason for our survival but it was a very special survival tool gifted to us by nature and it worked. We are still here.
Our primal ancestors lived in a very dangerous environment. Try to imagine living in a world where large man-eating predators were free to roam around and dine on whatever opportunity presented to them. Sometimes people were on the menu. So to survive, people had to have the strength and wits to either run fast enough or fight hard enough to survive. When suddenly faced with danger, the body needs a lot of energy very quickly. It adapted to this need by increasing the heart rate and blood pressure so that there was plenty of blood flowing to create extra energy for extreme exertion. Hormones are excreted which increases blood sugar. The body would

suppress non essential systems such as the immune system. Needing more oxygen, the body increased the breathing rate. And because the individual might be injured, the blood clotting potential increased so that they would not bleed out while unconscious or trying to recover. It was a dangerous world, yet we did survive with the help of the stress response.

While the stress response helped us to survive, it has now become somewhat of a hazard. Living in a modern culture, the modern citizen is no longer in danger from predatory beasts. Instead, the exterior causes of stress inducing dangers have been replaced by the human mind and imaginary situations that evoke the stress response. Anxiety, Fear, Anger, Rage, have all become part of the modern day experience. Not only has the stress source been replaced by mental perceptions, but the response is triggered many more times each day. Stress is created and follows us through the day until we go to bed at night, only to be repeated again the next day and the next. Over and over, from the morning commute to the stress filled job, the evening television drama, and the evening news hour, we are triggering the stress response. Years go by and one day you find yourself sick, tired and worn out, wanting to get your life back, yet not understanding exactly why life is so unfair.

Here is a typical scenario of western modern culture for many of us. If this is not your typical work day, then I offer congratulations. Yet you probably know someone who does have this kind of daily experience.

We wake up in the morning, and before we sit up in bed, we begin to think about the issues that plagued us from the day before. We rise and make our way to sit down in front of a television set where we begin our daily programming of what all is wrong with the world. Because we are sleep deprived and do not have enough energy, we over indulge in a very powerful stimulant called caffeine or then we skip breakfast. As we indulge in our constant need to be distracted, we finally realize that we are late for work and rush to get out of the house and head to the job we really do not like and be with people that we do not want to be around. Our drive to the work place is rushed. The caffeine expands the already increasing stress level. When traffic does not cooperate, we become even more stressed, yelling at complete strangers, giving obscene gestures, and causing others to become stressed. We arrive at the job we do not like, and begin another long day of stress related activities. At lunch, we over eat unhealthy foods, and return for an afternoon of more stress related activities. Having over eaten the wrong foods, we feel satiated and sleepy, so we imbibe more caffeine to stay alert. We leave at the end of the day exhausted and get into our car, tired but wired for the stressful trip home. We arrive at home, tired and wired, plop down in front of the television for more stressful programming, and eat more unhealthy food. We then sit there late into the night, tired but wired until exhaustion overtakes us and we crawl off to bed, if we haven't already fallen asleep in the chair. But the stressful day is not over yet. We temporarily found sleep due to exhaustion, but it is interrupted by stress and an over use of caffeine. So we wake up at 2:30 A.M. and resume our day worrying and agitated unable to sleep. A few hours later we fall again into exhausted sleep only to way up a little later to start the cycle over again.

I hope this is not your lifestyle. It was mine and I was very surprised to find so many others who were in the same boat. It is no surprise that I nearly had my first heart attack at the early age of fifty three. If you know someone like this, notice how tired they always are and much older they look.

The good news is that nature gifted us with the antidote to the that I will simply call a recovery rest. When the mind and body become quiet, the body will then respond inversely with a quiet state of relaxation. It is the opposite of the body's response to stress.

The recovery response is evoked by simply quieting the mind and the body for a short period of time. I consider it to be a form of simple meditation and include it in all of my guided meditation classes.

The Recovery Response

These areas of increased stress can lead to poor health and even chronic conditions. I know from personal experience about the effect of stress on heart disease. Spending years in a continuous condition of stress will cause serious problems. There is plenty we can do about it, but most importantly we must become still and quiet.

The body and mind will automatically begin to exhibit the qualities of the relaxation response when the proper conditions are put into place. The heart rate begins to slow which can be detected by a slowing pulse. The blood pressure will drop and breathing becomes slow and deep. Importantly, blood levels of Cortisol began to drop. The immune system comes back online and healing can begin. Very often, in my classes, students realize how much they have forgotten how to relax. When we rise from relaxation, they are almost always so relaxed that they do not want to stop. Many people spend so much time being stressed out, that it seems almost normal to be living with a rapid heart rate. Some characteristics of practicing the deep relaxation technique are better memory, better mood, better appetite, less jittery, slower to anger, less worry, longer periods of happiness, better and deeper sleep, and a reduction in the use of alcohol and drugs.
When practiced on a regular basis the mental and physical condition can dramatically improve. See the Relaxation Response Technique for how to do it or find a meditation instructor willing to teach you how. It is easy, does not take long and can be practiced almost anywhere you can sit or lie down.

About Caffeine

Excessive use of caffeine or other stimulants are not the friend of relaxation. Artificially stimulating your metabolism makes it very hard if not impossible to relax. What is the opposite of relaxation? Why it is being stimulated. So trying to relax while artificially stimulated is usually a futile exercise. I strongly recommend limited your caffeine and other stimulants to a moderate use, and only in the morning hours. It takes approximately seven hours (or more) for caffeine to leave the body, thus if you consume it anytime seven hours before bedtime, guess what? You will experience insomnia.

And here is another word of warning. Do not try to detox from caffeine cold turkey. It can lead to a headache that can make you feel sick. Some caffeine headaches reach the migraine category, as it was in my case, and it is something you do not want to experience. Try gradually limiting caffeine over a week or two.

How much caffeine is ok? It varies from person to person, but I would say that on average one should not consume more than about 200 mgs per day. That is equivalent of 12 ounces of coffee. Many of the caffeine sources are not as benign as one might think. Drinking Diet Cola or Iced Tea continuously throughout the day is just as bad as drinking coffee or any other caffeinated products. Caffeine is caffeine. It can have dramatic results in your ability to relax, fall asleep and to stay asleep.

Caffeine is such a part of our culture that it is almost impossible to imagine not having it. It is one of the many unconscious activities we do as a culture. Like anything, caffeine in moderation is not a problem for most people. Yet the average person is not really aware of how much caffeine they indulge in. If you are stressed out, have trouble sleeping, have trouble staying asleep, feel irritable, agitated and have unexplained headaches, then you should take a serious look at how much caffeine you consume.

Stress seems to be cumulative. It can stack up with event after event. Eventually it can build up to a point where it will force a venting action. I like to think of a volcano that builds up pressure until it finally has to blow. So suppressing stress is dangerous. Venting stress can be harmful. Letting stress go gradually through relaxation and meditation is the safest way for both yourself and those around. It can take many sessions to work your way through the pent up pressure of emotional pain. However it can be done, and once the excessive pressure has been relieved, then daily maintenance will keep excessive stress from accumulating.

I believe that nature has gifted us with a natural stress management system through sleep and dreaming. For some people, perhaps many people, this can be enough. Yet our modern lifestyle is such that for many more people stress is too prominent to let go during sleep alone. Plus there are so many people who do not have enough good quality sleep to handle a normal stress load. It may be due to too much caffeine or just too much sensation seeking and avoiding sleep, but they simply cannot let go of the buildup. Therefore it accumulates to the point of an explosive event or breakdown.

Along the way, people sense that they are deeply stressed and unhappy and seek distraction or satisfaction to an extreme level. A coping mechanism is either consciously or unconsciously sought to "take the mind off of the problems". It may be drinking, eating, drama television, books, drugs, sex and too many more to list here. The sensation seeking and distraction seeking becomes so dominant that it becomes the predominant activity in life. (See Chapter on Distraction and Coping)

It is a trillion dollar industry that serves up the items sought after by sensation seeking and distraction seeking individuals. Lost in striving, unconscious of what they are doing, they find ways to turn off consciousness and reality to find a quantum of solace by artificial means. Large companies engage psychologists to create sleek and elegant lures and traps to get these folks to use their particular sensation or distraction product. Psychologists team up with producers to create a commercial that will generate excitement, push emotional buttons, and create a sense of urgency so that hopefully the stressed out masses will rush to buy their product. They hope to program the minds of many people to see them as a source or "the" source for satisfying that subliminal need.

Television is probably the most powerful programming tool ever to pervade the senses. This medium uses both visual and auditory input to directly stimulate the ego. That sensation and distraction seeking, needy and never satisfied part of the mind, is always hungry for more. It is no wonder that it is called TV "programming", yet we seem to be unconscious to the effect and willingly surrender to it. TV commercials are purposefully loud so that they can drill through every other distraction and capture your attention by directly linking to your brain through optic and auditory nerves

When stress and unhappiness builds up to the point of misery, we get to the point where we will do almost anything for relief. We consume alcohol and other drugs to deaden the senses and the mind. The collective consciousness of our society realizes the problem and has enacted laws against the use and overuse of the various drugs available in our country. Yet when we have reached a point of imbalance of extremes we cross over the line. Once crossed, it becomes so easy to cross over again and again. Then one day karma (cause and effect) catches up to us, and we find ourselves in trouble.

In recent years the imbalance became so great that the world fell into a global economic recession. It seems apparent to me that the global obsession with seeking relief from stress through distraction and sensation seeking became so out of balance that the inevitable recession resulted. When over a billion people achieve debt that they cannot pay off, the system will collapse. It is the extraordinary case of so many people out of balance that they would drive themselves and their societies into extreme debt and not be aware of it. In the decades of the 1990's and 2000, we bought too much stuff, houses we couldn't afford with crazy loan agreements, borrowing more than the property was worth. Expensive cars, big screen TV's (better for sensation seeking), clothes, this, that, and just too much stuff. In the end, it could not be sustained.

Just in the few lines you have read here, it has come into your awareness the dangers of stress on only two levels. Health and Financial Wellness are closely related. And yet, there are even more areas where stress creates havoc. I think it is all due to too much stress and the unconscious, coping mechanisms we engage in. There is a better way. It requires detachment from sensation seeking enough to become aware of who we are and what we are thinking and doing. When we are able to bring awareness and doing into balance, we find harmony. It is the path to getting your life back. Free your Self from stress and live your true life.

Coping

"It's not the strongest who survive, nor the most intelligent, but the ones most adaptable to change' Charles Darwin;

There is a tendency with the egoic mind to perceive life as problematic. Before ego attaches to them, these events are simply just the world doing what it does. Each moment of each day life flows around us. Yet some part of our mind gives special and personal meaning to the detail in this changing world. That entity or part of the mind that identifies with events is called ego. If you have not read the Chapter on Ego, please do so now. If the detail of the content that is perceived does not meet the expectations of ego, the occurrence is defined as a problem. Ego struggles with these perceived problems with a reaction called coping. So one can see how the need to cope depends strictly on the meaning given by ego. Sometimes the coping measures compound the problem and things get even worse. Can you recall that old saying of "out of the frying pan and into the fire"?

Example: A problem is perceived. Ego experiences unhappiness or discomfort. To cope with these feelings, the person turns to the purchase of a new object as a form of distraction. For a time the source of distraction brings a materialistic joy that is short lived. Imagine that a new problem arises at work. Ego experiences a rough day and copes by eating thousands of calories of something to feel better. Momentarily satisfied, it looks ahead and decides "what I really need is another thingy, maybe a bigger and better thingy" But already maxed out on disposable income, ego needs a credit card to make the purchase, which is only the "small amount". As the cycle continues the financial debts mounts as well as the added pounds. The pain of juggling debt is coped with by eating extra calories; the misery of being overweight is coped with by spending more of the borrowed money. Eventually the individual becomes trapped in a downward spiral of coping and suffering. Often the situation just gets worse and worse. This is not uncommon and can be observed in almost every situation of imbalance.

So it follows that the meaning given by ego is many times just a conditioned response and not necessarily accurate. Therefore the coping measure will be inaccurate or unnecessary as well.

Through meditation and self awareness, we can observe ego responding to life's events and remain non-attached from reaction. (See the Chapter Action and Reaction).Being mindful we can stand off as the observer and observe. In awareness, choice becomes available. We can choose what action if any can or should be taken. In awareness many possibilities are observed and noted. A much wider variety of choices become available. The action taken, if any, is not a matter of coping but one of working with or avoiding the perceived problem. It is then possible and probable that a deepening of the crises is averted. In a previous chapter we talked about cause and effect. Understanding coping measures is to understand the initiating factor for cause and effect. Sometimes the outcome or the effect is a lot worse than it would have been if left alone. Yet it is important to notice how often ego feels the need to do something, to take action when the perceived problem arises. Coping is the neediness of ego. Awareness is seeing and accepting things as they are and avoiding the trap. (See the Chapter on Cause and Effect)

Living in awareness requires a kind of faith. This faith is based on the trust that we can try and refrain from interfering with the natural flow of life. The world is as it is and not accepting that reality is to engage in egoic coping. Christians have a saying of "let go and let God". Devout believers would not dream of interfering with God. If you are not a devout believer then just consider that as egoic humans we are not omniscient and cannot know everything going on all of the time. Thus it is impossible to know what your actions in coping will result in. This is just the practical application of having patience and taking time to get more detail.

As a spiritual being we can reduce ego's effort to try and control everything that happens. Ego, in its arrogance, believes it knows what is best for itself and may completely disregard what effect the responding action will have on others. Remember, with ego, it is all about "me".

To see coping gone wrong, one only has to consider in an honest way, the imbalance in their life. Make an honest self check to see how centered and in balance you are. What are the things you would want to change in your life? Try accepting things as they are. Look for the ego that you feel that it cannot accept things as they are. Now look at the things you should change and contemplate why you feel you cannot accept changing them.

Exercise

- How happy and content are you with yourself and where you are in life? (acceptance)

- What are your coping measures that you use when you experience an unpleasant event?

- What is your level of physical fitness?

- How healthy are you?

- When you experience problems, what coping measures do you practice to alleviate the unpleasantness?

- How do these coping measures cause or contribute to an unhealthy life style. For example, when you have "bad day" do you skip exercise and go eat "comfort food known to be unhealthy?

- Or perhaps observe your financial well being. Do you find yourself thinking and feeling that if you could just purchase something (fill in the blank), and then you would be happy. (ego)

- Do you like to go shopping when you are depressed?

- Have these led to an excessive debt?

- Is your credit card maxed out due to the purchasing of non-essential stuff?

Be honest and observe if these areas are in balance or not.

- Do you feel as if there is not enough time? (illusion of time)

- Are you over weight from over eating? (honesty)

- Do you stay stressed out? (Stress)

- Are you deeply in debt? (ego)

- Do you talk too much?

- Do people avoid you?

Now take a look an honest look how you cope with these imbalances. This can be hard work, and know that ego will fight you all the way. In fact, ego may be rising as you read this to urge you to drop this activity and go back to coping. Generally speaking, coping is sensation seeking and distraction. Ego sees the fulfillment of desire as the means to an end. The ego would see eating comfort food as a means for feeling better because it perceives a problem. It may be that an individual has reached a point of imbalance where there are multiple problems extending from too many coping measures. They often overlap and the coping will overlap as well, accelerating the pace towards some sort of collapse.

These scenarios are the result of an out of control ego. By waking up and becoming aware we can see things as they are and learn to let them go. We can head off problematic coping at the very start when we observe them rising. Suffering is a wakeup call. It is the red flag trying to wake you up.

The antidote of course is awareness. In Mindfulness Meditation we learn to quiet the mind and become self aware. Mindfulness practice is the sustaining of this self awareness as we navigate each moment of our life. In awareness we remain grounded in the present moment, the 'now'. In each 'now', each moment of perception we see events rise and fall. As they rise and we sense ego beginning it quantifying and judging and just let it go. What would have been perceived as a problem can now be seen as life just being as it is. If we have to take action we can do so through discernment rather than judgment. We do not have to let emotion control the decision making process. With practice we can learn to use the energy from emotion to accomplish a higher intention born in compassion. In awareness we can chose from a much wider variety of possibilities than the singular option of coping. In awareness we can free our "self" from the destruction of ego and its caustic coping measures.

Self Honesty

'Honesty is the first chapter of the book wisdom.'   Thomas Jefferson

We all know what honesty is. Most of us consider ourselves to be pretty honest. Yet the individual we deceive the most is our self. I talk about this a little in some of the other chapters. Here we can go more deeply into it. So for a few minutes, see if you can be honest with some self truths and perhaps a valuable new insight will present itself.

Self Deception is not a new concept. Most of the people who have not learned self awareness are primarily the ones most lost in self deception. Since it is the nature of ego to avoid the boring or painful present moment it thrives in the illusion of deceit. So from the perspective of ego, anything that does not meet the materialistic criteria, is to be avoided. When being honest is too painful to experience, it will create an illusion and avoid the truth.

Exercise

In this 'now', this slice of perception, look at the aspects of your life.

- How happy, healthy and content are you? Take an honest look at the causes you initiated that created these results.

- Can you take ownership of these actions or do you feel the need to blame someone or something else?

When you ask these questions, observe the response. One will be ego; one will be the higher self. One will dishonest and one will be honest.

- If you work for someone or an organization, ask yourself if you exploit your working relationship with your employer. Do you waste company time?

- Do you cheat by seeking distraction in all sorts of ways? How much time is spent doing your actual job to the best of your ability

- Do you waste company time on the internet, texting or making personal phone calls? Can you be honest in this assessment? Observe the responses within. One will acknowledge, accept and take ownership of the truth; the other will deny, not accept or blame something else.

Perhaps you were able to honestly answer those questions above with positive answers. If that is so, you are on the right path. If you are in touch with your higher self, you will not be afraid to explore other aspects of your life and look for any imbalances. So now ask "what areas of life are out of balance"?

Another way in which to have an honesty check would be to observe how television programming has influenced your mind? How has it effected your feelings about certain topics? Politics is a good place to examine. For the most part, the American Culture is a dichotomy of two value systems. They would be either Conservatives or Liberals. If you had to write a report on why you support one view or the other, can you support that view without the use of information you gained from television and especially cable news organizations? I am not saying one is right or wrong. I am challenging you to see if you came by that opinion honestly. If you are completely dependent on television programming for forming your views, then surely you must realize that they are not your views at all but simply what you have been programmed to believe. Television is the most powerful programming tool by those who create their fortunes by manipulating opinions. Their agenda is to control what you think but who you are. The alternative is to point your compass to your spiritual source. In awareness we can realize most of television programming or any other programming is sourced from other egos. In awareness we can be released from the bondage that ego or collective egos capture us in. Are you addicted to television programming? Be honest.

Exercise

Try going without television and or radio for one week. If you can free yourself from programming for one week, it will be revealing. You will begin to wake up and know life as it really is. If you cannot, it will be revealing in that you are addicted to living in an illusion created by the collective egos that do the programming, and rely on your addiction.

If you try the exercise and are successful and decide to return to programming, see if you can limit your exposure. Try searching for programming content that has a more benign agenda. Be honest in your assessment and bring your exposure to programming into balance.

These are just a few of possible areas where we deceive our "self". In every moment of every day we have a choice for being aware and being in the 'now'. We can consider other aspects of our life such as our lifestyle, our ability to manage weight, financial management, personal interaction, and any other areas for improvement that come to mind. Can you be honest and accept that the areas you know are out of balance? Can you take ownership of the circumstances of your life? You cannot make changes for the better until you can realize that in many cases you are the creator. For ego, being honest with your higher self is very hard and painful. Being in awareness, which is to realize and identify as your higher self, you can see and know the ego as the aspect of self that avoids honesty. In awareness choice is available. Un-attached and unidentified with ego we can transcend self denial and choose to be in alignment with truth. You should approach this insight as if your life depends on it, because in many ways it does.

Being honest with yourself is one of the most transforming insights that you can take up. It affects all areas of your life. Each minute of your life is filled with many of the smallest, most sublime decisions. Some of these have a very big immediate impact, but many are tiny and insignificant that does not reach the surface of our mind. A sudden impulse to send or receive just one text message can have massive and obvious consequences. As obvious as that is, there are still so many who do and cause crashes. It now happens so often, that it has now become a law in many states. So that is a biggie.

But what of the tiny, small and seemingly insignificant decisions we make without ever being aware of having made it? These can be just as tragic and destructive. People develop diseases slowly over time as a result of these tiny decisions. Many, if not most, are cumulative and seem mundane. So we kill ourselves calorie by calorie, minute by minute and day by day. Can you be honest with your "self" and ask "should I be doing this?" Is this the wrong thing to be doing?

Being unconscious (not in awareness), ego makes each of us vulnerable to those who purposefully exploit the weakness of egoic dishonesty. There are psychologists that team up with marketing firms to find innovative ways to take advantage of the weakness of ego. This constant sensation seeking and distraction can make you a target for your particular weakness, whatever that may be. (See Chapter on Manipulation and Being Manipulated)

Can you remain conscious and mindful of where your mind is as you become exposed to all of this sensation bait? Be honest with your "self". Next time you are in the checkout lane at the store ask yourself:

- Do you really need to read that magazine?

- Is it good for you?

- Can you admit your hunger for the drama?

When you are faced with the candy and must have doo-dads around the cash register, be aware of how ego begins justifying the acquiring of these non essentials.

- Do you really need them?

- Can you remain aware long enough and observe that desire arising?

- More importantly can you remain aware long enough to resist the crafty arguments by ego?

In awareness, we are awake and paying attention to what we are doing and why we are doing it.

Since most people are inherently honest once they realize what they are doing, the chose to do the right thing. Being dishonest with our self is ignoring your body and your higher self. Rather than just blindly plow down your life path in constant pursuit of the next pleasure you can wake up and exercise the choices available to you. It is so simple yet so hard … at first.

Even during the work day, some of us waste so much of our time in search of some distraction. Be honest and examine how much of your employer's time you waste? Managers constantly fight with productivity. The battle line in productivity is almost always in time management. At any given moment ask yourself is this the most productive thing I can be doing with this moment?

Also be honest and look deeper into the why you are wasting time on distractions. Many people simply hate their jobs. They feel trapped in this perceived prison because they believe this is all they can manage for any number of reasons.

Some people know what they would rather be pursuing but cannot figure out how to get there. Others have spent so much time in unconscious behavior they have never gotten to know their inner self or their inherent gifts. When years are spent lost in this crazy unconscious behavior, possibility gets reduced to only that which ego allows to rise. In awareness we detach from ego and the infinity of possibility of the universe becomes available.

Being honest with yourself you will see that should you give up so much of this incessant pursuit of material happiness and false fulfillment, then you would easily have the time and energy to get that college degree, certification, write that book, paint that picture, write that song or whatever that excuse is.

Being in awareness and being mindful of what we are doing, in each event we find ourselves about to make one of those impulse purchases, we can ask ourselves do I really need this.

In awareness the need for constant sensation seeking and distractions diffuses. You can suddenly see that you do not need near as much stuff. First you must be awake and aware, and then you must be honest. Ego will be the devil on your shoulder whispering in your ear about what a bad day you have had, or telling you that you deserve it, or how good you will look when you have it, or whatever. Being aware, you can choose to let it go. You will find you do not need as much money as you thought.

Being honest, you can take a look at your personal debt and see how much money your ego has borrowed to sustain itself. Can you be honest and agree with what has been going on in your unconscious mind?

So you can become aware that you are about to do it, but being honest is the true self remaining in control and turning away from ego and all the trouble it can cause. Remaining mindful is the hardest part, being honest tends to be easier because the calm abiding of the higher self is seeing things as they really are.

There is nothing to be gained in feeling guilty about mistakes made in the past. Learn from them. In awareness focus on what you did and why. Be mindful to watch for the same behavior to arise again and be ready for it. When it does, simply let it go. Feeling guilty is a poor use of resources. It is best to just let that go. Just go and sin no more.

Here are some exercises that can help get some traction on awareness and honesty.

- Do you ever feel that you do not have enough time?

- Do you cope with stress by eating?

- Are you aware of what you eat and how much you eat?

- Are you aware of what it is doing to your body?

- Are you coping by buying things impulsively?

- Is your debt out of balance?

- What other ways are you coping with stress?

- What other imbalances can you realize? Look at areas such as relationships, distractions, and feelings.

This list could go on and on. This is just a starting point. If you have been honest and you found that you waste money and time, if you eat too much and exercise too little, and if you have experienced stress of any magnitude this is your wake up call. It is now. Now is all you will ever have.

Your chances of success will be greatly increased many times over if you can find an effective instructor in Mindfulness Meditation. Learn how to detach from mind stream and ego and become aware. Balance awareness in your active life by being mindful of what you are doing and why you are doing it.

A new life awaits you. This can be heaven or hell. The choice is yours. Instead of choices controlled by ego, you have deeper, more meaningful choices available. Instead of choosing jelly filled donuts in the sensation seeking ego, you can chose life and longevity. Become aware of the choices being made for you and how ego is using you up at a rate faster than you can comprehend.

As you read the following chapters that discuss the negative virtues of ego, it is important to be honest in your discernment and acceptance. We cannot change the cycle of cause and effect until we take ownership of our actions.

 Our goal is to be honest with our "self" in every present moment. This is to be our authentic self. So be honest with your "self". There is no way we can ever be honest with others without first being honest with our self. Free your "self". Be the true self.

Patience

He that can have patience can have what he will. BENJAMIN FRANKLIN, Poor Richard's Almanac, June 1736

An invulnerable armor is patience. The Buddha

If you could pick just one insight to see and follow, patience would probably be the most profound. My definition of patience is the calm abiding of acceptance that things are as they are. It is the calm non-absorption into egoic reaction unless absolutely necessary. There are exceptions such as if you are about to be run over by a bus, then of course you should take immediate action and jump out of the way. The other 99% of the time, a person being in the present moment has a choice of letting go of egoic urges and responses. (See the Chapters on Ego, Self Awareness, and Action and Reaction)

First let us look at what patience is not. The opposite of patience is the living for immediate gratification. The ego which is trapped in many paradoxes sees the now as something that can only be tolerated with the help of a distraction. Ego wants its desires fulfilled right now but refuses to dwell in the now. Thus it creates the impossible situation. Ego strives for some future fulfillment for which does not yet exist but is demanding it in this now. It postpones enjoying the present moment with whatever is being experienced and looking to the future for fulfillment of some desire. Not satisfied with this 'now' it strives for a future that does not exist nor ever will. There is only this 'now'. The present moment that occurred in the past no longer exists and future 'nows' do not exist... yet ... and that is the paradox.

A typical ego statement can be heard stating "I'll be happy when... ". Always looking forward, ego can only remain in the now when it is fulfilling desire. Even then it will begin to look ahead for the next sensation and does not fully experience the very thing it was striving for. Patience is the dwelling in the now, awake and aware and accepting what is. Patience is the insight of accepting the now as it is, and not becoming attached to or becoming absorbed by the illusion of the being in future. *Being* patient is living fully, moment by moment, in full consciousness. Contentedness and fulfillment do not require the conditions needed by ego to arise. While ego feels frustration and says "I will be happy when…." The higher self is grounded in patience and realizes contentment. Awake and aware aligned with patience, consciousness observes and experiences unrestricted joy with what is right here and right now.

This insight is so very subtle yet so very powerful. As discussed in other chapters, in each moment (each now) we approach crossroads where very subtle decisions are made. Unaware we miss hundreds of opportunities to avoid future problems. Moment by moment in awareness we can make choices that prevent cause and effect from creating future problems. Unaware, in ego, we unconsciously follow the conditioning that ego is grounded in and just do what we always do even when it is harmful to us. This doing what we always do is a conditioning that happens while in the unconscious state of ego. Being in the unconscious and emotional conditioning of ego, our reactions create the cause and effect that will produce a future experience. Patience allows us to remain awake and aware so that we can be careful of cause and effect and the results we create. Not practicing patience, automatically reacting in each 'now' without using wisdom or consideration, we plant the seeds that will grow "problems" to be experienced in another moment of ego.

Example: While conducting weight management courses through meditation, I found that a lack of patience to be the biggest obstacle to being in balance. So I want to use weight management as the example in this chapter. *Being* overweight is a very clear indicator of an imbalance in life. It is also a very clear example of not being present or not being aware of what we are doing and why we are doing it. In all moments of perception we can seek balance and make good choices. Almost always the condition of being overweight is due to the individual not living as their true self. Being overweight is the physical manifestation of imbalance. The physical blueprint of all living creatures is determined mostly by their genes. When the environment is normal, their DNA will determine the physical characteristics to which they will become. So the imbalance in the mind, body, and spirit unity will manifest in a number ways which many times is reflected in obvious physical characteristic. It happens molecule by molecule, moment by moment, over days, weeks and years. Imbalance occurs when in each 'now', the ego, unconscious and unaware, seeks out either a distraction as a means of coping with "problems" or sensation seeking due to boredom. In the awareness of the now (full consciousness) we can observe these subtle (sometimes not so subtle) feelings and remain detached from reactions of the striving ego. Try being *patient*, and accepting what is, and to not give in to the automatic reaction of coping with the *conditioned* response. Being patient is to just let go of the feeling of needing to "cope" and just being. Being patient we can see what we are doing and why we are doing it. Instead of eating that half gallon of ice cream because ego is having a "bad day", we can break the fetters of egoic response and choose another course. Instead of responding to the perceived problem with egoic coping we can choose to take a breath and walk it off. Within awareness you can even choose to not accept the event as a problem and as the problem diffuses so does the neediness to eat something. Patience is the choosing to remain in awareness and not giving in to the whims of ego. With weight management in awareness we become patient and learn cease eating for the wrong reasons. Being patient we can choose when to eat, what to eat and how much to eat. In awareness life events are not necessarily defined as "problems". Life events are simply that, events that arise in perception. Defining and judging is a function of ego. So being in awareness we can choose patience and choose calm abiding over emotional response. If emotional response is a bit overwhelming we can still maintain control of ego and choose a correct action which will not have a negative result. Patience allows choice. (See the Chapters on Acceptance, Coping, Action and Reaction, and Cause and Effect)

Also and most importantly, we can be patient when eating. We can be very aware and enjoy food moment by moment, bite by bite so that the meal brings us satisfaction. In awareness we slow life down and become patient. Being patient is letting go of this business of ego always wanting to get to the next bite. Ego is not patient with each bite and wants to hurry up and finish the bite it has so it can get to the next one. Having finished the food without enough satisfaction, it needs more, so it goes for seconds. Sometimes ego is so busy while eating it cannot slow and down biting, chewing, talking and slurping. Suddenly things get jammed up and you become aware you are choking. This can be a moment of truth which could easily have been avoided.

Lost in unconsciousness and mindstream, we override nature's self regulating process of eating just enough. By consuming food so fast that the sensation of feeling full has no chance to catch up. You can run a quick search on the internet and find that it takes about 20 minutes for the stomach to feel full after undertaking eating. With unlimited food available a human can consume more than a day's calorie requirements in less than the 20 minutes it takes to feel satiated. This condition is easily met when attending an all you can eat buffet.

Sometimes ego combines sensation seeking with distraction by overeating while watching television. In this mode ego is feeding itself physically with food and emotional (drama) or intellectually (documentaries or instructions) and getting a double bang. Cause and effect will create a quadruple bang result with diabetes, heart disease, joint pain and depression among others.

Let's look at weight management while practicing patience. It begins with eating when you are truly hungry. When the urge to eat or especially to snack arises, become aware of the why you want to eat. If you are genuinely hungry, but it is not meal time, a small healthy snack will tide you over. If you are just stressed out and have no real need to eat, then practice patience and choose a different action such as calming down with an appropriate means. Try to be patient and wait until meal time. Be patient and consider whether you are thirsty rather than hungry. Be in awareness and pay attention with purpose why you want to eat and why you are about to eat. These moment by moment exercises in patience will transform your life. Being in the calm abiding of awareness creates the space for patience. Patience creates the opportunity for choice. Choice is what is present every moment of every hour.

Exercise

Let two hours pass without eating. Become still and quiet your mind by focusing on your breath. In the current now observe with your mind your physical state of how you feel. Be alert for signs of true hunger. When real hunger arises observe it and know it for what it really is.

- Now choose something healthy to eat.

- Make sure there are no distractions available such as TV, Radio or something to read. It is just you and your food.

- Slow down and experience each bite and take your time processing the food.

- Be alert for ego to want to rush through and gobble it all up quickly. Make the snack or meal last. Stretch it out. Don't rush.

- After each bite, consider what you just experienced. Look at your food. Observe the color.

- Observe the smell.

- Observe the tactile feel in your mouth. Is it crunchy or squishy?

- As you taste each bite, look for flavors. Experience the flavor.

- When finished observe how you feel. Can you sense the energy that will already begin to rise in your system?

- When a minimum of 20 minutes have passed, stop and observe how you feel. Note the feeling of not being hungry. File that away for future use. Be ready to compare a false desire to eat with the real need of taking on more fuel.

- During the day, be aware and observe if you are *looking forward* to eating.

- Be aware of the desire building and then let it go. Be aware of anticipation and do not let it take control through ego.

Weight management is just an example of practicing patience. We can apply patience to every aspect of life. By being patient we are accepting each moment as it is. By being patient we are saying, *right now in this moment things are what they are. In this moment I chose to remain calm, discern information or observe what happens next.* (Mindfulness)

To free your true self from the bondage of ego and mindless

living you must become aware and allow the insight of patience to rise and manifest. With patience comes wisdom and with wisdom comes patience. Get your life back, free your "self".

Finding Joy

"To get up each morning with the resolve to be happy...is to set our own conditions to the events of each day. To do this is to condition circumstances instead of being conditioned by them." Ralph Waldo Emerson

Joy is one of the most powerful emotions to be experienced. It is at once the ultimate goal of sensation seeking and once experienced it is never forgotten. Most of us experience some sense of joy early on. As children it seems readily available and at least a daily occurrence if not more frequently. Because of its power, it is additive. Yet that is not to say that when it arises it should be neither suppressed nor forbidden. Joy is to be treasured yet not attached to. Please refrain from being appalled when I suggest this. What is being suggested here is to allow joy to rise on its own, spontaneously, and to not let the pursuit of it be the purpose in life.

When I was a boy growing up in the South, my friends and I would spend early summer evenings chasing fireflies. In my part of the South, these little creatures were called "lightning bugs". They were available in two colors, mostly green, but sometimes amber. We would race around in the night with a jar and lid trying to capture one. Once we captured our prize, we would observe them for as long as possible and marvel at the incessant blinking of nature's spontaneous light. Later as an adult I came to realize that there was a resonate behavior in chasing after joy. In the dark night of adulthood where responsibilities and problems weighed heavy, I would find myself chasing after and hoping to capture that feeling of joy. Once captured, like lightning bugs, the joy could not be long sustained. It was soon to wither and die away, lost in the daily grind of life.

As we grow up, our egos mature into the purpose driven life of striving. Many times it is the striving for joy through sensation seeking. Somehow we come to believe that joy is found in the material world and ego has a way of becoming blind to the true sources of joy. In this blindness of ego, a paradox is created.

The joy we strive for remains disguised, hiding right in front of us and in great abundance. It is hidden because we do not realize what it looks like and thinking that it can be something found. The paradox is that this constant striving for joy is the very thing that blinds us from experiencing it. Because in the quest for joy, a great need develops. The greater the need one feels, the deeper becomes the blindness one experiences. The deeper the blindness becomes, the greater the need that grows from it. The ego becomes more and more desperate with yearning. Yet joy is ever present, ready to rise when the space for it is created in stillness. There is nothing we have to do to find joy. It is already there waiting to be experienced.

Think back and try to remember some of the silliest things that our egos have exhibited in pursuit of the fulfillment of joy. Look at the things we have bought, the relationships we have started and the stuff we have eaten in the quiet but urgent desperation of joy seeking. It is important to understand that it is the constant striving for joy and making it your unintended life's purpose that is at the heart of all misery and suffering.

In awareness and living the simple life, there develops the spontaneous fulfillment of joy. By ceasing from the constant striving and obsessions, we can create the space for joy to arise on its own.

Joy is subjective. As discussed on other chapters, ego is always controlling reality by how it defines everything that is perceived. As an event arises, emotion and mood filters it out as either good or bad. Life becomes good or bad. Events become defined as problems and thus life becomes one big complicated problem. So rather than allowing life to be as it is, ego must make a determination that it is either good or bad. In egoic unconsciousness the dichotomy of have and have not is created. Each perceived event is defined as either contributing to sensation seeking or distraction or it does not. Each moment is either satisfying or not satisfying. It either stimulates the pleasure center or it does not. In this setting joy cannot arise unless it meets the specific criteria of ego. Even when the illusive faux joy is found, ego will immediately begin to look for the next experience of joy, never becoming still to be in joy or to 'en-joy' this moment. The striving ego which is surrounded by negative feelings and conditioning cannot experience the very thing it is striving for. It may not even be satisfied with the current sense of joy because it already wants the next experience of joy.

The alternative to this is awareness. In the quiet state of pure being, the consciousness is mostly observing. It observes the silly activities of ego that come and go without being caught up in the emotional current. In this quiet and not busy space of expanded awareness, other properties and insights are allowed to rise and go as well. In awareness we can choose to let go of those things which may be inappropriate and allow those things we choose to experience. In awareness we can allow the now to be as it is and experience the wonder of it. We can choose to be still and in the quiet, joy will rise as surely as the morning sun. Striving is as if the morning sun was covered with dark and angry clouds. Above the dark clouds of egoic illusion, the sun is still shining. Above the egoic illusion, joy awaits us.

There is an age old cliché that has great meaning. You have heard it many times and probably dismissed it, being too busy in ego to experience the wisdom contained in the words. The cliché is simply this:

"Stop and smell the roses"

What does this mean? I choose to give it the meaning that when we become quiet in awareness we notice the rose. We observe the rose in a very special way and allow in the infinite space of awareness the full beauty of the rose to rise into a dynamic experience. Our gift of sight shows us beautiful colors. From the sense of smell we can detect a wonderful and unique fragrance. We can touch and sense the tactile surface of stem and petals. We can hear insects as they navigate around the blossoms. And most importantly in awareness we can sense the way the rose is woven into the tapestry of life. At once we can realize what the fragrance is and what it means to bees. We can know what the bees are doing with the pollen that they gather from the rose. We can wonder at nature's purpose for the thorns. We can contemplate the color of green and marvel at how chlorophyll functions in a relationship with our nearest star. We can observe how the light passes through the petals and the changes in color form plant to plant. We can contemplate how flowers use color to attract bees and humans alike to help them replicate. In amazement we can allow the spontaneous rising of joy and wonder. And this is just one moment with a rose.

In this experience a simple joy is found. When we are in awareness we resonate with life. Joy will rise spontaneously with no effort. Just be and be at one with the rose and nature.

Can you see how ego can be at work in the mind to be too busy and overlook the beauty and joy of experiencing the rose? Can you see how people around you, lost in ego, are just too busy to stop and be alive? In ego we are so busy pursuing the false trails to some temporary faux experience that we are missing out on life itself.

It is very important to be alert because ego is tricky and adaptable. Ego can quickly take the joy sensed in the rose and make it into the next pursuit. Ego immediately begins making urgent plans for going to the store and starting a rose garden. Ego is feeling that 'oh my, I must replicate this experience as soon as possible'. Ego is feeling that it does not matter what the cost is, it must have the roses and it must be able to go have the experience over and over again. Almost instantly the magic is gone, lost in the pursuit. The joy is lost because ego is already moving on to some future event that does not yet exist. Instead of just being in the now and en-joy-ing (be in joy) the moment is as it is, ego wants to become a rose gardner. So how should one handle this? They should return to awareness and in the infinite space of now allow possibility to arise. One can let go of the need to pursuit it and own it. In awareness we can allow the world to be as it is and point our attention to other observations. Trying to recreate the moment with the rose is living in the past. In awareness we can allow joy to arise from an infinite amount of other sources. Moment by moment we can experience the reality and its miracles where ever we find ourselves. So where ever you find yourself, be there in this now, observe the tapestry of life and realize the beauty of how it is woven together.

Note. This is not to say that you should not become a rose gardener after enjoying the rose. The point is to let the joy of the moment be. Let any action such as getting more roses or becoming a rose gardener happen after letting possibility mature in consciousness. While enjoying the rose, do not become attached. Do not react, define, judge and give in to the neediness of striving. Just 'en-joy' the moment.

We have plenty of recurring opportunities for joy. The most immediate and significant example that rises in this moment of writing is the observing and experiencing the family. When any one of my three children comes into my perception I tend to marvel at this miracle just as I would the rose. Experiencing moments with my wife and children are a constant source of spontaneous joy. There is something breathtakingly miraculous in interacting with the consciousness of those most closest to you.

Exercise

> If you are experiencing the gift of family, take a moment to "stop and smell the roses". In this aspect, take a moment and become quiet then observe the next immediate family member or loved one that comes to you. Try and remain in alert awareness and observe the things that your faculties tell you.
>
> - Observe what the senses tell you.
>
> - Observe your feelings.

- When the strivings of ego arise, simply let them go.

- When the joy of knowing your family member arises, let it blossom.

- Allow the moment to unfold without interrupting and simply be and experience.

- Know this person. See them for who they are. Accept them without the filter of ego and most importantly is when the love arises, bond with it.

- In this moment set the intention of sustaining this love.

- Be alert for ego to try and set conditions for love. Allow love in awareness to be unconditional.

  - Observe how the love and joy just is. This is the state of consciousness that is supreme.

  - Set the intention of not striving for this moment again and intend to allow it to rise again.

Can you imagine experiencing unconditional love and compassion for all beings? There are those who walk among us that have reached this level of enlightenment. They reside in awareness and have left the restrictions and conditions of ego far behind. It is the definition of being a spiritual leader. Their purpose in this life is to lead us on the path of unconditional love.

"Be the change you would like to see in the world" Mahatma Gandhi

Take a look at your life. Stop now, right here in this 'now' and contemplate the true meaning of joy. Wake up and become aware. In awareness observe the rising of thought driven ego and how it is impatient to go do whatever. Let that go, and turn your attention to the world around you. What do you observe? Where ever you are become aware of life and look for the flow of it around you. Observe this deep tapestry of connections and how it is all woven together. Now observe your place in it. In this moment you are free. This is life and this is living. Free your "self".

Gratitude

"Earth provides enough to satisfy every man's need, but not every man's greed" Mahatma Gandhi

One of the best ways to bring abundance into your life is by grounding your perspective in gratitude. Gratitude is a watershed virtue that covers and laps so many positive aspects of life. Gratitude is that state of mind where one accepts life as it is and feels gratitude for the all there is.

This is a really big deal. It really is the higher road and not many people walk it. Being able to accept the reality of a situation is one thing, but to accept it and be grateful for it is something very special.

At once gratitude embraces the virtues of acceptance, appreciation, and humility. Gratitude is a virtue realized by the authentic self. In awareness we realize how much abundance is in our lives and when we keep our attention on gratitude and abundance the cause and effect creates more abundance.

In ego, the other G word that is on the agenda is greed. Ego is ever satisfied with what it has, quickly tires of its gift of life and greedily wants more. Enough is never enough. Therefore the egoic perspective is one grounded in deprivation and the cause and effect result will always render a lack of abundance. Simply put, greed and dissatisfaction will always render a result of never having enough. (See the Chapters on Greed, Deprivation and Cause and Effect)

Gratitude has a way of expanding the beauty of that which is present. Because satisfaction goes hand in hand with being grateful, having enough is plenty. Gratefulness is a component of living the simple life. In the simply life joy spontaneously arises moment by moment. Being grateful opens the heart to relate to the flow of life around us. Since greediness and ungratefulness always demand more, there becomes a reduction in what is available. Greed filters out most of the simple beauty of life and Gratitude amplifies the beauty in all things. This creates a very fertile ground for the seeds of joy to grow and bear fruit. It is the nature of manifesting through the cause and effect of karma.

Think back to the last time you were recently disappointed. What were your expectations? Why did you feel less than grateful for what transpired? In what part of you is the source of the dissatisfaction?

Now think back to the last time you experienced someone showing you gratitude. How did that make you feel? Did it create a feeling of wanting to help or allow that person to show gratitude again?

Notice the difference in the two feelings. Remember the cold negative feeling of dissatisfaction. Now remember the warm feeling of satisfaction you felt when someone shared their gratitude with you.

Gratitude is a virtue that lives in the present moment. It gives meaning to the wide spectrum of aspects in our life. In any given moment, there is always something to be grateful for. Every moment of every day, if you remain in awareness there is something to which you should feel thankful for.

It begins the moment you wake up in your bed and know that your body is functioning. Every occurrence that happens to you until you shut your eyes again requires acknowledgement of being thankful. Everything from the air you breathe to the freedom you experience living as a free person. We take it all for granted, almost never being aware of our living experience. Every moment that we are unconscious in the pursuit of more stuff, we are ignoring the opportunity for being thankful and grateful. Being satisfied with what we have, takes the energy out of striving for more stuff. With the time and money you that you save by **being grateful** for what you do have, you **will create** even more **abundance** to be grateful for.

Exercise

Stop what you are doing and be here now. Be awake and

aware. In awareness, look around you and realize how much abundance you really have. If you have trouble realizing your abundance, then all you have to do is leave your surroundings and go into an area where the homeless people can be found.

Where ever you are right now while you read this, there is plenty to be grateful for. Who are the people around you? Are you healthy? Do you have any money at all?

The most important area of displaying gratitude is toward those who you have the good fortune to live with. If you are blessed with a spouse, partner or friend, then you my friend, are indeed so very fortunate. If you are loved, then you have been blessed with the greatest gift there is. To be loved by another human being is far and away the most abundant symbol that has ever manifested. Stop and consider this being that loves you and let gratitude arise in your consciousness. If you are with them right now, get up and go give them a hug and be conscious of what you are doing and why. If you cannot at this moment, make it your next thing in life to do. If you remember nothing in this book but this one piece of advice, remember to always be grateful for those who love you. You show your gratitude simply by loving them back and not taking them for granted.

Be honest with yourself now. Have you been ungrateful for the abundance you currently experience? Have you been striving for more than enough? Take a look at your wealth regardless of where you are and who you are. It doesn't matter if you are in a prison cell or sitting in a penthouse. Become aware in all aspects of life how and where you are blessed. Be happy with what you have and accept it with gratitude.

The crazy paradox is that the more you accept what you have and feel grateful for it; more will be on its way. Be sure to share it with others because there is more on the way. Only when greed takes over and striving begins does the flow cease and lacking sets in.

Gratitude is about accepting things as they are. I am always amazed at how often we reject the way things are and are never satisfied. A good example is the weather. It seems that we are never satisfied with the current weather and are always hoping for whatever it is not doing.

If it is warm and sunny, we desire rain. When the rain comes we complain because it interferes with our plans. When it is cold, we wish it was hot forgetting our complaints in the summer about the heat.

Weather is a great place to practice accepting the universe as it is. Nature just does what it does, and fretting about it not complying with our desires is just silly. The exercise here is to accept whatever is taking place and then feel grateful for it. There is absolutely no benefit in wasting energy being ungrateful for the weather.

Lastly, generating gratitude can begin by always looking for the good in every situation. If you can maintain a grateful heart then the positive attributes will arise spontaneously. We must understand that we live in a changing world. Change is a fundamental part of nature and has been since the beginning. Rather than let ego get established in trying to control reality and the changes that come, the being in awareness embraces change by looking for the good in all things. Seeing the good in all things develops gratitude and appreciation for life itself. Loving life and living in awareness is an aspect of the true self. Free yourself from the misery of greed and striving by appreciating the abundance you have. Learn to live the simple life of gratitude.

Serenity

"If you are depressed you are living in the past. If you are anxious you are living in the future. If you are at peace you are living in the present."
Lao Tzu

Awareness is serenity. If you have to be striving for anything at all it should be serenity, which can only be found in the infinity of the present moment. In allowing life to be as it is, acceptance gives rise to serenity. In refraining from being absorbed by ego and its manic reactions we find the calm abiding presence of *being* serene. In calm abiding we reside in this experience with serene observation. Serenity is the absence of striving for the fulfillment of desire.

Unconsciousness, that is the experiencing of life through ego, is the exact opposite of serenity. Not being happy with the present moment, ego creates a reality based on the fulfillment of desire. It rejects the present now as too painful, too boring or just not satisfying enough. Since there is only 'now', and a being can only experience in the present moment, the future will never arrive. Thus ego lives a life in illusion, postponing life until things are just right, and missing all of the true life in between. In the present moment, this 'now', and experiencing reality through the highest state of consciousness, we can dwell in a continuous state of serenity. States of agitation and unhappiness do not have to be present and only happen when ego is allowed to run free.

In this peaceful state of consciousness insights become present and are known. Insights which help us navigate life's path and develop a truer understanding must be preceded by serenity. In serenity, insight flowers, wisdom is realized and ignorance is dissipated.

Ego, famous for its compulsive behavior, detests the present moment and wants to get on with things. Immediately when ego arises, the problems arise with them. The impatient ego reacts impulsively, never giving wisdom a chance to be observed. Just a quick knee jerk reaction based on emotional definitions, and ego is dusting off its hands and later wondering why things did not work out. (See the Chapters on Action and Reaction and Cause and Effect)

In serenity, insights and intuition become the conduit or channel for our universal source to provide understanding. In awareness the most elegant and beautiful solutions to some of the most tangled problems can arise. Yet most often we never see them for we are lost in the torrent of mind stream and ego as the river boat captain struggling to move against the current. Imagine a wagon loaded with round wheels being pushed in a futile effort by ego that does not seem to know that the wagon is fixed with square wheels. Yet this is how many of us spend our lives.

Serenity is balance, and ego is imbalance. Serenity is flowing with life and having joy arise on its own, ignorance and unconsciousness is pushing that wagon with square wheels yet refusing to consider alternatives.

In meditation, when we withdraw to observe the mind, serenity will arise and our consciousness floats on the sea of tranquility. In mindfulness we pay special attention to the tricks the mind will play and continuously return to serenity and awareness. In the peace and stillness of serenity, you can free your "self".

Meditation

"Meditation brings wisdom; lack of mediation leaves ignorance. Know well what leads you forward and what hold you back, and choose the path that leads to wisdom." Buddha

There is a bit of misconception about meditation and what it is. When asked, one might get as many different answers as there are people who either practice or instruct it. Over the centuries individual cultures, sub-cultures and religions have produced their own definition and meaning of just what meditation is.

The intent in this book is to keep meditation as simple as possible so that the average person can use the practice to gain self awareness. Since self awareness and mindfulness are the states of consciousness to be realized, it is important to not have too many "rules" or "instructions" to cloud the path to realization. And most importantly, do not feed ego whether it is yours or mine.

Meditation and the practice of Meditation

Meditation is being and the practice of meditation is doing. Meditation is a state of consciousness and, not something you do. The *practice* of meditation is a doing thing. Sitting, breathing, and chanting are all doing things. They may or may not lead to the transcended state of consciousness. Being is not the same as doing. Being is experiencing life through observation and meditation is the state of awareness where observing is the condition. To remain grounded in observation, we can use the focus of observing the breath, the repetition of sounds, or the chanting as an anchor in being awake and conscious.

So Meditation is not so much a "thing" and it is not some thing that you do. The *practice* of meditation is the doing activity that one may use to focus the observation on that which is being observed. Therefore anyone may sit down and imitate the activity of meditation which would look like sitting quietly with the eyes closed for prolonged periods of time. Some cognitively astute people are great at multi-tasking so they can repeat mantras and chant, yet at the same time the attention of the observer is off and gone with the current of mindstream. It matters not that you can juggle bottles, chew gum and recite poetry at the same time, if you cannot keep from being absorbed by the activities of the mind. The difference between meditation and the practice of meditation is with the realization of consciousness as a state being and the practice at meditation as something we can do.

When the individual sits down to practice meditation, it is with the intention to wake up from the clutches or fetters of the mind stream. When a person is successful in no longer being absorbed by the constant stream of thoughts, they become awake and aware. This transition from being "lost in thought" to being in awareness is commonly known as transcendence. Being "lost in thought" is a type of unconsciousness. Being lost in thought, the individual is not really aware of what is going on around them. They are not very much aware of where they are going, or what they are doing or why they are doing it.

Example

One example of being unconscious and unaware is the state our minds descend into when we watch television. Totally engrossed in the virtual reality streaming into our minds, we become unaware of what is going around us in the real world. I would be so engrossed in the program that I would not even hear someone speaking to me. My wife would have to walk in between me and the television to interrupt the flow and to get my attention. Sometimes she would say outrageous things to me in front of other people and I would not be aware until I realized that people were laughing.

Awareness is being awake, aware and knowing that you are in the present moment. Being aware in each "now", or each moment of perception is to be in pure consciousness or in a complete state of awareness.

Meditation is the state of consciousness of being absolutely awake and aware. Awake and aware, it is our higher self, the observer, that is observing the observed. The observed can be sourced as internal or external. Internally observations might be of emotions, feelings, thoughts, images and phenomena of memory. External observation can be information presented to the surface of the mind by the senses. Note the specific use of the word *observation*. Observing is not judging. (See the chapter on Judgment) In observation, we are just paying close attention to the event unfolding in our perception, without taking any action. The observer uses intention and discernment to maintain the focus of awareness of the subject of observation without getting caught up or being absorbed in what is being observed.

In the instant the observer begins defining and judging the observed, the attention is absorbed. In that instantaneous shift from neutrality of discernment, to placing meaning of good or bad to whatever is being observed, we move from awareness back into thought stream. So meditation is the sustained presence of being. The practice of meditation is the activity used to focus and *anchor the attention* as the observer, to awaken and to sustain awareness.

The opposite of being conscious is of course being unconscious. Most people think that they understand what being unconscious is. Yet when someone is in a state of unconsciousness it is like being in the sleep state and not realizing it. In this book, on this path, being unconscious has very little to do with having the eyes open. This type of unconsciousness involves having your eyes open, not asleep yet not being aware of what you are doing and why you are doing it.

Example

Observe someone while they are watching a television program.

- Notice the rapt unblinking state of rapture they seem to be in. If there is a drama taking place then the attention and full focus of consciousness is captured.

- While they are in this state, notice how they are unaware of what is going around them.

- Frequently they will also being doing other things at the same time that they are unaware of. People whose consciousness is captivated by television programming will:
  - eat all sorts of things, scratch themselves until they bleed,
  - Chew their nails, pick their nose, cover their eyes, and hide their mouth.
  - People lose track of time, and often forget to do very important things they have promised.
  - Talk to the characters on the TV
  - Drink too much alcohol
  - Ignore their crying children
  - Ignore their pets

While in this state of unconsciousness they really do not know what they are doing or why they are doing it.

This is just scratching the surface. There are a myriad of things that surfaces upon the mind that humans get lost in. We become our thoughts and thus become prisoner to our thoughts, moods, emotions and feelings. Meditation is awakening from by those currents of the mind stream. In the case of television, we are unconscious with our eyes wide open. If we wake up and return to awareness, then we are no longer absorbed by the television programming.

Thinking and Observing.

There is a common misconception about mindfulness meditation that the goal to stop thinking. Understandably this can be very difficult if not impossible to achieve. The practice in mindfulness meditation is about observing and being aware of the thoughts. Trying to stop a thought can be very frustrating and a futile effort. If you have tried meditation and became agitated and frustrated with the struggle of trying to stop the thoughts, then I urge you to not give up the practice but to just let go of that struggle. In mindfulness meditation, thoughts will arise, yet you learn to not get caught up in them and carried away. You will learn to not be absorbed by the thoughts and mindstream. They arise, and they play out. Observing means just that, only observing. It is paying attention without becoming absorbed by the thoughts or mind activities.

Being alert to the emotional content that we are conditioned with, we can observe the thoughts and emotions as they are without losing our point of observation. That is to say, we can observe thoughts and emotions without being absorbed by them. More importantly, we can observe without responding with a spontaneous reaction. Some emotions, feelings and thoughts are easier to remain non-absorbed in than others. Some can be downright demanding for egoic attention. Letting go of resentment because it is raining is a lot easier than not being absorbed by the grief of a loved one. Not being attached to emotional stimuli is the objective. Since we are usually just everyday people, the degree to which we can resist many of these emotions and feelings can vary on a scale of being very sensitive and easy to be distracted, to being strong in awareness and not easily affected by emotions. Meditation is a return to being and finding balance.

Suppressing thought. It is very important at this juncture to draw the distinction between suppressing emotions, thoughts and feelings and observing them. Suppressing thoughts and emotions is even worse than being caught up in them. Being caught up in egoic emotions can lead to trouble and often does. Yet suppressing emotions, feelings and thoughts will create a subconscious pressure that will eventually vent itself in destructive ways. Observing these thought/feeling activities as they arise yet remaining as the observer, allows them to play out without being caught up in a knee jerk reaction and it vents the emotional content. *You can be aware of your feelings without being absorbed or controlled by them.*

Since we spend years in building layer upon layer of conditioning which are the behaviors created by reaction, it can take a long time to process or let go of the accumulated emotional memories. The subconscious may be the repository of the stuff we experience. During lucid dreaming and deep meditation the observer can be aware of the stored experiences through images and feelings. Some of each day's experience is processed during the nightly sleep cycle, but when there is too much to be assimilated, they just continue to bubble and brew in the caldron of sub-consciousness. Thoughts and feelings with heavy emotional weight can affect us on the surface by experiencing moods and feelings that we cannot quite be aware of. Unresolved emotional issues may never go away or take a long time to diffuse. Observing these subconscious thoughts, feelings and emotions during meditation can be very powerful in allowing resolution by allowing them come and go. By sustaining a heightened state of consciousness we can let these experiences arise, acknowledge them then allow them to pass on without getting absorbed by them. It is like taking out the trash that has accumulated over a long time.

It will serve a person well if they can devote a length of time to allow the momentum of the mind to slow or to prevent the mindstream from becoming over active. This activity of mindstream can wake up you in the middle of the night, or it can become active as soon as you wake in the morning. As our mind merges or becomes absorbed by the increasing mindstream, the cognitive momentum increases. Since it takes energy for the brain/mind to perform these activities, the body responds by increasing metabolism. It is part of the reason why it can be so hard to go back to sleep in the middle of the night. Most importantly, if the nature of the thought stream is experienced as "stressful", then the body responds with the stress response. The more energetic the mind, the more momentum is created. So it becomes important to prevent this ramp up of momentum as soon as it begins. Often that is in the middle of the night or first thing upon waking in the morning. In either case, you should use the practice of meditation to keep the mind quiet. I strongly recommend that you begin meditation as you rise from sleep. Mindfulness begins as soon as you begin observing the waking aspect of life. As you become aware of mindstream beginning its swirling and turning, focus on your breath or mantra to keep from being absorbed. If is in the middle of the night, the circadian rhythm will take back control and you should fall asleep again. As the relaxation response resumes, Melatonin in the brain will induce sleep again. If you are waking in the morning and ready to rise and start your day, begin immediately with meditation and mindfulness to start your day awake and aware. Before the current of mindstream can take you away and create stressful momentum, you anchor in awareness and maintain a balance all day. If there has been too much mental stimulation from the previous day and deep sleep did not eliminate it, the egoic mind stream will bring it up first thing. Your subconscious is repository of stuff that needs to wind down. Sometimes we accumulate too much emotional memory and we need a sustained down time to process it all.

Meditation retreats are great for this concentrating on what is lurking below the surface of the unconscious mind. Especially effective are "silent retreats" where you remain focused without speaking for several days, while you strengthen the observing focus and allow years of emotional pressure to play out. It is also why when we sit down to meditation sometimes it's like opening the door to an over packed closet. All that emotional content rises to the surface of our mind and it is just too much too fast. It is like trying to drink from a firehouse when we have years of accumulated emotional feelings and layers of experience to deal with. If you are a beginner, and you do not have access to a retreat, find a good meditation instructor who can teach you how to begin the process of sustaining the concentrated focus without being too overwhelmed.

So if you have tried meditation but gave up because you could not stop the thinking, that can be the first thing that you let go of. Thoughts will rise and fall as surely as your breath. Yet just like breath we let them go only observing, not reacting and not becoming absorbed.

Transcendence

Transcendence is defined as rising above or going beyond. This rising above the prison of the alter self or ego, that lives in frustration and misery is to transcend to the true or authentic self.

From a philosophical perspective, transcendence is that rising above ego and mind stream and becoming the knower. It is the detaching from the ego based identity and orienting as just being. Transcending thought is to realize that you are a not the thoughts. It is the letting go of "I" and "me" and just being. The egoic self is one which is grounded in the materialistic nature of sensation seeking and distraction. Transcendence is a state of pure consciousness.

The modern cliché of 'being at one with universe' might be a useful way to bridge the leap from knower to known. As implied there is no separateness between the observer and the observed. You are the universe, consciousness or awareness.

All of this can be heady stuff the first time you are exposed to it. It may take a while to absorb the meanings so it will take patience. Do not go seeking transcendence, rather find and become stillness and transcendence will find you.

Meditation begins with relaxation. The practice becomes the alert observation to realize the gap between busy activities of the mind. Using a focal point such as breathing or mantra, use those gaps to become awake and aware. The gap is found when we remain alert and watchful for the next thought. In that space from being focused on breath or mantra until the next thought arises, is the gap. When one continues this practice the gaps between the thoughts become longer and more sustained. In these gaps, that is, during awareness, you begin to become alert for the next thought. Awareness is found in that gap. You, the observer, expect and look for the next onslaught that will carry you away. As you are floating away in the current of thought, it will become apparent and you use your focal point to pull your attention back out and to the present again. This is the primary effort for the first few months. It is simple but it is not easy and it is hard work. Who would imagine that doing nothing could be so hard? But slowly, almost imperceptibly, the gap widens and you the observer, the knower is able to sustain awareness. As you created a beachhead in awareness, as you get anchored in being awake, you set an intention or dedicate yourself to return to awareness as much as possible. At some point you realize that you do not have to leave for very long. This beachhead or sanctuary is only a breath away. It is as simple as stopping your busy mind to determine if you are still breathing or not. In the instant that you focus your awareness to breathing; you are out of mindstream and awake again. You are here, now and present.

In our meditation class we use various techniques to help beginners remain unabsorbed by thought stream. It can be helpful to set the intention to be alert for having your attention being absorbed by the current of the mind stream. You may try seeing how long you can focus on your breath or even count each breath until your attention wanders. While repeating your mantra, see how long you can be alert and focused before being interrupted and carried away. With practice you get better and better. With practice eventually your mind will settle into stillness. The mind activity will sooner or later become diffused and relatively quiet. With continued practice the transition from busy mind to tranquil will become shorter and shorter. When your meditation session is over, remain mindful of the mind and its current of activity. As you engage your daily activities balance stillness and awareness with the activity at hand. Be aware of what you are doing and why you are doing it. In this way you can avoid being consumed and absorbed in egoic reaction. In this quiet stillness insights and choices are available. Moment by moment you can choose the true path and not the one determined by ego.

The first moment where I became awake and aware was very special. I realized for the first time, that I had spent most of life in a state of unconsciousness. Even after I realized what to do, it was very hard remaining awake and aware. Every so often I would wake up and realize just how long I had been gone. At first it was weeks. Even though I loved the relaxed state of meditation, I would soon become lost to it and go for a long time before something would cause me to "wake up". Finally in a desperate attempt to return to being no matter what, I devised a system to wake myself up. It occurred to me that I needed a personal alarm clock. So I set my digital watch to chime every hour. I set up strict instructions that whatever I was doing, when the alarm went off I would stop and wake up. The most amazing changes began to happen. Each hour I would take a few minutes to just stop and watch my breath. I would become aware of what I was thinking and feeling. I would realize what I had been unconsciously been doing. Sometimes I would be on the phone and would hit the snooze so that I could not get lost when the call was over. As zany as this system sounds, I found that it worked very well. Pretty soon I developed the habit of anticipating the hourly charm. At some point I didn't need the alarm. So I went for quite a while with my hourly quickie meditation. Then it occurred to me that perhaps it would be alright to wake up twice per hour. I resumed my alarm for every thirty minutes. Later, I dismissed the alarm having developed the sense to just constantly return over and over to be awake and present. This ladies and gentlemen transformed my life.

My routine became to wake up in the morning and immediately practice meditation..I would observe what the mind wanted to churn up and quietly let things go until a sense of peace settled in. It became the practice to remain grounded in stillness before I started my day. My Buddhist teacher once called this state of stillness as "calm abiding". After meditation I would study some form of spiritual development by reading or watching a video. Even while reading or watching, I would constantly return to presence. Existence has become the most wonderful place. Time has slowed down and only a tool for perception. Each experience became just that. An experience. A meal was an experience involving not just the senses, but a higher sensitivity but how the body was responding to the food. By being conscious while I was eating each bite slowed down the eating process. I would be aware of being full and realize that I needed less. During the day, in awareness, I would *know* the difference between being hungry and thirsty, being hungry and sensation seeking. I lost about 50 lbs by doing nothing and have never gained it back. Weight management can be as simple as paying attention to what you eat and why you are eating it.

The Buddhist groups I studied with primarily used breathing as the foundation of mental focus. While I had studied various types of meditation, I slipped easily into being able to quiet the mind by focusing on the breath. The most helpful and powerful lessons came when we practiced insight meditation.

During insight meditation, I could observe the truly amazing things that would be perceived on the surface of my mind. So for me, this meditation along with a few others that the Buddhist practice became very meaningful and transformed my life

Once a person can sustain awareness, other possibilities arise. Concentrated meditation enables the deeper understanding of emptiness. You may have to learn concentrated meditation to get your mind around that concept.

In concluding this chapter on meditation, let me summarize.

Meditation is a state of consciousness, not something you do. (The doing would be the practice of meditation). Meditation is awareness.

In awareness one is able to be sense aspects of the self. That would be Self Awareness.

Being alert and paying attention on purpose to the state of the mind you are in and remaining absorbed by its activity, is called Mindfulness.

In the following chapters we will discuss the insights that will enable you to understand the illusions, also known as problems, arise from. Meditation, self awareness, and mindfulness are the path of freeing you to be your true self. On this path you can free your "self" from unconsciousness and egoic ignorance.

Setbacks

"The definition of Insanity is doing the same thing over and over again and expecting a different result" Origin Unknown

"Develop success from failures. Discouragement and failure are two of the surest stepping stones to success." Dale Carnegie

In the introduction, I stated that I was a regular guy who had made many of the mistakes that you may be experiencing. Along the way I have and still do experience some setbacks. As mentioned before, I am no enlightened guru. I am a regular guy who got his life back and is now enjoying every minute of it. Having setbacks is just part of the learning experience. We are not born wise, but we may become wise by learning from our experiences. The main difference between ignorance and wisdom may be found in learning from our failures rather than continuing to suffer by repeating them.

Managing Ego and reducing its influence over us is not easy. Notice the use of the word managing. Eliminating ego completely may be too challenging, so at first you may just want to simply find balance. Please understand that transcending ego is such a worthy goal that just moving a little beyond where you are now can transform your life. As stated several times in this book, you may want to manage ego as if your life depended on it. For sure, your quality of life and those who are close to you depend on it.

At first it will seem impossible and some will give up too quickly and go back to the old ways and continue to suffer. Others of you will become determined to stop the cycle of ignorance and set an intention to persevere. To transform your life you must realize that it takes patience, learning, setbacks, and determination.

Ego is very tricky. It is sneaky and it will cheat. This alter identity of will seem defeated only to sneak in the back door when you least expect it. It is an aspect of you and therefore it knows all of the secrets. Heck ego was born from your secrets and has a way of coming back from the grave with a vulnerable spot that may sneak past your alert watching. So to put this in perspective, try to remember that you spend years developing this conditioning of ego and thus it can take years to undo it.

You must realize and accept that you are going to have setbacks. Unless you are one of the rare beings that completely transform and become released from it completely, instantly, you are going to have days where you have failures. Our ever changing and unpredictable universe will zig when you may want to zag. So even though your path may zig-zag you can accept it as it is and avoid attachment issues. Deliverance from egoic suffering is found in acceptance and the return to awareness. Accepting your failures allows you to see what happened and where things went wrong. Accepting failure with humility is a step toward enlightenment, because it is ego that cannot stand up in the light of truth and honesty. Be alert for ego tricks and try not to be become attached to outcome. Patience is a virtue of awareness. To get well you must be able and willing to learn from your mistakes. Getting frustrated when ego gets temporary control is just ego getting frustrated with ego. So wake up and return to awareness and let go of frustration. You have to be honest and be willing to accept things as they are, including your setbacks. The power of acceptance is manifested when we can embrace a self truth.

Ego is so tricky that it can even silently assume the role as the agent seeking yet more attention. As you work towards living the life of balance and harmony never stop observing what you are doing and why you are doing it. Ego can create a self image where in its imagination you are admired and envied by others no so enlightened. Ego will have you daydreaming with visions of grandeur and before you know it, the illusion you will be living is one as an ego centered spiritual advocate. (Yes ego can even pretend to be spiritual). By being in the present moment, aware and mindful of the true intention behind your feelings and actions you can remain humble and side step the tricks of ego.

Ego gets attached to outcome, so when an emotional storm is experienced it becomes frustrated because it believes that transcendence should be easy. Even in transcendence ego seeks instant gratification by becoming impatient for it (enlightenment) to happen. When you are meditating and sense the rise of impatience, boredom or frustration, know that ego is sneaking in. Focus on your mantra or breath, remain in awareness and just let the emotions go. Without the energy of attention they will diffuse on their own. In awareness, patience and other insights will anchor you in peace.

The reward for managing ego is tremendous. Even with setbacks the turnaround in cause and effect will smooth out a lot of bumps in the road. The more you eliminate decision making based on ignorance and illusion, the less you will perceive problems on your path. When we take ownership for the pain that we have caused ourselves we can begin to change. Constantly looking to place cause (blame) on the something other than your own actions only creates more negative karma. When we take ownership of our actions, we accept our failures and become centered in truth. From truth we can release ourselves from the behaviors and conditioned responses (actions) that lead to "problems".

If you are having a hard time owning your mistakes, you must look inward at the reason why. In awareness look for that part of you that resists the truth. It may be too painful to contemplate. If you cannot untangle this knot on your own, then please seek professional counseling. For if you cannot accept your actions, you cannot let them go. If you cannot let them go, you will not change and you can expect the same results.

Mindfulness

"What are you doing? And why are you doing it?   S Beasley

Mindfulness refers to being completely in touch with and aware of the present moment, as well as taking a non-evaluative and non-judgmental approach to your inner experience. A mindfulness approach to one's inner experience is simply viewing "thoughts as thoughts" as opposed to evaluating certain thoughts as positive or negative.

The term comes from Eastern spiritual and religious traditions and make up a core belief in Buddhism. However, mental health professionals also recognize that mindfulness can have many benefits for people suffering from difficulties such as anxiety and depression.

In Meditation and Self Awareness we learned about freeing oneself from the prison of mindstream and ego and into awareness. And because we cannot spend all day everyday in meditation and enter into the world of thought and doing, there must be a means of being where we can have both at the same time. This would be the practice of mindfulness. Mindfulness is about being alert and watching or "paying attention" from the point of awareness of what you are doing and thinking at any given time. When we can balance mindfulness, doing our path becomes so much smoother.

Let's use the metaphor of driving the car as a continuing example. As discussed before and also in the chapters on balance and self awareness we looked at how we become unconscious while we were driving the car. Being unconscious, we start the car, put it into gear and immediately become "lost in thought". Our attention completely captivated by mindstream and all of the activity within that single domain we are not aware of so many things as we operate a heavy steel vehicle to our destination. Once reaching the destination, we do not know if we stopped at red lights or stop signs. We cannot remember many, if any, of the other cars encountered. We listen to talk radio, or talk, or text, or put on makeup, and many other mind captivating activities rather than *know* what we are doing.

Mindfulness is being in the 'now'. It is being in this moment aware and paying attention to what is going on with both inside and outside of your body. Being mindful of driving the car, you are checking your mirrors and where other cars are. You are mindful of how much fuel you have, how the vehicle is functioning, the driving conditions and traffic flow. Inside your body, inside your mind, you are aware of how you are feeling, where your thought drift away to. Being mindful you continuously bring your attention back to now at hand to what you are experiencing.

It may sound simple but for most people this can be very difficult to do. Having spent a life time of being unconscious in thought stream, it is the natural tendency to dwell in this preoccupied state. After years and years of being conditioned for distraction, it becomes our natural state of non awareness and we seek it constantly. While any reasonable person would readily tell you that life is precious and to be lived to the fullest, they will also immediately resume avoiding life by avoiding the present moment. As mentioned before in this book many times, many if not most of us spend vast amounts of time seeking something sensational as a distraction. It is my observation that ninety percent of people are unconscious (unaware/distracted), ninety percent of the time.

I used to be so unconscious while driving that I would frequently wake up only to find myself on the wrong road in the wrong part of town. I have even missed my exit on the interstate and had to drive 20 miles back to get on track. This example is just while driving a car, yet we do it so much of our entire existence.

Right here and right now, stop, look up, and be aware of where you are, what you are doing, and why. Welcome to the 'now'. For this instant you are no longer part of the ninety percent. How soon will you become lost again?

Take any situation where there is an imbalance in life and you will find a state of unconsciousness. See the chapter on balance and harmony. Balance and harmony are a must for a healthy life. Broader awareness is broader mindfulness. The mind is capable of multi-tasking a lot of activities at one time. But generally we can only hold tight focus on one or two things in each individual moment of perception. So even though I am aware of the smell of jasmine, the feel of the warm spring Georgia air flowing over my skin, the sound of kids playing in the background, my focus is on the message being conveyed. The focus in awareness is like the beam of a flash light that high lights things in a dark room. Because of some ambient light, you may pick up other things in the room but the ray of light brings the things within its beam into focus. My mind is focused on the phenomena coming into awareness. It is a kind of creative part of me that is spontaneous whenever awareness can focus on that intuitive insight. In awareness I am observing in this special way the flow of words. I do not have to think about typing or that the brain is doing something it has been taught to do. I don't have to think about breathing, as it is an automatic response from the autonomic nervous system. But being mindful, I am paying attention in this special way to what I am doing as I do it.

Writing reminds me of the practice of Tai Chi. Aspects of the mind learn how to move the hands and feet in a specific choreography that is synchronized with breathing. With lots of practice, the movements become as natural as breathing. They all come together in a singular flow. It is like a maestro who guides the different melodies of each group of musicians into a combination of sounds creating something beautiful. Sounds become a song. The special concentration found in Tai Chi is an ancient and beautiful form of mindfulness.

Mindfulness is the special observing of what we are doing in all aspects of our life. We become mindful of what we are doing and the intention behind our actions. The higher self manages the balance of being and doing in a harmonious manner by being mindful and paying attention in a very unique and concentrated way. The path to a balanced and unlimited life begins with mindfulness. The moment the mind enters into a waking consciousness, mindfulness is alert and watching in its special way. Upon waking, thoughts begin to fill the mind. If we are aware and mindful, we can observe what the different entities of the mind are up to. We can observe feelings and moods that begin to arise. And in awareness, we can observe the conditions of the body. Notice the sense of urgency that arises when the bladder is full. I really advise paying attention that one.

We pay attention and become mindful of aches and pains, thirst, and energy levels. More importantly, mindfulness will allow the higher self to observe and pay attention to any egoic reaction to the information coming into awareness in this 'now'. Thus choice begins the instant, the 'now' that we gain consciousness after sleeping. We can start our day by paying attention to how we feel, and make choices because we know what we are doing and why we are doing it. This ability is very powerful.

For many people, waking on Monday morning means an automatic moodiness because of the realization that is time to return to work If the weather has been defined as undesirable by ego, there may be an automatic sense of gloom. And this is even before we get out of the restroom. Being mindful of these feelings, emotions and moods is to allow the self to accept things as they are and to remain un-absorbed from ego moodiness. Awake and aware we can choose from the infinite possibilities in each moment. We find when it comes to how we view reality, options are available. One *coula choose* to be cheerful and find joy in anticipating the work they have chosen do. Or they *coula choose* to ignore the weather defined as gloomy and feel happy accepting that the cycle of weather is on its own schedule. None of these alternatives is an option without being mindful of what our mind is thinking. Mindfulness is being vigilant to avoid becoming a captive prisoner of an emotional response. Mindfulness is being aware of what the mind is up to, and that is a mind-full.

Exercise

Set an intention to begin your mindfulness practice.

Look with your mind to see if you are breathing. In this instant you are here in the present. You are awake and aware.

Pay attention to how you are feeling right now. Fill in the blank   "I am feeling _____" Remember, you are not your thoughts, and try to become the non judgmental observer, observing the feelings and emotions.

As the non judgmental observer, discern what you are feeling and why you are feeling that way. If you are feeling joy, happiness, and fulfillment, then reside in the calm abiding.

If you are feeling negative or experiencing inappropriate feelings or in a bad mood, then observe and discern what is going on and why?

- Now ask these questions:

- Can I change this?

- Can I move it or remove myself?

- Can I accept it?

- Why not feel something else right here and right now?

- What are other possible feelings to choose from?

- What obstacle is preventing my choices of how to feel?

As you become awake, that is aware in the present moment, try to realize (to use insight) to recognize that when you (the higher or authentic self) have been away, unconscious and not aware. In its absence, notice, how you may have been lost in the mind stream of ego and reaction.

Set the intention of remaining awake and aware of where you are and what you are doing/feeling.

Learn to explore ways of putting reminders in your daily life, to stop and become aware of what emotional state your mind is experiencing. Set your watch alarm, put up sticky notes, and get a friend to help monitor your absences.

This *will* take many efforts, and there will be set-backs, so don't let frustration take you away again. Be aware of egoic frustrations and perform the above listed exercise. Just realize and accept that it happened and resume being awake, aware, using intention and choice to work on the balance of being and doing.

When I made a commitment to practice mindfulness, I started exploring ways to wake myself up to do a check on my mental condition. What I came up with was to set my watch alarm to beep every hour. The alarm would sound off and where ever I was, I would stop and observed my breathing. I would check to see what I was thinking feeling and doing. I would just bring myself to awareness and hold it for a few minutes with an intention to come back as soon as possible. At first it felt pretty silly. But soon I really noticed how much less stress and anxiety I was carrying around. Pretty soon I became watchful for the alarm to go off and would find myself calm and centered before it beeped. So I moved the cycle up to every half hour. When it beeped, I would engage in a mini meditation. I would step back from thought and wake up. In awareness I began to see trends in my own behavior. Most importantly, I begin to pay attention to the stressful thought activity as it began to happen. Being aware, I was then able to choose to let the stressful reactions go and to choose some other action and feeling. It worked very well. Over time the balance has become a constant monitoring.

At first being mindful may seem like hard work. Meditation,

self awareness and mindfulness are not necessarily easy. Yet when it becomes engrained, it becomes an effortless way of navigating the path through balance. As your life comes into balance, you will notice that a lot of bumps in the road have smoothed out. There will still be events that require a lot of attention. And they are best addressed through awareness. Being mindful is the path to the balanced life. Free your "self".

The Illusion of Time

"I'm late / I'm late / for a very important date. / No time to say "Hello, Goodbye". / I'm late, I'm late, I'm late.' Excerpt from <u>Alice in Wonderland,</u> by Louis Carroll

Time. We think that we either do not have enough of it or need to kill it. We waste it, make it, or even manage it; yet time is only a useful illusion. The illusion of time is created in the mind brain conceptualization of each moment of perception. Within this illusion of time, ego is busy creating the problematic life.

As discussed in the chapter on Ego and Self Awareness, we came to understand that ego is never satisfied with things as they are. To cope with this dissatisfaction, ego looks to avoid the present moment by coping. (See Chapter on Coping). Coping is done by seeking distraction and sensational experiences. And since it can never be fully satisfied it spends all moments in this pursuit. This creates the illusion of not having enough time to do all that it desires. In other instances, if ego feels trapped in a boring 'now', then it seeks distraction also known as "killing time". These impossible situations create a paradox that can only be eliminated by becoming aware and detached from the mind stream of ego.

This brings us to the topic at hand, which is of course Time. So what is this illusion we call time? Immediately a part of your mind is probably insisting that time is an actual thing. Try as we might, we cannot touch or feel it. It is not tangible for it has not substance. We cannot capture it so we cannot save it, even though we constantly think we are "saving time". So no matter how hard you look for the time you "saved" you will not find it.

The illusion of time is experiential. Since it is not something we can touch or feel it must be something we experience. And how do we do this?

The illusion of experiencing time can be understood by thinking of "motion pictures". If you were to take your favorite movie, and look closely at the film, you would see a series of still pictures. When these still pictures are flashed before your eyes in a serial cascade, the illusion of motion begins to develop. As the progression of pictures flashes faster and faster it becomes more and more realistic. When the flashing of streaming pictures reaches a point that is synchronized with the moment by moment perception speed of the brain, the illusion is complete and the moving pictures look like reality. It looks so real that it is no longer questioned about how it is done; we just except it and become mesmerized by the content. It does not matter if the experience happens in an IMAX 3D movie theatre or the small screen on your smart phone, the illusion is accepted by the brain as reality.

This is how the brain experiences reality. Each small moment of perception that are so many milliseconds long, connected to the next moment of perception. The brain, organizing the senses, views life as one continuous movie. To experience time, devices were created to track each moment of perception. Even though life is actually continuous, humans live in a world of dualities. As creatures still experiencing some of our animal nature, we synchronize our existence with the rotation of our planet and its orbit around our star. Each rotation is subdivided into equal increments of 24 hours. Because we evolved with sleep and wake cycles known as circadian rhythms, night and dark divide our waking life and the 24 units can easily be divided into two halves of 12.

As humans began to evolve, they perceived the need to orient themselves to their location in this rhythm so they could organize their lives. Perhaps with the advent of ego, early civilized humans were not satisfied with how things were and sought out advantages by controlling their new discovery of time. Early humans regulated life by joining life and its experiences with daylight and night. Longer periods were segmented by the changing moon. Later as intellect grew other means of measuring existence came into being. Perhaps humans were simply practicing intellectual sensation seeking and exercised their growing intellect by building the first sun dials and water clocks as long as 4000 years ago.

Whenever it was, people's perceptions begin to change. Existence began to be defined as good or bad and experience was to be perceived as past, present and future. Clocks measured each increment of life in minutes, hours and days. A new perception was born that created the sense that experience and time were joined and that they flowed. The sense of flow is one where experience is linear. Somewhere along our intellectual evolution the illusionary sense of time evolved. It probably began with early humans who lived by the rise and fall of the sun and moon. Later the illusion grew with the ticking movement of clock hands the arrow of time came into consciousness. In modern times time has become the central regulating feature of ego into which all life must be confined.

Centuries ago, the Buddhists knew that this spooling out or flowing of time was just an illusion and there was only the now or one moment of perception. Through the deep insights found in meditation they were able to escape the illusion of time flow by observing the brain and mind as it creates snapshots. In meditation which is observing all things and especially the mind, they realized that the brain/mind would reset itself moment by moment. By becoming present in awareness and outside the flow of time they could realize what was actually happening. They observed the illusion of perceived *now's* created by the brain, and how it reset its perception every partial second and how change occurred in each partial second creating a false sense of flow. Thus life does not move, only the mind moves.

Then along comes the advent of Quantum Science. Scientists like Albert Einstein begin to realize that the components of the universe did not operate along the set of rules from the Newtonian era but followed something entirely different. Einstein figured out that space and time were not separate but joined in a continuum called "space-time". Previously all space was viewed as three dimensional. Space-time added the fourth dimension of time. In a continuum with three dimensions plus time (fourth dimension) events were plotted not where but when. If one views the universe as a large oval that could be dissected into slices it become apparent that now is the same no matter where in this universe one is located. Every point in the universe shares the same now, therefore there is only now.

Tonight go out and look up at a star. We can observe the star because of the light that travels from its location to our brain here on our planet. Cognitively we know that this is light that took many light years to arrive here. Our brain extrapolates this knowledge of travel as time spent. It does this because of how we evolved to record change in each moment of perception. Our brain concludes that the light from that star left 1000 light years ago and therefore happened in our past. Yet when we remove the illusion created by change (remember the illusion created by rapidly moving pictures to create a movie) we can realize that that star and our brain share the same now continuum. The brain creates the illusion of then and now because of this cognitive tool developed when we begin to measure time. Early humans, not having acquired the illusion of then and now would just assume that up there in the heavens the gods were doing what they do right now. Before humans developed the flow of time sense they, like other sentient creatures, only experienced 'now'.

The importance of understanding the flow of time being an illusion is in shifting your grounding in perception. Ego is enslaved by the clock as simply the device that regulates opportunity for fulfilling desire. In another chapter we looked at this paradox of ego where it wants to experience fulfillment right now, but resists being in the right now. Ego must and will always seek the past or future for everything it needs.

Ego senses that there is not enough time. This means that ego needs to spend more time pursuing fulfillment than there is time available. It creates an impossible situation that often leads to deep problems. The more stress and anxiety it feels for not getting fulfilled, the more it pursues sources of fulfillment. The more activity spent on this pursuit creates less opportunity for little else.

In other circumstances, ego which cannot experience patience, cannot abide the doing of nothing (meditation and just being). It must be doing something. Impatient to be doing something it finds ways to "kill time". Since life is being the true self, killing time is killing the self. Killing time is the separating oneself from being to become lost in sensation seeking or distraction. Just consider the nature of distraction. It is purposefully removing attention from experiencing what is. People cut out whole segments of life with distraction. Yet when they reach the end of the life experience, they so desperately cling to that which they tried so hard to avoid.

These illusions are the heart of all suffering and problems. Time is just a tool. Like a compass, it can orient us in our experience as a convenience. A compass can be a useful tool yet we would never consider letting the compass control us. Imagine that you are crossing a desert and you are out of water and tired. Your compass tells you that you must continue in a specified direction to reach your destination. Then you notice an oasis which is adjacent to the direction the compass is suggesting. Would you be willing to ignore the compass long enough to drink water and save your life or would you continue on in servitude to the compass? Time and clocks, like a compass are just tools.

It is not necessary to completely understand the quantum aspects of now to be in the 'now'. Being in the 'now' is found in self awareness. In fact, it is only in self awareness, in being your true self that one can experience the eternal now. In the unconsciousness of ego, we become obsessed with striving. Since ego will never be completely fulfilled it will constantly strive. The nature of ego is that its hunger grows within the illusion of time, and can never be fulfilled. We can observe the illusion of not having enough time by observing morning rush hour traffic in any city. Just notice how many people that are frantic and rushing to their place of employment because they are under the illusion that time is working against them. Hurry is a great indicator of being in the illusion.

Accepting life as it is, is accepting the 'now' and placing the tool of time back on the shelf. Trying to force a life too busy with distraction into a finite amount of time is a function of ego. It will lead to stress and anxiety. Stress and anxiety cause sickness, disease, and death. You should practice self awareness as if your life depended on it. Life is the conscious experiencing of living in the now. By practicing meditation, self awareness, and being mindful of what you are doing and why you are doing it, you can be your true self. This is life.

Love and Compassion

"A human being is a part of the whole called by us universe, a part limited in time and space. He experiences himself, his thoughts and feeling as something separated from the rest, a kind of optical delusion of his consciousness. This delusion is a kind of prison for us, restricting us to our personal desires and to affection for a few persons nearest to us. Our task must be to free ourselves from this prison by widening our circle of compassion to embrace all living creatures and the whole of nature in its beauty."   Albert Einstein

"Father forgive them, for they know not what they do".   Jesus Christ

Perhaps the most dynamic universal law of all is that of love and compassion. As a positive motivating force it drives one of the single most powerful motives for survival and that would be peaceful cooperation. Peaceful cooperation alone, among any and all organisms can create the fast track to harmony. But love and compassion added something to cooperation that may have resulted in the rapid growth to our current modern form. In recent years experts have drawn new conclusions as to how mutual cooperation and pair bonding led our species to assume a higher evolution. Emotional emergence may have helped to create relationships which in turn may have stimulated growth in all areas of human development. Somewhere along this path, humans attained sentience and became aware of their emotional state. Seeking out love and attachment has become so necessary that it is believed to be impossible for humans to succeed in life without it.

Most reasonable people will agree that cooperative behavior is more successful than self serving aggression. So on a very practical level, love and compassion is just a better way to live than being grounded in self (ego) serving aggression. On an even higher level, love and compassionate cooperation even for those not in our "inner circle" or "pair bond" can create even more success. The wider and more far reaching we can expand our love and compassion, the greater the success story. It seems so simple and pragmatic, yet why, as the most sentient specie on our planet can we not transcend loving only ourselves or our groups?

Perhaps it is due to our enslavement to ego. As discussed earlier, ego is the serving of the illusionary self. Egos that join in and love only their own kind can be considered to be a collective. On our planet, almost every collective group has this component. Many of us claim to follow spiritual paths that are centered on having love and compassion yet only sometimes practice loving and compassion of others. Or we may practice some degree of compassion for others, but draw a line very close in. Not only do many spiritual paths and religions teach love and compassion, but they emphasize the importance of loving and having compassion for those who are different or hate us or even harm us. And, on a transcendent level they direct us to live with love and compassion *especially* for those who wish us harm or are simply different from us. Yet all of us fail at this to some degree on a regular basis.

This concept begs the question of why? Why would we as sentient creatures be called to be compassionate for anyone who hates us or would harm us? The answer lies in being in awareness and detached from ego. For it is ego in both individual and collective states, that thrives on the negative emotion and conditioning. Hatred and fear, lead to the motive states of vengeance and destruction. In awareness and full consciousness we are in tune with the universal consciousness which is the source from which all universal laws are derived. When we are at one with the universal source, when we are fully conscious, we know that those of us in ego are unconscious and unaware of what they are doing why they are doing it. In awareness and in alignment with pure consciousness or true source we can be aware of what is happening and why. Grounded in love and compassion we can understand the quotation by Jesus Christ who said *"Forgive them Father for they know not what they do"* as they tortured him.

Returning to the practical application of love and compassion, when we can transcend our emotional attachments of ego, cooperation is seeded and something very special happens. We can stop and ponder where we are earth bound specie with relation to being in alignment with the love and compassion of our universal source by noting how often we kill each other.

More than any other sentient specie, and being the most sentient specie, we (in the collective sense) practice murder. With a little concentration we can realize this because as a sentient specie we have the most developed egos. Even though ego can be observed in smaller degrees with other species it can also be noted that the murder rate among these non human species is far less. Less sentient species kill for a number of reasons, but probably not for reasons of emotion. This is purely a human ego trait.

Perhaps the saddest revelation is that we may one day manage to cause our own extinction due to the uncontrolled action of singular and collective ego. The potential for us to cause our own genocide is now very apparent. There are stock piles of nuclear and biological weapons stored, primed and ready to be disseminated with only the cooperation of a small group of individuals. All it will take is for ego either in its individual form or a small collective to cross the line. If you think that is not possible, just think back to the last time you saw someone or some group cross the line. "Going postal" is one description for disgruntled egos who have crossed over. Terrorist groups are another example for ego collectives to cross over into insanity. Look to history for examples of killing by collective ego in large context. All it takes is for an individual or collective with authority to reach their threshold for egoic insanity and the end begins.

This state of affairs for which we find ourselves is not the way it is supposed to be. And the solution while simple to comprehend is quite difficult to actualize. All it would take is for all humans to wake up and become aware of what they are doing and why they are doing it. All it would take is for all people to slow down, become still and aware and release themselves from the chains of ego. It is Simple but very difficult to do. It is so simple and so necessary. It is nearly impossible because most people are so conditioned to their egoic perspective they will fight to the very end to be free to live out their delusions.

What if humanity could postpone all purposeful killing of each other for just one day? Imagine if all of humanity could for just one rotation of our planet resume the cooperative bonding that initially caused us to evolve so rapidly. Imagine if we could all let go of ego and share love and compassion with each other regardless of previous conditions. There is no limit on the abundance and prosperity that is possible. Quantum science has shown us that all of life, the entire universe is a field of infinite possibility. There is only one thing standing in the way. That one thing is ego.

We would not even have to "love" one another to transform our world. It could be as simple as respecting others. Accepting others, as they are, allows other cultures to be who they are. Acceptance creates the opportunity for respect to connect the various cultures. By respecting one another, we can put aside our differences and focus on common interests. There are many interests that are common as well as practical. Imagine if we, humanity in collective awareness worked towards having inexpensive sources of energy. Imagine if we could put aside our collective narcissism of ego and worked together to eliminate hunger. Imagine if opportunities for higher learning were shared. Imagine if our collective motive for life was not oriented towards greed but rather mutual benefit.

Respect for others is a powerful concept yet it is nowhere near as powerful as love, compassion and the sincere devotion toward others. Respect is an allowing process where compassion is a nurturing empowerment. Some of our species greatest achievements have been realized as the result from effort to promote the common good. Some our greatest disappointments have been spawned by greed and the obsession of profit. The degree of imbalance in the world's interpersonal relationships is directly related to the abundance or lack of cooperative love and compassion.

On a personal level, imbalance really can be reduced to the motivation from one orientation or the other. In each and every moment, we can be aware and ask if what we are about to do is motivated by compassion or is the motive sourced from egotism. In each and every 'now', we can be awake and aware of what we are doing and why we are doing the action we are undertaking. And as we learned in the chapter on cause and effect that our actions create results, it is important to explore the source of the causation. This becomes quite important when we compare compassion to greed. It was mentioned in the chapter on cause and effect that many of these primary laws over lap each other. Such is the case with love and compassion and cause and effect. Orienting an action based on service to others will result in something very different from an action whose source is meant to serve the ego. Simply speaking it creates an imbalance. Whenever there is an imbalance suffering will arise. It matters not whether one is thinking about money or food or political power, imbalance creates suffering. Balance is a singularity with unity as its core. Imbalance is a dichotomy with separation between the two parts. Economic and political imbalance creates the dichotomy of very rich and very poor, with little in the middle. Political imbalance creates a polarization where in the dichotomy; they oppose each other to the point where gridlock is inevitable.

Polarization is the result where unity and balance is lost. It is always apparent when it can be observed that one side has too much and the others have too little. The degree to which societies do not love or have compassion and respect for others determines the amount of separation. The more separation between views, then the stronger the polarization will be. Another way to look at this set up is to realize that the more loving and compassionate a society is, the more sharing becomes apparent. More sharing creates balance and harmony. Love and compassion reverse polarization because these virtues are not grounded in ego. Love and compassion is about caring for someone other than the self. Ego is self serving and loves only itself. Awareness, love and compassion are oriented in serving the greater good of all.

Our greatest spiritual leaders have not only taught us this, but have commanded it. Ask yourself what your spiritual path or religion says about loving others. Are you living this reality or are you letting ego polarize your life.

Exercise

- Here are some questions to ask yourself. Be absolutely honest.

- Do you ever find yourself judging others?

- Are there other people that you avoid or even hate?

- Can you cooperate with someone who is different? (Differences such as skin color, ethnicity, gender bias, age, or socio economic level)

- Do you feel that you and the group you belong to are better than others?

- Do you ever feel like hurting others?

- Are you able to compromise to reach a solution that will better benefit all?

- Do you ever feel that there is no good reason to share your abundance with others?

- Do you ever feel privileged?

- Do you ever think that you are separate from any others?

- Can you forgive others that want to do you harm?

- Can you find a way to respect others who believe differently from you?

- Do you feel there are some people who are beneath you?

- If you belong to a spiritual path that advocates loving others, why are you not able to follow it all the time?

It is important for each of us to become aware of how we are feeling. In awareness we can observe that we are not feeling the love. We can observe that part of our mind that only wants to serve itself (ego). It is even more important to understand that when we refuse to work on being released from ego and self serving, that we are not only part of the problem, we are the problem.

Being is experiencing as the true self. The true self is a loving being. Everything else is illusion and ignorance. Everything else is the reason that there is unnecessary suffering and death in the world. If any of us would want to transform our lives and become who we were meant to be, we must detach from our egoic part of the personality. There must be balance in our views and interactions with each other.

If we want to not only survive as a species, but actually prosper, then we must wake up and let go of the unconscious egoic life. It begins with the simple action of becoming still and being able to *know* what we are doing and why we are doing it to free your "self".

Altruism

"Every man must decide whether he will walk in the light of creative altruism or in the darkness of destructive selfishness". **Martin Luther King, Jr.**

We have discussed so much about ego behavior it is time to shift focus. Altruism is the practice of love and compassion in everyday life. In the previous chapter on love and compassion we talked about how it was a universal law and that the aspect of cooperation led to our rise as sentient specie. Those creatures we previously were, evolved into sentient beings through the process of natural selection. The universal consciousness experiences life through physical beings and the more sentient the higher the expression. By cooperating with each other our distant ancestors were able to affect, through the process of natural selection, the rise towards sentience. As self awareness developed, so did the concept of love and compassion. Cooperation, love and compassion seem to be the agent for which beings can further experience unity with consciousness. Thus the more any being can orient in love and compassion, the higher the level of consciousness can be realized.

Being self aware, humans have the ability to recognize this self organizing emergent property and consciously maintain its stability. This living each 'now', awake and aware as loving compassionate beings is altruism.

If altruism is so important for spiritual development why do we not all practice it more? The answer lies in the state of consciousness of each moment or each 'now'. Awake and aware, we can observe our feelings as they arise and follow a path in alignment with altruism. Unawake, unaware and unconscious we are grounded in ego which finds altruism boring. An individual completely given over to the narcissism of ego will look at you and ask "why should I care about anyone else but me?"

But it is fair to ask, why altruism? To understand the answer, one has to realize that we, humanity, are all connected. Separateness is an illusion of ego that allows it to pursue its own unrestricted course without regard for anyone or anything else. In ignorance, ego does not understand that what happens to another being will in some large or small way come back around. There is a saying, "what goes around, comes around". In the most obvious of ways, we are connected by sharing the same planet, almost identical DNA, the same environment, and the same source. Our bodies are made from the same materials; we breathe the same air, drink the same water, and walk on the same land. Spiritually we are from the same universal consciousness, which is the source for all things everywhere. So why then do some of us think we are different? It is the illusion of "me" that constitutes ego. Ego identity is derived from memories which become experience. Ego knits these cumulative experiences together in a story that defines who and what we *think* we are. This is a good time to read the chapter on Ego if you haven't already.

When we are experiencing our lives as our true self, our true being, we understand and *know* that we are all connected. Being grounded in love, compassion and respect, we follow the altruistic path of caring about the welfare of others. By doing so, we come into alignment with the cooperative element of natural selection that elevated humans to sentience.

Altruism is the most relevant action for any specie that wishes for survival. On a personal level, a person living with altruistic behavior will find their path much smoother with less suffering. Because of the law of cause and effect, what you put out into the world will return with interest. If you live a life of self serving egoism that is what you will create. Eventually everyone needs help from someone else. Because change is an inescapable component of reality, all things will change including and especially that false sense of security found with material possessions. When trouble comes to the egoic mind where does it turn to for help? It turns to materialistic solutions which are typically grounded in distraction or sensation seeking. The altruistic person who has devoted a life to caring for others will be surrounded by other caring and loving people. So we all have choices about the reality we create. We can create heaven or hell depending on our path. The only difference between the two states is how we treat each other.

So before you scoff and turn back to ego, consider the world you may be creating for yourself. The seeds you plant today will bear fruit down the path. Learn to be mindful of your mental state and what your heart is feeling. Learn to avoid the self serving path of egoism and turn to helping others. The best time and place to start is right here, right now, wherever you are, whatever you are doing. Start with your family. Love them as if your life depended on it. Love them, care for them and be present with them. Then visit with your close friends and find ways to care for them. Next move to the level of those you do not even know. Find ways to be loving and compassionate. It may only be a kind word, and often it is just listening to them. Share your abundance with those less fortunate. And when you really want to experience the exceptional life, find a place in your heart and love those you might consider to be your enemies. When someone does you wrong, remember they are probably driven by ego. Freed from the ego you can forgive them and understand that they are lost from consciousness. So love them anyway. Turn the other cheek and don't get caught up with egoic compulsions. This path is transforming yet necessary to free your "self".

Balance and Harmony

"All things in moderation, even moderation."   The Buddha

Balance

One definition of balance is to have experience, mental steadiness and emotional stability. I remember learning to ride a bike when I was a child. I remember the excitement of this new sensation of balance while in motion. It was tricky at first yet soon became something that could be done unconsciously. That first sensation of trying to balance the bike on the fraction of an inch of tires seemed almost impossible. Yet soon enough there was nothing to it.

Perhaps we can apply this metaphor to the balance of being and doing while moving forward on life's path. When we take a leisurely bike ride and have the intention of enjoying the experience, we move along slowly but steadily observing things along the way. But as soon as we lose that perfect balance we began to wobble. If we let too much of our weight go to one side then we can tip over and fall. If we are going too slow or need to stop we can always put our feet down and stand. If we go too fast, events can occur much too rapidly for us to be able to maintain balance or stop safely. When we crash the fall can be quite painful. I can recall some skinned knees from having experienced a couple of such falls. Metaphorically speaking in life, I have gone too fast, doing too much, lost my balance and crashed. There have been some times where my egoic pursuit of the greener pastures resulted in a bit more than just "skinned knees".

As discussed in previous chapters. Our constant striving for the next satisfying thing also known as sensation seeking can drive us to extremes. Ego, that part of our mind which is never satisfied, and never will be, is constantly and with a kind of desperation driving us faster and faster along the way to find some kind of fulfillment. These illusions are like a mirage in the desert. The individual hungry, thirsty and seeking relief perceives the illusion that what they need is just ahead. Fulfillment is just ahead. Constantly striving for the greener pastures is a function of ego. See the chapters on ego and conquering ego.

Finding balance in your life sounds simple but you may find that in practice it can be quite the challenge. It requires being awake, aware and mindful. Once we are awake or conscious we are able to see things as they really are. Seeing things as they really are is a self truth that is mandatory for transcending the suffering brought on by ego.

The first step is to become aware and observe in your life what is the most out of balance. What habit or behavior is causing the most harm, the most problems, a danger or the unhealthiest conditions, whatever that may be? Start with just this one for now. Through meditation and self awareness be honest with yourself and unpeel the source of your behavior like you would an onion. If your situation is just too difficult or chronic, then I adamantly advise you to seek professional counseling. Psychologists' can be very good at helping you get to the heart of things. They are committed to helping you bring your behavior and life back into balance. If the first visitation does not feel right, try another, but be fair about your judgment. I especially recommend those who specialize in Transpersonal Psychology.

Through the practice of self awareness and mindfulness, you can learn to observe those aspects of self, or that part of your decision making process that is behind the causation of the imbalance. More specifically, in Mindfulness Meditation you observe the activities rising in the mind. Practicing mindfulness is paying attention to these risings as they occur in daily life. When you become aware of that tendency beginning to arise, yet remain outside of it as it arises, then *choice* becomes possible. In the instructions for mindfulness meditation, the distinction is made to not "stop thinking" or try to suppress these activities in the mind. That is a futile battle that will lead to even more frustration. The work here is to simply observe activities that arise, not become absorbed and then let them go. "Struggle" is just another imbalance that leads to frustration.

As an event unfolds before you and you feel the frustration arise, just be aware of it and let it come and go. You may also sense the need for coping to arise. Letting go is a type of acceptance. Without being swept away in mindstream, see if you if you can accept the event as it is and let it go. If the event obviously requires some kind of action, try to practice patience to see what possibilities present themselves and what the appropriate action might be.

You may even choose as often is the case, that no action is required. In Taoism, there is a term called Wu Wei. Wu Wei is simply the action of no action. This requires awareness and patience. It requires faith in consciousness. When one realizes that all things are connected and part of the great tapestry of life and following a greater design and flow, many times it is simply best to just let things work themselves out. The most elegant solutions or possibilities can sometimes present themselves without ever doing anything. In fact, being that the nature of the universe is such that it is constantly changing, sooner or later, the issue will dissolve itself. Often the biggest struggle is to resist the impatient nature of ego to meddle in the natural flow of life. By being in awareness, you sense the rising of ego, this false need to interfere, and allow it to come and go.

However if action is obviously needed, then consider which action is most appropriate. Is the action a function of the needy ego? Who will benefit from this action? Is this an action based on compassion? Does the action need to be immediate? If you are about to be run over by a bus, that would require immediate action. If you perceive a worry arising about something to happen a week from now, practice patience and see what solutions present themselves. Try to not become absorbed in egoic worry. Place your attention on your breath and return to awareness. In awareness all sorts of possibilities will arise. In awareness you can place an intention that the solution should present itself and just let it go. Have faith in consciousness, awareness, God, the universe, the Tao or whatever you want label it. Each time an inappropriate need to worry begins to arise, acknowledge it and let it go and return to awareness.

In this way we can maintain balance. When too many worries, fears, anger, greed, and other negative feelings accumulate, so does the need to cope with them. This constant striving and coping will lead to an imbalance and suffering due to cause and effect. It becomes a downward spiral. The more you give in to striving and coping, the more out of balance you become. Then you need more coping and striving resulting in more imbalances. Life goes by and one day you find yourself in an extremely out of balance condition. You may be overweight, smoke, drink, watch too much television, not sleeping, have anger issues, aggressiveness, stressed out and miserable. You can feel trapped and cannot see a way out. I used to find myself in impossible situations where there was this illusion of having no choice. Or let me say, it seemed there were no good choices. This comes from the very narrow view of ego.

In awareness, specifically in mindfulness meditation and the practice of mindfulness you learn to pay attention to these feelings as they arise. Before you become absorbed and before these feelings can create an imbalance you just let them go or consider appropriate action. The emotional baggage that comes with perceived problems does not have to rule your life. Ego does not have rule your life. You can break the imprisoning chains of egoic mind behavior and free your "self". I am not saying it is easy. When trapped in Ego, doing nothing (self awareness) can be the hardest thing you have ever tried to experience. But dedication to the practice and learning to sustain awareness can put you on the path of balance. Releasing your "self" from the prison of emotional egoic bondage brings forth *choice*.

There is a great power in choice. Whereas before you might be a prisoner to your emotions and the automatic behavior or response to something that causes stress and unhappiness, awareness allows you to be awake and conscious of what is happening so that choice is possible.

Here is an example. Recently I became distracted and not being mindful I left my singing bowl at a park where were practicing meditation. When it was time for my next class and I wanted to use it, I could not find it. Being mindful of the irritation and agitation arising, I observed thoughts such as *"I hate when this happens to me"* and *"the class will not be as effective without the bowl "*. As these feelings begin to arise, I was able to let them go. The stress went with them. I placed an intention that I would like to either get the bowl I was using back or have another one come into my life. Preferably it would be one that did not cost too much. I placed that intention and then let it go. The whole issue dissolved, and I did not think of it until a few weeks later. While conducting Tai Chi Demonstrations at a Wellness Fair, I ran into a lady I knew through meditation classes. I noticed that she had a well used and older looking bowl sitting on her table where she was selling her merchandize. The bowl appealed to me because it was handmade without a lot of decorative nonsense. The sound quality was not perfect, yet it made what I thought was a smooth tone when struck. I asked her about it and she told me that she could not seem to get rid of it. A former customer had returned it because of the inferior quality of the sound. That person could not get it to ring or something. My friend wanted to find a new home for it and offered me the bowl at a very reasonable price. This is a typical event that can come and go. They can either be allowed to become personal and create agitation or they can be accepted and allowed to resolve themselves. Wu Wei, the action of no action, created an elegant solution. I acquired a bowl at a reasonable price, my friend was able to get rid of the bowl for a reasonable profit, and we were both quite satisfied. This story has a kind of resonant irony to it. I use a singing bowl as a call to awareness, to wake up and be conscious. In the guided mindfulness meditation, sometimes I will gently strike the bowl every couple of minutes to help the beginner students to realize they are captured by thought and to return to focus on observing the breath. This beacon of sound must have called out to me through awareness and by being conscious and giving the issue over to what will be, this bowl, this symbol, found its way into my life. Bin g g g g g g g. It's 'now' again.

When you bring all of the aspects of life into balance, the many become unified into a singularity of harmony. Let's define harmony as an agreement, an accord, and harmonious relations. It can be perceived as a simultaneous balance and pleasing arrangement of parts.

Harmony is often seen in team building as synergy. From my days attending corporate team building exercises, synergy was defined as the interaction of a number of participants whose contributions or efforts produce more than what each alone was capable of. It can be an amazing thing to see happen. Our world is full of wonderful products and innovations that are a result of synergy. You only have to look as far as the smart phone in your pocket to find a miracle of modern technology. At the same time you can view this device as either a miniature computer that also has communication features, or you can view it as a pocket-sized computer that has many other functions such as a phone, music player, document keeper and so much more.

Let's take a closer look at harmony or synergy. Where and how does this seemingly act of magic come from? From a given number of parts or activities come even more when brought together in unity. It is hidden in plain sight, and available to any who can become free of ego, self aware and mindful. This function of the becoming greater than itself, the pieces and parts is a potential miracle waiting to happen. It just needs a channel or space to be realized in.

This is what happens when we are able to break free from the prison of mind stream. Consciousness being the source and potential of possibilities is manifested when the parts come into harmony. The single biggest obstacle to balance and harmony is the mind. When aspects of the mind such as ego take over, and capture our awareness, the doorway for possibility is closed. We become who we think we are. But that is not your "True Self". This false identity and egoic prison is discussed in a chapter all to itself. (See the Chapter on Ego). But here right now, let us remain focused on balance and harmony.

Consider your favorite orchestra or band. Think of beautiful music. It is music that resonates within you and evokes feelings of joy. This is a very dynamic actualization. Let's look at what is going on.

In a given group of musicians and their leader, there are sections that specialize in certain sounds. An orchestra may have many sections. When you listen to them as they play their part separately and on their own you hear some pleasant sounds coming forth. It is pleasant in itself, but not all that it could be. Pretend that you are listing to just the wind instruments. As they play alone, it sounds fine but not especially moving. They are doing their part as they should. Then you listen to the instruments from the brass section. It presents the same perception, but you instinctively know that it can be more. As you move around the orchestra, you the maestro, listen and observe what they are doing and how they doing. You make adjustments to the performance and a few refinements where necessary.

Then you tap your baton and everyone begins *to play together*. Now each of the sound sections are joined and become as one. And in their harmonious joining something wonderful and beautiful is created. It is far and away more than each musician doing their individual performance. Together in harmony, as they become something greater, the sound moves you and brings forth wonderful feelings of joy and warm sensations. As they blend together, you allow your perception to change so that you now see through your ears and your mind. On a deeper level you perceive and *know* the intention of the music in a form we call a song. It has an individual nature that was born from consciousness in one mind, and manifested though the harmony of many minds. The sum of the many parts is greater than individual contributions. Imagine what could be accomplished if people were living in harmony, worldwide.

In summary, when you can become aware and become just a being of pure consciousness, the summation of possibility can arise. When individuals become harmonious in consciousness something miraculous is realized.

This path of awareness is found through the practice of meditation, self awareness and mindfulness.

Exercise:

We are going to make a list, so get something to write with.

Now let's take a quick review to see how things are going for you. How in balance or out of balance are you? Let's split your life up into the three basic components of Mind, Body, and Spirit. One thing you will notice is how these areas overlap. And do not be too hard on yourself; this is about being out of balance. You should be fair but honest.

Mind Body Spirit

Mind

How stressed is your life?

How often do you experience: some of the negative feelings of anger, fear, deprivation, greed, or jealousy. This list can go on and on, but just think over your life recently and get a feel for how often you remember feeling unhappy, depressed or negatively. Be honest with yourself and determine if it feels out of balance.

- How often do you relax for a few minutes?

- How often do you seek having fun?

- How often do you seek distraction because you are bored?

- How often do you have a negative interaction with someone else?

- How much TV do you watch?

- Would any of your family or friends say you are obsessed with something?

- Are you a workaholic?

- How often do you *do* something for someone else?

- How often do you forgive yourself?

- How often do you feel loved?

- And the most important question, how often do you feel love and compassion for someone else?

Body

How in balance is your body's health?

- Do you know your weight and or BMI (body mass index) and is it normal?

- Is your blood glucose level normal?

- Is your cholesterol normal?

- Is your blood pressure normal?

- Do you have continuous aches and pains that interfere with the quality of your life?

- Do you use intoxicants or stimulants (legal or not) that are more than the daily recommended allowance?

- Do you use something illegal or something that interferes with your abilities to maintain a normal life?

- Are you ignoring warning signs? (Painful joints, headaches, dizziness, heart-burn etc)?

- Do you have unexplained sores, lesions, bumps or pimples or dark spots in the skin?

- Do you expose yourself to harmful amounts of radiation? (Sun and Tanning Beds)

Again, be honest and fair, is something out of balance?

Spirit

Even if you are an atheist this can apply to you. All people are spiritual beings whether they are religious or not. Being spiritual does not mean that you go to church or chant to another being. "Beingness" is spiritual. Being is your essential self. Transcending ego *is* spirituality and realizing your true spiritual self.

Not being in touch with your deeper spiritual self is to be lost in ego and thought. Forget about what Descartes said, and realize you are not your thoughts. ("I think, therefore I am") Thoughts are just phenomena that rise in the continuum of your mind. When you identify with your thoughts, you are identifying with whatever phenomena. In this mind experience, you are caught up in your thoughts and held captive by ego. The essential you, that is your essential self, gets lost and forgotten. Ask your "self" these questions.

Exercise

- When did you last wake up from thought and realize where you were and what you were doing? (Remember the example of the car, how we get into it and immediately our minds go off somewhere else and we unconsciously drive a large heavy vehicle without being aware of what we are doing?)

- When was the last time you were able to just be?

- Did you try meditation (being awake) only to give in to the unconsciousness of thought?

- How often are you able to be mindful of what you thinking and doing? (Paying attention to what you are thinking and doing, and why you are doing what you are doing)

Being in spiritual balance is to be able to guide your "self" in your daily life through a balance of being spiritual (awareness) and using thoughts as the means to accomplish what you have intended to do.

When Mind, Body, and Spirit are in balance, they are in

harmony. In harmony, life is so simple yet so beautiful. Will power is the means for bringing about balance and harmony into this existence we call life.

Awareness and your Body

"To keep the body in good health is a duty, otherwise we shall not be able to keep our mind strong and clear". The Buddha

In the earlier chapters of this book, we have given a lot of attention to the psychological aspects of awareness. In this section, the body and all of its wondrous aspects are brought into awareness. One of the beautiful gifts of being a sentient being is the ability to be and to be aware of your body. Our living experience is about being alive in a body. Our body is the physical manifestation of the self and the vessel in which can life can be experienced. We spend so much effort only using our body as a tool for sensation seeking and pleasure, ignoring and abusing our body, that we submit it to excessive wear and tear. Miraculously it will repair itself over and over again until it falls apart from use and misuse. Our single-minded obsession of fulfilling egoic desires through physical experiences has caused us to ignore the more important role that we play as the steward of this magnificent product of nature. The only thing worse than having a bad relationship with your body is to have no relationship with your body.

So what does that mean to have a relationship with your body? When we think of relationship, we can consider it as a connection between people. On the individual level, we can and should have a relationship with this living organism we know as our body. A healthy relationship requires the two parties to stay connected to each other and good communication is a feature of any good healthy relationship. When we have a good relationship with our body, we are in tune with it. We listen and respond to what it is telling us and we support it. Just as importantly, we must communicate with it and work with a shared agenda. First let's look at the communication we have through our senses between us and our body.

The notion that we should communicate with our bodies may be something you have never considered before and may seem a little bit hokey. You may be wondering how you would have a conversation with your body. The conversation with your body is a little bit different than one you would have with another person in that it is more intimate. You must listen with your mind and more importantly you must especially listen with your senses. Your body is the first and last thing to be aware of. When left alone, it's just you and your body. Your body is constantly communicating with you. If you don't believe it, then skip the next meal and see how you feel. Your body can be very direct in the way it sends a message. If you think it is too subtle to pick up on, just remember the last hangover you experienced when you consumed too much alcohol. Weakness, headache and nausea are not subtle in their nature and the message is very clear. Your body does not like it.

Our senses are informative devices for giving our cognitive mind the necessary data needed to navigate through life. The senses are truly miracles that we take for granted until we lose one of them. They can take environmental conditions and relay them through various electrical signals through various means. These are external conditions.

 Internally your body communicates through the senses and especially through the sense of touch and sensation. Combined touch and sensation produce a state we can call feeling. It may be the surface of your skin feeling warm, or the lining of your stomach feeling the burn of acid. We can feel tired, nauseated, dizzy and a number of other sensations. You may perceive symptoms through the use of eyes, detect issues by sense of smell, or hear things that just do not sound right. Strangely we can almost always respond and point our attention towards an emergency siren when a fire truck comes up our street, but we have little patience to pay attention to an inconvenient pain in a joint. When one takes the effort to look closely at the ingenious way nature has crafted our sense organs, the wonder and amazement of our body becomes apparent.

It may be apparent what the senses do for us externally. But what about what our senses can tell us about what is going on *inside* the body? When we turn to the inside, the outward senses are of less use to us. Our vision, hearing, taste, and sense of smell are a bit limited in what they can tell us about things going on internally. Our sense of feeling though can play a big role. However, even the sense of touch does not always pick up on issues that have subtle characteristics. In this, our sense of awareness can play a vital role. Many times there is a feeling of something just not being quite right. For most people this just brings on more sensation seeking or distraction. Instead of becoming quiet and focused, we pursue that which might "take our minds off" of feeling bad. Impatient, we do not consider cause for very long, and quickly remove the issue with a pain pill. And if one pill does not do the trick, then maybe four will get the job done. Being lost in mind stream and not paying attention we just become irritable at the interruption in our busy lives.

In meditation and in awareness we can listen with the great care. In awareness we can note our feelings about what may be going on. We can disregard the fears and anxieties of ego and allow the truth to surface. In awareness intuition can play a big role in helping us to "get a feel" for what might be right or wrong. The subconscious, acting as an agent between our body and our cognitive mind can give us visual clues. We can pay attention to images that arise during meditation or dreaming and consider what they mean through intuition. Please see the chapter on intuition to further understand and develop this sense.

We can also be aware of other aspects of our inner health by allowing ourselves to be mindful of normal bodily functions. We can note when we use the toilet the nature of the elimination processes. Through our outer senses we can determine color, quantity, texture and other unpleasant but informative details. I am not suggesting that you become obsessed with this activity, just to note and be aware of how things are functioning. If you are not sure, ask your physician next time you have an appointment. There is also a lot of general information on the internet. However, I would advise *caution* as you bring more information into awareness. Ego, always seeking attention, can quickly become a hypochondriac and go off on tangents created through fear, worry, or the need for attention. Through cause and effect, ego can create the imbalance experienced as sickness.

In awareness you can note how your sleep cycle is performing. What is the quality of your sleep and how much are you really getting. It is important to be honest with yourself. Ego, never wants to look bad, so it will be in denial if you may have been practicing bad habits. Be honest and take a look at how much down time you have and how much good restful sleep you have. In an earlier chapter I discussed the negative effects that caffeine has on good sleep. Become aware of how much you take in and what it is doing to you. In my own experience, I resolved an issue with ongoing really bad headaches that I was calling a migraine. They could be incapacitating, and I could not figure out what would trigger them. Later, when I was taught how to practice meditation and self awareness I was able to observe how caffeine withdrawal was causing me so much pain and anguish. All it took was becoming aware of how much I was consuming. With a small effort, learned to manage it successfully, and the headaches went away and sleep returned.

Along with sleep and rest is the awareness of how stressed and anxious we might be. Please do not under estimate the destructive power of stress and what it does to our bodies. Stress is a killer and becoming aware of it in our lives can be a very illuminating experience. (See the chapter Stress Kills.) Mindfulness is the special way of paying attention to things, and it is the best tool for managing stress. Our body communicates to us when it is suffering from stress. We can sense the physical symptoms of stress by being aware of the signals. Some of the symptoms of the Stress Response we can feel are rapid breathing, rapid heart rate, a rise in energy, shaking of the limbs, dehydration, and many others.

Pain is an acute attention getter that the body uses when something chronic is occurring. Pain is a message that communicates through the nervous system and can be like one of those burglar alarms that will not shut off. Once it gets your attention, you begin telling yourself, "ok I get the message now please stop". However, maybe there is a reason that pain is persistent. Remember how many times we ignore symptoms in the body and just cover it up with a couple of pills. The pain subsides and is forgotten about. The cause of the pain is left unchecked only to get worse. Maybe pain, as one of those signals, decides it is not going away until the problem is fixed. Of course sometimes we cannot fix the problem and pain only adds misery to the condition. So I am not suggesting that pain is good. I am pointing out that pain is a messenger and should be paid attention to, at the earliest onset. One of the clichés that really causes me pain, pardon the pun, is the one stating "no pain, no gain". That is a message straight from ego. Pride is the currency of ego and being able to endure pain is ignoring your body. Yet in all things balance can be used to place things in harmony. Sometimes we (our egos) are very sensitive to our changing conditions and label something very minor as pain and suffering. A little soreness after taking on an exercise program is a message from your body that it is repairing muscle fibers and please give it chance to rest. Should you chose to ignore this and allow ego to push you into ignoring a required rest and repair stage, problems will arise. On the other hand, if you allow ego to get in your head and tell you that the little bit of pain is not worth the effort, you will be ignoring the body's need for exercise. Use awareness and right thinking to find balance in what you do and listen to your body. Know what it is telling you.

Your body has an agenda. You have your own agenda. You two must get together and form a close working relationship. Your body is here to support you within reason. You in turn, have to support your body by nurturing it and not being too demanding.

Once in a meditation group I asked the participants, if you were the mayor of this city, would you purposefully have trucks drive around and dump piles of toxic waste in the streets and neighborhoods? Would you overuse the resources until they are depleted or would you deprive the department of city services the necessities they need to perform life saving duties such as fire and policing? Would you cut off the power to the hospitals and clinics? Would you turn off the phones in your office and just go off on a vacation and ignore the needs of the citizens? No you probably would not. Yet many of us do exactly that with our bodies. We ignore the incoming messages about the status of our internal systems. We consume toxic substances that destroy cells and organs. We over indulge in resources to the extent that our blood becomes toxic, and we experience system failures. And through continuously indulging in the sensation seeking and distraction of egoic desires, we ignore what is going on. We seek the unconsciousness of distraction and yo-yo between stress and the bliss of satiation. Then, when we have abused the body too much, we get sick and sometimes we die.

It was not meant to be this way. We know this by the way nature has gifted us with the wondrous aspects of the body and its ability to repair itself. Somehow our ability to preserve our true self became over ridden by this mind entity known as ego. When we become our ego, we lose touch with our spiritual core and we lose touch with the precious beautiful body we all have been given.

Stand up and go look in the mirror. If you for any reason do not see a beautiful body standing before you, then you are in ego. Ego is that part of you making a judgment about being too short, too tall, too skinny, too fat, too this or too that. The craziest part about this is how ego blames the body for the condition it is in. Now that is crazy. If you are sensation-seeking to the point where you are consuming five thousand calories per day then you are unconscious and need to wake up. If you are paying someone to expose your body to the cancer causing radiation (tanning beds) just so you can look good, then you are unconscious in ego and ignoring your body. This is your wake up call. This is your chance to become aware of who you are, where you are, what you are doing. Please, for your body's sake, for your own sake, wake up. We must be aware of our body as if our life depended on it, because guess what? Your life absolutely depends on it. So hello, wake up. It is 'now' again. And in this 'now', while you are awake, try and realize this insight. Right now, set the intention to remain awake, and mindful of what you are doing in your life. Free your "self" from the bondage of ego and know and love your body.

Physical Fitness

"Exercise is a dirty word. Every time I hear it, I wash my mouth out with chocolate" Author is Unknown

Our body is the living miracle for which our consciousness experiences life. It took the study of Tai Chi Chuan for me to become intimate with the human body. Like so many people, there was a disconnect between mind, body, and spirit. And I resided in the illusion of living as an egoic entity. At age 51, I found myself on a table in a cardiac unit having a stent put into a vein leading to my heart. It was a moment of truth for which I experienced a traumatic awakening. I realized my own mortality. The cardiologist had a frank discussion with me about the limit I was putting on my life span. In that moment of truth I promised myself and my body that I would change my ways. As the saying goes, "when the student is ready, the teacher will appear". I devoted all of my non working time to the pursuit of fixing my mind, body and spirit. Through the practice of mindfulness meditation and Tai Chi Chuan (tie – chee – chwen) I was able to free my "self" and get my life back. You can too.

We learned in earlier chapters that ego does not understand nor care that *all things are connected.* The understanding of this connection begins with our relationship with our body. It would seem that ego would appreciate the body more since it is the primary device for experiencing sensation. Yet ego takes for granted having a body. It does this because it does not reside in the present moment, the now. The closest thing to experiencing the now is when it is experiencing a dramatic level of sensation such as pain or physical ecstasy. It will even submit to or allow the creation of pain just to be able to experience the ecstasy. To the ego, the body is just a tool or device for which to experience sensational pleasure. Not caring and not realizing the connection, it abuses the relationship up to and sometimes even unto the point of death. If nothing else written in this book helps you to see the nature of ego, then perhaps the way ego takes the body for granted, will bring the message home.

While it is true that we (our higher or true self) are not our body, our consciousness cannot have a physical experience without it. The relationship with our body is the closest one we will ever have in a physical existence. One would think that since we experience all physical events by means of our bodies we would treat it with more reverence. Therefore it becomes glaringly apparent that the fitness level of our body is extremely important.

Being fit physically is extremely important on several levels. First of all, the degree of fitness is one determining factor in life span. Those people who live their life in a poor physical condition can suffer a lot before they die. Note, this is not directed at those whose fitness level is poor through no fault of ego. This tongue lashing is aimed at those whose unchecked ego ignores the body and treats it wrongly.

The body is a living miracle of nature and while physical organisms found in nature are mysterious and wonderful, the human body is light years beyond that. This is because being sentient we can realize the miracle through the mind, body, spirit relationship. As highly sentient beings we can realize pure consciousness. When these three aspects of living are in harmony something beyond miracles becomes the central element of life. This is something no other known creature on earth but humans can experience. Notice I use the term *can experience.*

In awareness we become in tune with and become part of the universe (universal consciousness, god etc). Our bodies are the vessels for which these things can be experienced. Within our body, other organisms live and thrive. There is a plausible argument that states that even the very cells that course through our body have purpose and strive to be alive. These basic life forms are part of us and make up a macro neighborhood, town, city, state, country, planetary body and even a universe unto its own. The top decision maker is our consciousness; our true and authentic self. Or it should be, but alas for probably 80% of us, ego has taken over and is calling the shots. It is like a gangster took over the White House and began ruling the world. Egos live an existence of desire seeking and exploitation. This especially includes the body. When we learn meditation and become self aware we detach from ego and kick the gangster out of the White House. Through awareness we learn to listen to what the various bodily entities have to say to us. They speak to us in a special language that nature has provided to get our attention. However if we are so caught up in narcissistic sensation seeking, we either do not hear the messages or we just ignore them. Natural body sensations are messages that give us a status report on how thing are and what is needed. We just have to become still and listen. We have to pay attention in a very special way, called mindfulness, and then we can better realize what is going on. Getting to know your body takes time. It is just like learning anything else, you have to do it, practice it and grow strong in it. We have to nurture our relationship with our body just like any relationship to develop and maintain a good healthy balance. When we are able to shift our life into balance, we return to being our true authentic self, and the body returns to its own authentic design.

Exercise

As you read this book, stop and go look in the mirror and contemplate what you see. Is your body exactly as nature intended? Most of you, if you are being honest, will have to say no. The glaring question becomes "why not?" And as always, the answer is always …ego. Living in ego, we would rather postpone this most important of relationships so we can either pursue some sensation or some distraction, which is often at the expense of the body.

The body is also the up close and personal example of cause and effect. (See the chapter on cause and effect) Since the body evolved to absorb much of what is put into it, then what is put into becomes part of the body. The body is saying "Duh", and in the mirror the image of you is tapping you on the forehead saying "hey… this is us you're messing with!" The aspect of self we are calling ego only wants to fulfill desire and will often ignore the consequences.

The body needs to have an active physical purpose or it will suffer atrophy. You can take this bit of information to the bank. You use it or you will lose it. There is so much we can do to restore our quality of life once we engage the relationship with our body.

When examining the concept that *all things* are connected, it is important to include the body and its myriad of systems as part *of all things*. So when we abuse one item in our body, many other parts of the system are affected also. The body is so complex that modern medicine is still trying to sort out why the body and nature does what it does. In the mind, body, spirit triangle, these connections are extremely important. The mind affects the body in every second of every day. Make sure to read the chapter on 'stress kills' to appreciate just how important this aspect is. When ego is having a bad day, the body will always suffer the consequences. The condition of the body can greatly affect the mind which is also connected to spirit.

We should treat our relationship with our body as if our life depended on it, because guess what? It does depend on it. Since perception requires data that comes through the senses, the body plays a major role in information gathering. How can we perceive anything if the body has stopped working? The answer is we cannot because we are dead. And that conversation about what the consciousness perceives without the body is one for another day. This conversation is about staying alive and sustaining life as it is meant to be. Ego is so nihilistic that when it has a really bad day, it can even try to end it all by destroying the body. How crazy is that? So you can see that ego does not have good intentions. The solution to all of this is just simply waking up and realizing who you and what you really are. Awake and aware, we can nurture the relationship with our body so that it will carry us through many years of joyful experiences. It is now again, time to wake up and free your "self" from ego. Love your body.

Healing our "self"

"To keep the body in good health is a duty... otherwise we shall not be able to keep our mind strong and clear." The Buddha

This chapter is about healing. It begins with healing the relationship between the body and the self. If you are sick and are hoping for healing to happen, it must begin within awareness. Nature has gifted us with the most amazing body for which our consciousness can experience a physical life. Much of our physical sickness originates with an imbalance between the mind and the body. There are belief systems and cultures that believe all sickness results from having a sick mind and being out of balance. In ancient Indian and Chinese practices this was and still is to some extent the basis for healing. In many of the previous chapters of this book, imbalance has been created by the problems we experience in our modern culture. (See the chapters on Honesty, Balance, and Awareness and the Body)

We have discussed at length how being unconscious in ego creates an imbalance due to the constant and incessant pursuit of sensation seeking and distraction. If by some chance you are reading this chapter before having read self awareness, ego or balance and harmony, perhaps you will best be served if you go read those now.

Having read those chapters you know now that experiencing life through the unconscious ego will lead to misery and sickness. You should also understand now that being in awareness and mindful of what you are doing and why you are doing it, offers true choice. Living a life out of balance creates sickness emotionally, spiritually and physically. So the first step in healing is to begin your path back to your true self.

There are some powerful healing meditations that can restore health and happiness. As discussed in meditation it takes practice. With practice and dedication you can learn to reside in a sustained awareness. For healing to take place we must be in awareness and remain in the calm abiding of consciousness. For in this state, true balance is found. Only through the quiet stillness between the thoughts can the space for healing begin to arise. The mind is very powerful and can instruct through imagery and intention for the body to heal itself. But for this to happen, the individual must be detached from the currents of mindstream. One cannot concentrate on healing while being swept away by the heavy current of mindstream and ego. When a stressful mind state has captured consciousness, not only can you not heal, but the stress of more thinking can make you even sicker. It is in that stillness of awareness that we find sanctuary and create the environment for healing to become powerful and effective.

Stressful living and destructive behaviors are the source of many of today's common sicknesses. Just by reducing stress we can empower the immune system to become more effective. By being aware of what we are doing and why we are doing it, we can change the behaviors that drive the sickness causing activities. By being aware and mindful we can let go of thoughts, emotions and feelings that initiate and sustain the stress response. By being in a relaxed state, the relaxation response can take over and normal body function is maintained. It really is that simple. Much of the sickness can be avoided by learning to live a relaxed life without stress. If you are already sick as a result of a stressful and chaotic lifestyle, then the sooner you begin a meditation program, the sooner your body will begin to return to balance. Hopefully it will before you reach the point of no return where there is too much damage and is irreversible. Even if that has occurred, it is never too late to slow down, to become aware and live what life you have left, moment by moment.

Healing of the self can happen best when we give our mind, body and spirit the opportunity to return to source. Everything else is just a hindrance. Where ever you are on your life path, whether you are young or old, it is never too late to find your true authentic self and reside there.

It is my full belief that while our genes may dictate how the body responds to the environment, it does not include a definite expiration set point. While modern medicine is winning some battles with heart disease and cancer, there are still remote cultures that do not experience the level of diseases that we do here in the West. They live long healthy lives yet have no access to modern medicine. The reason is being shown that with the spread of the modern culture, aka materialism, so does the spread of modern diseases. It appears that the conditioning of ego (ignorance) is contagious and those cultures who begin a life of materialism that is sensation seeking and distraction seeking, the modern diseases soon follow.

If you ask centenarians what the secret to longevity is they all have several common pieces of advice. They will tell you to remember to laugh, to not take yourself too seriously, moderation in food and drink, and surround yourself with loving people and family.

So healing begins with a returning to your true and authentic self. Knowing exactly what is wrong may be illusive so intuition can be a perceptive tool to help understand what is going wrong. In that quiet stillness of awareness we can "listen" to our body and "feel" with something other than the mindstream of ego. Ego, always impulsive and subject to fear and worry, creates conditions that can make matters even worse. By being able to sustain awareness we can create the space for "knowing" to arise. This is as important in us as it is in attempting the healing of others. Dr. Wayne Dyer PhD, says that "you cannot give away what you don't have".

Good listening skills always make a better healer. Listening with intuition and empathy along with being tuned in to what the sick person is feeling, seems to be the road less traveled these days. Yet studies show, that healers that take time to really listen often get better results.

As balance to your life returns, so does the opportunity for a healing miracle to occur. Being your true self is being in balance. Being in balance is being happy and healthy in a natural way. Being in awareness we avoid those pitfalls of behavior that are the cause of needless misery. Being balanced, aware and mindful, our happy healthy state prepares us best for the challenges that life can throw at us.

There are a lot of factors that make up the reasons why some people get sick and others do not. Sometimes people are both happy and healthy and still die of disease. Medical science may one day solve those mysteries. For those of us who cause our own downfall this can be a wakeup call. Even if you are reasonably healthy and strong, the flu virus is awaiting in the next cold season to take you down. If we enter the next flu season weakened by stress, anxiety, bad habits and poor health that are created by ego we can make ourselves vulnerable to sickness. We can prepare ourselves best by coming into balance through the calm abiding of self awareness.

There are specific meditation techniques that we can learn for healing. They are most effective when we can learn to sustain our awareness in the transcended state of consciousness. However they require a degree of practice. So find a meditation class in your community that teaches self awareness and mindfulness. Devote yourself to your practice as if your health depended on it. Join a group who practices regularly and reinforce your practice with shared insights. Take charge of your ego and learn to be awake and aware. Be mindful of stress and learn to let it go. Let go of destructive behaviors and habits and allow your body to return to health and vitality if possible. Free your "self" from ego. This is your life, so live it in wellness

The Law of Attraction, Manifestation and Ego

"Manifest plainness, embrace simplicity, reduce selfishness, have few desires." Lao Tzu

'We are what we think. All that we are arises with our thoughts. With our thoughts we make the world.' Siddhartha Gautama

You are not your thoughts. Yet when we become absorbed by our thoughts, what we think about becomes our reality. The concept of the "law of attraction" is about being able to manifest things of this world by thinking about them. The "Law of Attraction" is a modern era striving. The concept goes by different titles and has been around for some time "Think and Grow Rich" and "The Law of Success" were some common examples about how we manifest what we focus on. There is a kernel of truth to this concept which is what the Buddha discussed during his day. One can read many testimonies of how people watched the movie 'The Secret' and had their wishes fulfilled. Obviously the creators of that movie have managed to give credence to the concept and are still enjoying wealth from its launch in 2006.

Yet there are still many average citizens who found that it did not work for them. And of course there are always reasons why, which bring the fault back to the individual who did not *do* something quite right. So for those of you who can manifest whatever you want by focusing on' it', then I extend a hearty and sincere congratulations for your success.

That leaves the rest of us mortals just trying to keep our mortgages paid on time. This chapter is about having a slightly different understanding about the law of attraction and the manifesting of desires. Before we get all involved with how to manifest, I think that the more important question to ask is why do we desire to manifest something?

By now, the message in this book has been repeated many

times. And that message is, in awareness we are aware of what we are doing and why we are doing it. If we are grounded in awareness we are unified with the source of all things and all possibilities. Since all things are manifest through and from source (consciousness), then that is where we must begin with our wisdom. In consciousness we are aware of what we are doing and why we are doing it. Manifestation is simply the process of fulfilling desire. Only in awareness can we distinguish the difference between desire of ego and the intention of our true self. So before we get all ramped up to manifest, we must know whether this is just more sensation or distraction seeking by ego and thus striving.

In awareness we are in alignment with source and we are connected to the fabric of life. In awareness we can accept things as they are. Aligned with our true self we no longer need to manifest the material desire of ego and the need to manifest dissipates.

However in awareness there are times when we seek to fulfill intention when it is in alignment with the flow of life. When we are setting intentions to relieve the sufferings or to bring fulfillment to others out of love and compassion our desire is sourced from other than ego. Even then, we must release the outcome and solution to the greater power, to pure consciousness and be willing to accept what is. So manifestation is not just the fast lane to getting what ego wants. That is just another word for striving. Striving or coveting leads to suffering and problems.

As the Buddha stated "*We are what we think. All that we are arises with our thoughts. With our thoughts we make the world*". And since most of us spend all of our waking moments in the continuous striving for sensation experiences and distractions, then that is what will be manifested. This quantum process creates more striving and more sensation seeking because ego is never satisfied..

It is important to observe the motivation of striving to manifest material abundances. Usually it is ego, and ego is not being in alignment with the fabric of life. When in pure consciousness and experiencing life as your true self, the need for striving falls away. Being in consciousness the self serving need for material objects is gone. The true self does not need to strive for material wealth. Being in true consciousness (non-ordinary) it is understood that it, consciousness, is the source of all things and the "ground of all being". So ultimately being in consciousness is realizing the simple life through cause and effect, can create abundance. When you strive for material gain, the only thing you will ultimately gain is suffering. When you let go of the striving and just be and live the simple life of being, abundance will pour forth in ways you cannot imagine. Living the simple life transcends neediness and requires little. In awareness gratitude will realize abundance.

Exercise

Sit quietly and focus your mind on the breath for a few moments. Each time, your attention and focus are drawn towards being absorbed by your stream of thoughts; return your focus to your breath. When the mind is relatively quiet bring your attention to the thoughts you may have been having about manifesting something. One hint may be seeing that you said "I wish _____fill in the blank_____. Ask the following questions and discern the true and honest answers.

Why do you wish for this thing to happen? (Desire, Judgment)

Why can you not accept things as they are? (Acceptance)

What part of you is it that is longing for or striving for this thing to have or happen? (Ego)

What emotion or feeling is behind the desire?

Who benefits from having the desire fulfilled? (Ego [me]?)

Is it ego? (See chapter on ego and conquering ego)

Is the desire grounded in love and compassion?

Can you accept the outcome to be in alignment with source

(the flow of life)?

Are you experiencing a feeling of neediness? Is this just another attachment?

Does fulfilling this desire create balance?

Is this striving and just more sensation seeking or distraction?

Another insight to be mindful of, is to accept things as they are. When the desires are pure and sourced from consciousness they are in harmony with the greater consciousness or the flow. Dr. Amit Goswami states that we must accept and give over to the pure consciousness is the solution as it must be. *"Thy will be done"*. Quantum Physicist and Author of The Self Aware Universe, Dr. Amit Goswami gives an example where a traffic light is set up to regulate traffic. Understandably both directions of the traffic cannot be green for go at the same time because "pandemonium" as he calls it, would result. So the source of all downward causation is regulated by some inherent law in consciousness that keeps the flow of life in balance. Thus the desire and its fulfillment will fall into the framework of consciousness. And since we are all connected, as we discussed in earlier chapters, balance is maintained.

Also to be considered is the law of Karma or cause and effect. The Buddha taught that all phenomena (defined as a fact, occurrence, or circumstance observed or observable) are a result of cause and effect. This is also known as Karma. The law of cause and effect is one that is absolute and supersedes all other and lesser factors of causation (law of attraction). (See the chapter on cause and effect)

A simple way to view this is to think about seeds that we plant. If you plant seeds from weeds, then weeds is what you will get. If you plant weed seeds and expect sweet fruit, then you are living in illusion. The law of attraction (downward causation) results in a realized effect. Many times if not most of the time, it is not what we thought we would get. True manifestation requires a special state of consciousness, that is to say true consciousness not unconsciousness and ego. And going further the desires of ego are synonymous with the planting of weed seeds. They are not in harmony with the consciousness of the true self (pure awareness) and thus are not pure. The desires of ego are not born out of compassion, and are only self serving. This goes against the grain of the traffic light rule, where we are all connected, and must be at one with the flow of traffic (flow of the universe).

Karma as a non-tangible insight has to do with the product of ignorance (egoic thinking and striving). Thus what we think about does come to reality, only the downward causation (manifestation) is strongly affected by a mindstream, which is disconnected from source.

Example:

In ego a person may have the strong desire to be rich. The person may even achieve a grand wealth and the illusion of abundance yet still experience an illusion of not having enough. They can quite literally achieve fame and fortune yet obsess on more distraction seeking because they live an unfulfilled and unauthentic life. This can be observed when famous movie and rock stars seem to have it all only to die an unnecessary death. The person strove to manifest fame and fortune while what they really wanted was fulfillment. True fulfillment can only be realized by the true self. True fulfillment cannot be purchased.

A person who is living the authentic life does not define rich as having something to do with money and financial well being, although many times financial abundance is present. They perceive being rich by other standards such as being surrounded by loved ones. They find fulfillment moment by moment in the world around them and do not need to seek riches outside of the self. Usually when people are fully conscious the need for manifesting for themselves does not arise. What they focus on and desire to manifest is peace and abundance for others. Knowing their connection to others, being in awareness, they are connected to source and being

273

resonant with the flow of the greater consciousness, their seeds tend to bear the sweetest fruit.

Also it is important to realize and observe how ego will have a very specific outcome that it desires. If the exact egoic solution does not present itself, ego feels frustration, disappointment, or a sense of failure because it did not get what it wished for.

In consciousness, we set forth the intention of that which we wish to manifest. In awareness we can see the outcome and know that it is on its way. We let go of time tables and expectations and assume that the perfect solution is on the way, and *accept whatever that may be.* Many times the universe or God acts in very subtle ways. Only when we are mindful and oriented in the stillness of awareness are we able to sense the answer when it comes. We must be alert at all times for the subtle voice of consciousness and the things that manifest before us. Each time we open our eyes in the morning it is a new day with new possibilities. These are possibilities from the "conglomerate of possibilities" and must be observed to become that which is sought. We must be awake and aware, free of ego and able to accept what is and what will be.

Hopefully you can see the fallacy of striving for material solutions to the perceived problem of ego. Yearning and coveting material objects (especially money) as a means to happiness is the path to the dark side of ego. Perhaps you are ready to let go and let the "ground of all being" be your guide. Be in stillness, and observe. In pure consciousness, as your true self, observe that which comes forth from intention. Free your "self" from the dark side of ego and see what the law of attraction really holds for you.

Inspiration

"I never made one of my discoveries through the process of rational thinking" Albert Einstein

Authors' Definition: *To produce or arouse through communion with our true self.*

Inspiration is one of those insights that has been captured and copyrighted by lots of institutions over time and history. So when you hear the words inspire and inspiration there is no telling what comes to your mind.

This chapter is about perceiving insights and ideas that arrive through alignment with source. When the word "inspired" is used to describe the motivating force for a negative idea that is not what I am talking about. One has to consider the root meaning of inspiration as a condition of *being in-spirit*. In this regard it means that to be in spirit is being pure consciousness. It means that when fully tuned to God, the Tao, the Universe, or however you view the creative source, you are in spirit.

In awareness and present as the observer and the knower, the true self, the true spiritual core is in that infinite space in which all possibilities are realized. Inspiration is not an insight found in mindstream and ego. That is unconsciousness. That is a mind state in which awareness is pushed away and all focus is on the fulfillment of desire. In ego, a brilliant and even elegant notion may arise in how to fulfill the coveted desire, yet this is not inspiration. For inspiration to arise, one must be in true consciousness and not absorbed in egoic mindstream.

Essentially our true self is a spiritual being having a physical experience. Yet this basis of reality is soon lost in childhood as our young minds are captured by devices meant to ensnare and influence them. To see what this means, watch some Saturday morning cartoons and pay special attention to the advertisements that are woven into the programming. This unconscious programming starts early in our society and has been imbedded for several generations. Yet being unconscious was not spawned with the advent of television and movies, it has been around since before modern history began.

In the 1970's there was a popular television commercial that demonstrated the high quality of cassette tape by the brand name of Memorex. In the commercial Ella Fitzgerald sang loudly enough to break glass. Then the recording on a Memorex tape was played and it too broke the glass with sound vibrations. To the human ear, the two were indistinguishable. The consumer could not tell the difference between a live production and a recorded version. Sometimes this same thing can be experienced with true and faux inspiration. Ego has even snatched the term inspiration as its own and uses it to give validation to its self serving insights. The term inspired has been abused by religious egos since before the Common Era. One case of extreme misuse can be viewed by considering the "inspirational notions" of the Reverend Jim Jones. His ego was able to convince people to follow him to South America and sadly to the end of their lives. The motivating force behind some of this behavior had to have been that they believed that he was "inspired".

So the litmus test for determining if the inspiration is from ego or awareness is by observing who and what is to be benefited from the idea. What is the source of the motivation? It is necessary to be able to observe freely the source of the inspired notion. In awareness, discernment can separate egoic source from the universal awareness. With honesty the individual can discern whether the motivating force manifesting the inspiration is based on compassion and love or ego serving narcissism. In the consciousness of true self, we can use wisdom and knowing to side step ego based compulsions that arise. If the central purpose of the inspired insight is *primarily* about benefiting 'me' regardless of others, the insight is only another self serving scheme. However, in awareness and stillness we can take the insight back and ask how this inspired thought could serve others in a loving compassionate manner. In stillness and being identified as our true self we can open ourselves to the alignment of the flow of the universe to that inspired thought and see if they resonate with each other. If it is counterproductive to the helping of others and primarily serves itself (ego) or only serves the group (collective ego) and especially if it harms or manipulates others, then the warning sirens should be going off.

Ego can take the purest and most divine inspiration and turn it into a method of control. Our lives are full of examples, and I invite you to look around and see what is at work and why. You might start with our greatest information resource, the internet. There is an old archive video of Arthur C. Clarke being interviewed in 1974 about the future of the internet. It is quite obvious that he saw the use of an internet for the purpose of increasing communication and productivity for all peoples. And it came to be as he envisioned. However it also came to be that ego personalities and groups took this inspiration and turned its purpose into serving only the ego (and collective ego). Consciousness based inspiration can use all this information for inspired new insights and education or ego can use this information resource for the exploitation of child pornography. As in all things, awareness and true self are aligned with the light of spirit, the flow of the universe and ego based compulsions are evil and self (ego) serving.

In Albert Einstein's quote "I never made one of my discoveries through the process of rational thinking."Pperhaps he is telling us to detach from the materialist world of form and to be open to the true source of things. The mechanical world of science that was launched by Sir Isaac Newton was one where there was a strict set of rules into which all things must be defined. While it was a fundamental insight in his time, the higher insights of quantum sciences have moved from thinking inside the box to awareness outside of the box. The new Common Era that began around the time that Albert Einstein and others were making new radical discoveries is one based in infinite possibility. In an astonishing coincidence it appears that the ancient teachings of Buddhism on consciousness has found some common ground with Quantum Physics.

The ancients traveled the higher road of consciousness and in this 'now' we find that it merges with a different perspective of consciousness know as quantum physics. What this means is that inspiration is sourced through the awakened state of consciousness. This insight can only be experienced by letting go of egoic intent and following the flow of the universe. There is a Christian saying to "let go and let God" and "thy will be done". Being conscious in the higher self is the following of your true path. Let ego go and let consciousness be your compass. Only in this manner can true inspiration be experienced. Free your "self" from ego and realize true inspiration.

Intuition

"The only real valuable thing is intuition". - Albert Einstein

One way of understanding intuition is to consider it as directly perceiving information rising onto the surface of the mind. The most common means of obtaining information is the through the five senses. (In my opinion) Intuition is different than ESP in that Intuition is passive and ESP is an active pursuit of information to be gained by means other than the five normal senses. One is active and one is passive.

Intuition and ESP are such very similar insights and can be a gift available to any being that can transcend the mind chatter and sustain awareness. Perhaps the distinction between the two can be thought of as a kind of prophesy and intuition.

What does a "sixth sense" mean? One dictionary defines it as a power of perception beyond the five senses. Another defines it nearly the same as extra sensory perception. The term has been manipulated by egoic minds for a long time now. Ego loves this insight because it is at once ambiguous enough that almost anyone can claim it, yet also mysterious enough that it can almost be used to gain attention. There are many opinions about whether humans possess a sixth sense or can display extra sensory perception at will. My opinion is it depends on which meaning of the verb "to sense" is used. For simplicity many of us use the verb sense to mean to perceive. The mind can perceive information from origins other than the five senses and that would be extra sensory. So as hokey as that sounds, to me, extra sensory perception has a better accuracy than to say that people have a sixth sense.

There is information on the term extra sensory perception which was brought into the social consciousness in the 1930's by a Mr. J. D. Rhine as they made an effort to "develop psychological research into an experiential science". The term ESP became a part of the American vocabulary and the subject of much speculation since then. This chapter is about understanding how in awareness and detached from the current of mindstream, we can observe other phenomena that are perceived from sources other than the five senses.

Before you get excited, it is important to be aware of ego and how it is already leaning over your shoulder thinking of ways to exploit this attention getting concept. Because the phenomena that arises in the mind is extra sensory, it can only be perceived by the self when in a pure awareness. As is much of life that happens around us, there is much apparent yet not perceived. Perceiving insights or to sense information that arises from other than sight, sound, taste, touch, and smell requires that you be "tuned in" or "logged into the network". And even then when something does register, the novice will be pushed aside by ego and the true understanding is lost within the current of ego and its shenanigans.

Yet the most interesting of worlds awaits any of us when we can tune out ego and tune into to the greater consciousness. These moments of clarity have been experienced and noted by sages since earliest days of recorded history. In some sects of Buddhism, the term is called "Samadhi" (defined as *"an abiding in which mina becomes very still but does not merge with the object of attention, ana is thus able to observe ana gain insight into the changing flow of experience*).

In Zen Buddhism the term Kensho applies where insights are perceived by "seeing into one's true nature".

Again, try not to let your ego get too excited because this level of sustained awareness takes years of dedicated practice to accomplish. While there are some who arrive at it instantaneously through a profound moment of truth, most arrive with years of hard work. The moment of truth is more of a flash of understanding of the true self and the way things really are. Perhaps it is like tuning the radio band looking for that a particular station on a particular frequency. And then the components of the radio reach the resonant frequency into which the radio and the broadcasting station become resonant with one another. They become one and as the listener you become one with the activities of the station, the information coming forth, the radio and the content being transmitted. If we continue on with the metaphor of the radio and radio station, it is like the radio station cannot sustain the resonance for very long and soon the station is lost. It is like the tuning knob cannot stop tuning and the station is lost. When our minds are in pure awareness, they become resonant with all that there is. Meditation practice is sustained concentration of an alert observation to what is. In meditation the concentrated focus becomes resonant to the tapestry of the universe and the phenomena within it. The moment the mind goes back into mindstream and the prison of ego, the radio becomes unplugged and turned off. This being turned off is defined in the earlier chapter on self awareness as being "unconscious".

Yet once you have experienced this very special moment of being tuned into the universe, or God, or the Tao, you will be changed forever. This profound experience will give you the determination to keep working with diligence on your meditation practice. Becoming self aware is the moment of tuning in, and practicing mindfulness is the continuation of staying tuned in. Each time the radio drifts off frequency (becoming absorbed by thought stream); your true self realizes it (mindfulness) and turns the tuner (awareness) back to being in tune or back into awareness. With practice, we can create a "saved" button which makes it easy to return to the special point of focus. Focusing on breath is a common method for doing this. As soon as you realize that the mind has drifted off station (become lost in thought and ego), quickly focus on breath and instantly be back on station (in awareness and observing).

Just like being tuned to the radio station, in awareness, more information is perceived. Imagine that each of the five senses as different stations. As you move up the spectrum of frequencies, you can observe content being perceived by sight, sound, touch, smell and taste. When we are lost in mindstream, it is like walking out of the room and not being able to hear the radio. It is broadcasting all sorts of information yet no one is there to perceive it. As soon as you return (come back into consciousness) the information is available.

Now imagine that not only are there five stations that represent the senses, but there are other stations on a different bandwidth (different and higher frequencies) that can be tuned into where other information can be perceived. These other stations could be called extra sensory because they are not part of the same bandwidth as the big five. Expanding the bandwidth of the radio is synonymous with expanding awareness of the mind. In this bandwidth some stations could be thought of as intuition, inspiration, and creative ideas. Intuition can be perceived by paying attention to feelings. In awareness, using discernment, we can separate egoic feelings from inspired feelings and pay close attention.

Here is an **example** that you may have experienced.

You are busy in your life doing whatever you are doing and typically lost in thought. Somewhere in the steam of busy thoughts, in the gap created when one cascade of thoughts ends and before the next cascade begins a very subtle notion arises from out of nowhere. Let's pretend that suddenly for no perceived reason you perceive thoughts or memories of your college roommate, who is someone you have not heard from in five years. They have been completely out of mind and then suddenly you picture them. You may remember a moment you shared together, or hear them say a word, or something even more subtle. For a very short moment of perception you pause and ponder it. Then very soon afterwards, the next cascade of thought catches you and away you go again. Then later, perhaps a few hours or a few days, the friend calls and you have a conversation. Way back in the recesses of memory you recall just thinking of them recently and think … "hmmm, just a coincidence" You may even have the presence of mind to consider how interesting it would be if you were able to develop this trait. But soon even this is lost in mind stream and gone until the next coincidence.

Now let us look at this from another perspective. What if you were a serious meditation practitioner and were adept at staying "tuned in". In a time of stillness the notion of your old friend arises. Yet in this state of consciousness where notions are like a single cloud on a clear horizon, this notion is very obvious. Eventually the stream of thought becomes diffused. Each thought is more like a single cloud crossing towards you from the horizon. In the timelessness of awareness, your true self is able to examine much detail. Much like being able to see the shapes of animals in clouds, consciousness is able to find insightful meaning with the data being perceived. Unlike the unconscious person who barely has the ability to perceive the insight between the current of mind stream, consciousness can focus on the insight as it crosses the continuum of the mind. The unconscious person barely records it, but to the awake and fully aware person it is an event filled with information. When those thoughts or feelings about the old roommate arrive, you should pay attention.

Developing intuitive perception requires concentration and practice. One cannot be able to create and sustain the empty space necessary for intuition to arise without practice and commitment. Being free of the currents of mindstream, that sweeps the unconscious person away, the concentrated focus enables us to develop the space necessary for intuition to arise. Within concentrated focus we can tune in and observe all sorts of feelings, thoughts and information that is not available to the unconscious mind.

To the skeptic, extra sensory perception is the substance of science fiction. But then, so can the concept of awareness be a subject of skepticism. To the awakened person it is the reality of being the true self.

Exercise

- In this present moment, stop and become aware

  and sense your feelings.

- Is part of you getting excited and already striving to become proficient with ESP? (Ego at work?)

- Is part of you already having visions of grandeur as some kind of a "sooth saying sage"? (Ego again?)

- Are you able to observe your mood and feelings without being absorbed by them? (Awareness)

- Are you able to realize your higher self as the observer and the feelings and moods as the observed?

- Can you sustain your concentrated observation long enough to discern the nature and source of the feelings or mood.

- Are they generated by ego?

- Or are they sourced from the greater consciousness, or source, or the fabric of life?

- Can you tell the difference?

Be honest with yourself and recognize ego when it quietly slips in the back door. When you realize that you lost concentration and become lost in thought stream again, just become quiet, focus on your mantra or breathing and return to observing. With practice you will become better and better. The better you become at staying grounded in awareness the more sensitive your awareness becomes. In sustained awareness you will be able to notice intuition for what it is and gain great insight from it. Sometimes these intuitive insights are a subtle as the brush of a Butterfly's wing. Other times they will be fairly prominent. You will sense neither when lost in the mind stream of ego.

Intuition can be a powerful friend when used with compassion and empathy. We can learn to quiet our mind and observe what is going on around us especially when it is in regard to others. In the stillness of awareness we "listen" to our feelings and gain some insight as to what others are feeling. This deeper connection to each other can remove obstacles and can develop strong trusting relationships. Whether it is between two people or two organizations, set aside ego and see how you can serve others in an effective way. Listen to their words and listen to your heart (intuition). Seek out awareness and use all means of perception to "see" others and to "know" them. When you can be empathetic, you can provide meaningful compassion supported by love. Anything else is fake and the work of ego.

When we are tasked to help someone solve a problem, intuition can be vital in understanding the person and the nature of why they perceive a problem. In healing, one must be able to listen on a deeper level that combines empathy and inspiration. Effective healing requires a kind of knowing that only comes from that source other than ego. It is the ultimate source of pure consciousness. Free your "self" and realize the insight of intuition.

The Authentic Self

This is another profound insight and important chapter of this book. If I can reach your heart and give you hope this will be the place. The first time I heard this term, "The Authentic Self", I wondered what it really meant. As the discovery of consciousness manifested, so did the remembering of the authentic self. Simply put the authentic self is the consciousness expression to whom we have always been. The un-authentic self is ego. In many of the other chapters where ego is discussed there is a continuous call to detach from ego and wake up. This waking up is the returning to our true or authentic self.

The question was asked earlier on (the chapter on The Self), "who are you?" A lot of that chapter is devoted to understanding what you are not. When we ask ourselves who we are, most if not all of the answers are not it. So for a few moments just let go of *needing* to define who or what you are. This chapter is realizing who you really are aside from ego.

First and foremost, you must understand and then remember that people are happiest and most fulfilled when they play. Like many of the things we lose in childhood, we came into this physical experience motivated into action by the joy of play. Hopefully you can remember happy moments in childhood where play was central to life. Then as we "matured" which I believe to mean that we succumb to egoic pursuits, we are finally assimilated into the ego collective. When we allowed ego to take control, we lost the joy of play. The joy of play was hijacked like so much else, and turned into the pursuit of sensation or distraction. Somewhere early on, when life became problematic, we sought out distraction as a means of coping with unacceptable life events that arose. Instead of finding our natural or authentic joy, we found artificial and superficial stimuli to ease the burden of life. And that becomes the issue; Life becoming a burden and why we feel that way.

As children we are naturally happy. Conditions do not have to be just right. Happiness and play are spontaneous. As children we begin our life as our authentic self. Most of us were pure, loving and unrestricted. Then as we merge into our local cultural main stream, we lost our "self" or rather we lost our true identity or became lost to our true self. We forget who we truly are and merge or become absorbed by ego. In the chapter on Ego we learned that we lose our self to a false identity based on memory and the story of me. Read the chapter on ego to fully understand the impact of ego as a barrier to consciousness (our true self).

As children we (most of us) start off just as nature intended. Children learn so much of life through play and doing what they enjoy. However, even though our bodies were young, underlying is the eternal connection to all there is. Perhaps that is what was meant when in the movie, "The Legend Of Bagger Vance", a grown up version of the character "Hardy" said: "God is happiest when his children are at play". I so solidly concur with this remark and am urging each of you to take an honest assessment of your life as it is *in this 'now'*.

If you are not happy at play, then perhaps it's time to reevaluate your life. The most common assessment that I often hear is that something along the notion that "I have to work so I can make a living". What this really means is that ego has taken over and it feels that it must have plenty of money to find happiness in stuff and status. Working for egoic pursuits simply supports sensation seeking and distraction. There is a cliché about "working to live, or living to work". Young children rarely worry about stuff and status when at play. Grownups can release the concern about stuff and status when they wake up and find their authentic self.

This chapter started off with the quote that each and every one of us has a very special game to which only we can play and that it was what brought us into this world. You can best understand this concept by considering it to be saying that each of us has a special something to share with the world. As you consider this, any negative feelings that arise are just ego. Or this may inspire a sense of hope. Hopefully you can remain detached from that feeling long enough to explore what your special something is. And because you may have been in ego for all of your adult life, you probably have forgotten who you were as a child, what you loved and what it is like to play. There is good news, the search for your special something is fun in itself. Discovering your play and your special something is absolutely transforming.

Here are two ideas that you should seriously consider. One is to imagine what it is like to do something fun that you love, and is good for you and those around you. This is something that you love is so much that you will suspend everything else just to engage in it. It must meet the criteria of when you are doing it you are alert and aware and experience each moment as being in pure joy. This is not to be confused with sensation seeking and being in distraction.

Secondly, imagine if you found this special something that you loved so much that it wouldn't seem fair if you were paid to share it? There are a few of us in our world culture who have found this niche and live lives in awe and wonder. The rest of us are on some treadmill pursuing egoic rewards of sensation and distraction. One is heaven the other is hell. If you are on a treadmill, you should get off. When ego whispers in your ear "I can't" you must understand what is happening. Viewing life from the trap of ego is living life fettered by chains of attachment. Consciousness is the field of infinite possibility. We must be awake, aware and in tune with our authentic self to experience the "field".

When we are at one with the field, we are connected to all there is. When we are connected to the field and being love, happiness and play, life is so very sweet. Connected and unrestricted, life flows through us, and we flow through life. We are not only connected to the field, we are the field. When we are fully connected to the field of possibility all things are possible. When we are grounded in the field, when we are the field, all of the beauty and grace of possibility can flow through us and be shared with others.

Being your true self is being in unity of mind, body and spirit. These are aspects of living the balanced life. The most immediate way to discern balance is to just look at your life with honesty. When we are honest, we can observe where harmony is disrupted. Look at some of these areas of your life and be honest about the level of balance.

Exercise

- Look in the mirror and stand on the scale. Is your body overweight? How much?

- Look at your debt ratio, is it out of whack?

- How often are you truly happy, content and accepting of the condition of your life?

- Are you always sick?

- Do others dread seeing you coming?

- Do you talk too much?

- Do you talk too much about yourself?

- Do you change jobs a lot?

- Do your coworkers trust you?

- How often do you have fun?

- How often do you play?

- What is your gift?

- What is the game you were meant to play?

- What do you love to do?

- What is the reason you were sent here?

Now be honest with yourself and look at some of these questions again. Remember the old saying "to thine own *self* be true" DO NOT LIE TO YOUR SELF. (See the Chapter on Honesty). If you are having a hard time accepting the true state of how things are, let this be your ego meter. It is in the red zone. Ego does not want to face up to the reality it has created. You, your true self has to take charge, and starve ego's power by remaining in the stillness of awareness. This is done by learning meditation; strengthen your self-awareness and becoming mindful as you experience life. In the space between the episodes of being lost in mindstream, the true self will arise. You should practice this as if your future depended on it. Because having a physical experience while chained to misery of the egoic existence is not life. Life is living as the true self. Awake, aware and present in every moment. As ego rises up and absorbs your attention and carries you away to the next pursuit, the essence of who you really are is being hijacked. In meditation, we awake from this illusion and become one with all there is. We rejoin our place in the tapestry of the universe where all things are connected.

Free your true self. Detach from "doing" and just be still. Find a meditation instructor that teaches mindfulness meditation and begin the process of getting your true life back. Real joy and contentment are waiting for you.

Play and the Authentic Self

"We don't stop playing because we grow old; we grow old because we stop playing".

George Bernard Shaw (essayist, playwright and novelist) July 1856 – November 1950

When is the last time you remember having a genuinely good time? When did you last *play*? As children, play is as spontaneous as breathing. For adults play is many times forgotten, and is at best a very low priority. And that is where we make our biggest mistake.

It is not that unusual to have forgotten what play is. It is quite common to not even remember how to play. Play is doing something you love to do just for the sake of doing it. Play is a most positive form of synergy; bringing together fun, amusement, intent and joy realizing your true gift and purpose. If you do not know your play, then consider different things to try. Keep trying until you find it. Do not make the mistake of putting a time limit on how long you will pursue your play, because finding your play is finding your purpose. When you're in alignment as your true self and your true purpose, you begin to live your play. You must experience play in the now (present moment). For the 'now' is all there ever is.

Be alert for ego to infiltrate play just as it does other aspects of life. Ego, always seeking opportunity to build its esteem, will hijack play and use it to promote itself. Telling everyone you meet about your play so what you will look good is a fast track to losing the joy. Ego will hijack the purpose behind play and try to use it to make "me" look better. Play is not about that. Real play is the authentic self in alignment with life.

If you take up tennis because your ego thinks that you will look good and appear in a good position for everyone in your circle to admire, then I can almost promise you that soon tennis will lose its charm. You must play tennis because you find it the most fun thing to be doing.

Play has more to do with being in alignment with your special gifts that are unique to you. Typically it is a connection with a skill, knowledge, gift, or special talent that is as natural as breathing. Often you may not know how you do it, you just do. Sometimes it is something you developed and became very good at and just like doing it. Each of us has a special something that we love as we connect with it. It may have been lost to us over the years and our job is to find it.

When you are at play, sensation seeking will often take a back row. I remember when I was a child, I loved playing baseball. I loved playing baseball so much that I did not even want to stop to eat. I did not want to watch much TV or almost anything else. I wanted to play baseball. I do not know whether I loved it because I was good at it or if I was good at it because I loved it, or both. I lived to play baseball. Later I found that I loved all things about radios. I was just utterly fascinated with radio waves. It became my joy and my more grown up play. As I got older, I could not believe it when the United States Navy not only agreed to send me to Radio Schools, but also paid me to operate and repair the equipment. I became a Navy Radioman. As an operator and technician I did very well at it because I just loved it. I was living my dream. Through ignorance I allowed my "self" to become disconnected to that gift and play only to spend many years until I found a new gift and a new play. I can state that in finding my true self I was able to connect with my true play again.

Finding your play is the unification of mind, body and spirit. When these three aspects of self come together, a sense of joy will arise that is like no other. It gives purpose. When we join our play with helping and serving others with love and compassion, we live life with a sense of purpose that develops purity in our self that is beyond words. If you can find your gift, share it with others and get paid for it, the word "job" loses all meaning.

I love sharing Meditation and Tai Chi with people who are

searching for their true self. When they find happiness or get well because of these ancient practices, it makes me feel sustained. When I see a senior citizen stand up from a wheel chair for the first time in years from learning Tai Chi it warms my heart. When we can help fulfill the hope that someone else has, we have become unified with our creative source. We do these things because we love doing it and we can bring something very special to others. Through our own gifts we can help others. What stronger calling is there?

Somewhere in the dark halls of your heart there is a forgotten joy that has been put aside. Take time, that is, be in stillness and let go of ego and the chains that bind us to that which we really do not want. In the stillness allow the heart to soar with hope. Remember who you are and the things you love to do. This book is telling you to throw off the cultural conditioning of working yourself to death and remember how to play. There is an old saying, "all work and no play makes Jack a dull boy".

Following egoic desire that creates scenarios where you have to work to pay for all the stuff you don't really need is being on a treadmill that never stops and you only get off when you fall down. That faux joy of ego is just sensation seeking. Seek your true self and experience your true gift. If you can find that gift that not only brings fun and joy to your life, but also to others, then you truly begin to live your life. Being in the joy of your own play is living each moment as a moment of truth. Letting go of all the things that deter us from our true self will allow balance to be restored. With balanced comes harmony. With harmony we find bliss. Free your "self" and find your bliss.

And now it's now

There is no time like the present..." Originally from Proverbs, since amplified by others.

After all the discussion about living in the 'now', this 'now' is at a crossroads. It may be the most important choice you have ever made. If you have read this far, perhaps ego has lost its grip and you realize that you can choose your own true way. Going forward, cause and effect will either send you back into the egoic path of problems or the path to the higher road of being who you were meant to be. As you read the last word, the next step will determine whether you return to your life of mistaken identity (ego) or whether you find and free yourself. In this now, as you read this, you can set the intention to wake up and be free of old habits, bad moods and self destructive behavior. Or you can turn on the television and resume unconsciousness and ignorance. You can move forward and know the world as it really is with all of its wonder or you can return to the materialism of ego and suffering. It's your choice. You can choose balance and harmony or striving and misery.

If you have tried meditation before, you can resume your practice. If you never practiced meditation before, find a good mindfulness instructor and commit to becoming self aware. While awake and aware, set the intention to pay attention to what you are doing and why you are doing it as you live moment by moment. Awake and aware, be alert for egoic neediness that will arise before you. At first being mindful to remain awake and aware can be hard work. Remaining vigilant to ego and the tricks it will play will be a bit tiring. Yet soon enough, with diligent practice you will begin to realize that things are going smoother. You will notice a trend where there is more happiness and more contentment.

The more moments where you can just accept things as they are, without the grinding struggle to control the flow of life, the less the burden you have to carry. You will find that life is really quite simple, there is not so much you have to do, and certainly not so much material stuff that you have to have. As

Wayne Dyers says "There is no way to happiness, happiness is the way". Just let go and live.

Here are some actions steps to practice:

- Begin a meditation practice.

- Learn to identify as the observer, the true self

- Learn to observe without becoming absorbed into egoic thought stream

- Allow the true and authentic self awareness to blossom (transcendence)

- Extend self awareness into daily life through the practice of mindfulness. (that is paying attention to what you are doing and why you are doing it)

Be mindful of

- Jumping to conclusions and automatic reactions

- Practice discernment over judgment

- Refrain from reaction and practice acceptance

- Recognize the infinite possibility of choice when action is necessary

- Be mindful of feelings, moods and behaviors, and do not become absorbed by them

  o Judgment

  o Fear

o Desire, Greed and Lust

o Disappointment, Deprivation, and Jealousy

o Apathy

o Desperation

o Embarrassment

o Be very alert to Fear, Rage, Hatred and do not become absorbed by them

o Be mindful of old habits and be aware of automatically feeling or doing. (conditioning)

o Be aware of how you cope with a life that is not meeting up to egoic expectations (sensation and distraction seeking)

o Be aware of how easily your ego is manipulated and how it seeks to manipulates the ego of others.

o Be Honest with your self

o Examine your current path and take ownership of your own creation, your life. (Cause and Effect)

- o In the infinite space of awareness base your decisions and actions on love and compassion.
- o Allow honesty, joy, gratitude, and serenity to become present.
- o In awareness reconnect with your body and seek balance.
- o As you reconnect with your authentic self
    - Find your play and play (your gift and service to community) Do and Share what you love to do and were meant to do.
    - Understand the true meaning of the law of attraction (not striving)
- o Find the purpose of spirit through inspiration
- o Create the space for intuition to be a faithful guide
- o Understand, allow and accept that there will be setbacks and failures. Know that these are learning experiences that will

either continue ignorance or grow into
wisdom

o Understand the illusion of time (live in
the present moment)

o Set your compass and follow the path of
love, compassion and altruism.

o Practice and be patient, be vigilant and do
not give into ego.

o Seek balance and moderation in all things.

Follow these ancient insights and you will transform your life. You will be your true and authentic self. The being you were meant to be. Now it is up to you. Step forward and Free Your "self".

Index

Glossary

Authentic Self	The higher aspect of the self not dominated by ego. Who you really are.
Coping	how one deals with perceived problem that are unpleasant or painful
Discernment	observing life as it really is without influence of ego
Ego	Aspect of self that is grounded in emotions and feelings.
Ego Identity	Who you think you are when absorbed in ego
Judgment	defining aspects of perception as good or bad
Karma	the result of cause and effect
Meditation	The state of pure consciousness, the state of being and observing.
Mindfulness	being alert and paying attention to thoughts, emotions and feelings that come and go in the mind.
Mindstream	the current of mental activity that captivates and absorbs the attention of self
Now	this moment of perception
Play	Doing what you love to do aside from the influence of ego
Problems	defining aspects of life that are defined by ego
Self Awareness	Awake, aware and not unconscious in mindstream and egoic activities
Source	Consciousness
Thought	mental activity

Transcendence   The shift from unconsciousness to
                  awareness (from egoic state to higher self)

About the Author

Samuel Beasley is a Certified Meditation and Tai Chi Instructor living in Augusta Georgia.

He teaches Sun Style Tai Chi and studies and practices Sun Style, Yang Style, and Chen Style Tai Chi Chuan as well as Monkey Style Kung Fu under the guidance of Master Chun Zeng.

He is a student of Buddhist, Taoist and Christian philosophies.

Correspondence can be directed to
sbeasley@augustameditation.com

Made in the USA
Charleston, SC
31 October 2012